Collective Bargaining
and
Impasse Resolution
in the
Public Sector

COLLECTIVE BARGAINING
AND
IMPASSE RESOLUTION
IN THE
PUBLIC SECTOR

David A. Dilts
and
William J. Walsh

 QUORUM BOOKS
New York • Westport, Connecticut • London

Library of Congress Cataloging-in-Publication Data

Dilts, David A.
  Collective bargaining and impasse resolution in the public sector
/ David A. Dilts and William J. Walsh.
    p.   cm.
  Bibliography: p.
  Includes index.
  ISBN 0–89930–247–5 (lib. bdg. : alk. paper)
  1. Collective labor agreements—Government employees—United
States. 2. Employee–management relations in government—Law and
legislation—United States.   3. Arbitration, Industrial—United
States. I. Walsh, William J.   II. Title.
KF3409.P77D55   1988
344.73′018904135—dc19
[347.30418904135   88–4063

British Library Cataloguing in Publication Data is available.

Library of Congress Catalog Card Number: 88–4063
ISBN: 0–89930–247–5

First published in 1988 by Quorum Books

Greenwood Press, Inc.
88 Post Road West, Westport, Connecticut   06881

Printed in the United States of America

The paper used in this book complies with the
Permanent Paper Standard issued by the National
Information Standards Organization (Z39.48–1984).

10 9 8 7 6 5 4 3 2 1

This book is dedicated to the man whose inspired teaching, professional competence, and sincere concern sparked our interest in labor relations—arbitrator and friend—

Professor Fred Witney
Indiana University

Contents

Exhibits

Preface

Man's flight through life is sustained by the power of his knowledge.
Inscription on "The Eagle and Fledglings" statue
at the United States Air Force Academy

USE OF THIS BOOK

This manuscript is written with the practitioner in mind. Little or no background in the fields of labor relations or negotiations is necessary to benefit from this book, but it is hoped that those with either an academic or practical grounding in these subjects will find the book interesting and a useful guide to both bargaining and impasse resolution. The full range of topical coverage from the labor law through the impasse procedures also make this book a viable alternative text for those instructors who wish to teach public sector collective bargaining from the perspective of impasse resolution. It is hoped that this book will also prove a valuable reference work for academics in the field of public sector negotiations.

Personal experience as a professional arbitrator and fact finder brings some natural biases to this work. The authors are neither anti-union nor anti-management but are neutrals. That does not mean the book will be free of the authors' own particular views on how the world works. It simply means that one should not expect the authors to side with either labor or management in the presentations contained herein.

The plan of the book will offer some discussion of the topic areas to be covered. The discussion of public sector employer-employee relations is intended to develop a basic understanding of why unionization and collective bargaining in the public sector are such controversial topics.

Discussion of why unions were late bloomers in the public sector also provides some insights into the nature of public sector collective bargaining as well as its environment.

AUTHORS' INTENT

The public sector has seen significant unionization in recent years despite some retrenchment in the private sector. Much has been written concerning labor relations and collective bargaining in the private sector. There is also a wealth of published knowledge on grievance administration and grievance arbitration. There is, however, very little written on the subject of public sector collective bargaining and virtually nothing, in any organized sense, on the topic of contract negotiation impasse resolution.[1]

The general purpose of this book is to fill that void—to provide a complete reference guide to negotiations and impasse resolution in the public sector. Fact finding and arbitration are presented with an emphasis on both the procedural aspects of each and the decision rules applied in each. Mediation, a first-level impasse resolution procedure, also will be examined. The examination of mediation will offer, among other things, practical suggestions so that the parties to collective bargaining may make better use of this most effective of all dispute settlement mechanisms.

Since the impasse resolution procedures utilized in the public sector are an extension of the negotiations process, discussions of the art and science of table bargaining will be offered as a prelude to the examination of impasse procedures. The discussion of bargaining will be based on a brief examination of public sector collective bargaining laws. This organization offers a complete package for the negotiator or academic interested in the subject.

PUBLIC SECTOR BARGAINING AND IMPASSE RESOLUTION

The public sector includes many levels of government and a vast array of occupations. The focal point of this book is the state and local governmental levels. There are differences in the collective bargaining observed at the federal and state levels, but for the most part these differences revolve around the sizes of the respective agencies and the nature of the legal environment. Much of what is examined in this book is fully applicable to federal sector negotiations but is packaged to be most useful to those management and union negotiators representing such public employees as firefighters, police officers, teachers, state highway employees, and the agencies in which they work. This does not limit the sections on impasse procedures and collective bargaining to these groups, and those negotiators representing federal employees and agencies will find these discussions useful.

It is the negotiators operating in the public sector who have been largely ignored by the authors of labor relations texts and arbitration texts. At best, a chapter may be found that gives a general overview of the public sector or discusses a specific, often technical point, in either the labor law or collective bargaining. But these single chapter treatments offer little in the way of practical and useful information in preparing for either contract negotiations or impasse resolution procedures.[2]

With the exception of a few articles in the academic literature and even fewer in the trade literature, little has been written concerning fact finding or interest arbitration in the public sector. Mediation has been largely ignored as well except for a few academic studies that provide little useful information for the practitioner. In the majority of public sector collective bargaining relations, at all levels, these impasse resolution mechanisms are extremely important. The public sector resolves most of its impasses through these mechanisms and not through tests of economic power—threatened or actual strike or lockout—typically resorted to in the private sector.

PLAN OF THE BOOK

This book is divided into two major parts. Part I is an introduction to public sector collective bargaining. Part II is an in-depth analysis of the impasse resolution procedures used in the public sector.

Chapter 1 establishes the framework for discussion of public sector collective bargaining impasse resolution. An introduction to collective bargaining and its historical basis are presented. This is followed by a description of the public sector and how it differs from the private sector. The chapter concludes with an overview of impasse procedures.

Chapter 2 begins with a brief overview of state collective bargaining statutes. This chapter examines why it was left to the states to enact their own collective bargaining laws and compares the coverage of varying state statutes. This chapter then proceeds to examine election policies, scope of bargaining, employee rights, unfair labor practice provisions, and other provisions of the various statutory schemes important to an understanding of collective bargaining.

Chapter 3 focuses on collective bargaining. This chapter examines two models of bargaining: the economics of collective bargaining as well as the behavioral theory of negotiations. The basic concepts of these models are presented in such a manner as to provide a useful guide to the negotiator.

Chapter 4 addresses the strategies and tactics employed in collective bargaining. The intent is to identify an approach to bargaining that enhances bargaining strength and increases the likelihood of "winning" at impasse. The fourth chapter concludes Part I—the introduction to public sector collective bargaining.

The fifth chapter begins Part II: seven chapters dealing wth impasses in bargaining. Chapter 5 introduces impasse procedures. The various steps typically found in statutory impasse resolution procedures are examined. The neutrals who serve as mediators, fact finders, and interest arbitrators are examined to determine who they are and what backgrounds a negotiator can expect these people to have. Short discussions on netural selection and impasse minimization are also to be found in this chapter.

Chapter 6 examines mediation. The techniques utilized by mediators will be examined and the situations in which these techniques most often prove successful will be offered. A discussion of what the negotiators may do to enhance the effectiveness of mediation is also presented.

Chapter 7 details the procedures utilized in fact finding and interest arbitration hearings. The structure of the hearing and the details of the presentation of a fact finding or arbitration case are discussed.

Chapters 8 and 9, respectively, examine the decisional standards employed by arbitrators and fact finders in cases involving economic issues and in cases involving language issues. Chapter 9 concludes with a short discussion of how arbitrators weigh evidence and a brief presentation concerning the decisional thinking of fact finders and arbitrators.

Chapter 10 is an examination of the effects of statutory impasse procedures on collective bargaining. A practical guide to what a negotiator should do with a fact-finding report and an interest arbitration award is offered. Attention is then turned to the long-run effects of impasse resolution procedures on the nature and conduct of the parties' collective bargaining relation.

Chapter 11 is the final chapter in Part II and is an examination of experimental techniques in impasse resolution. The experiments are examined for two reasons. The first of these reasons is to determine what other approaches to impasse resolution have been utilized in the public sector. Once this has been ascertained, the second reason is to determine if any insights into the effectiveness of the traditional approaches to impasses resolution can be gained.

Chapter 12 serves as a summary statement presenting the conclusions of this book.

The appendices to this manuscript offer examples of "real world" situations. Appendix A is a fact-finding report dealing with five economic issues. It gives an insight into how fact finding is handled and how a report is typically constructed. Appendix B is an arbitration award previously published in *Labor Arbitration Reports*. It too deals with economic issues at impasse. Appendix C is the Code of Ethics of the Federal Mediation and Conciliation Service, American Arbitration Association, and the National Academy of Arbitrators. The Code of Ethics is included for several reasons: It is referred to several times at various places in the book but, more important, it is the document that is supposed to govern the behavior of fact finders and arbitrators. It is appropriate for practitioners to understand the professional code followed by those they employ.

NOTES

1. One notable exception is Arnold Zack, *Understanding Fact Finding and Arbitration in the Public Sector* (Washington, D.C.: U.S. Department of Labor, 1974). This monograph is a quick structural guide to procedures in fact finding and interest arbitration. Even though rather dated it is an authoritative guide to procedural issues in these forums.

2. For example, see Benjamin J. Taylor and Fred Witney, *Labor Relations Law, Fifth Edition* (Englewood Cliffs, N.J.: Prentice-Hall, 1987), chapter 21; David A. Dilts and Clarence R. Deitsch, *Labor Relations* (New York: Macmillan, 1983), chapter 15; Frank Elkouri and Edna A. Elkouri, *How Arbitration Works, Fourth Edition* (Washington, D.C.: Bureau of National Affairs, 1985), chapter 18; and John A. Fossum, *Labor Relations: Development, Structure, Process, Third Edition* (Plano, Texas: Business Publications, 1985), chapter 15.

PART I

INTRODUCTION TO PUBLIC SECTOR COLLECTIVE BARGAINING

1

Introduction to Public Sector Bargaining and Impasse Resolution

> Knowledge is of two kinds. We know a subject ourselves, or we know where we can find information upon it.
>   Samuel Johnson, in Boswell's *Life of Johnson*

This chapter introduces the institution of collective bargaining and briefly describes its evolution in the public sector. By the chapter's end, the reader will have a basic understanding of the nature of the collective bargaining relationship in the public sector and how public employment differs from private employment. Moreover, the reader will understand the controversial nature of unionization in the public sector.

WHAT IS COLLECTIVE BARGAINING AND WHERE DID IT COME FROM?

Collective bargaining is a system of labor-management relations to determine wages, hours, and other conditions of employment. The actual negotiations typically take place between representatives of the employer and employees rather than the principal parties themselves. The current collective bargaining system has developed from the historical experiences of the early practitioners (as described in this chapter). The current system has been shaped by the legislative, executive, and judicial branches of government (as described in the next chapter). It is continually modified to respond to the needs of the practitioners (as described in Chapters 2 and 3).

Today's collective bargaining structure is the result of an evolutionary process. The evolution has not been a smooth one. It has often followed a start-stop scenario, and that has been a source of frustration for the parties and occassionally for the general public. The 200-year history of organized labor and collective bargaining in the United States is testimony to the viability of the process and its ability to serve the parties.[1]

Collective bargaining predates the U.S. Constitution in America, but the modern period begins with the twentieth century. The early modern history of collective bargaining was marked by strife and conflict. Small businesses were largely owner managed, and these owners considered it impertinent (at best) that employees would attempt to tell them how to run their enterprises. Labor was treated as any other commodity—to be bought and sold or, more precisely, to be rented. The employer thought that the "take it or leave it approach" was a fair method of dealing with labor since that was the approach the employer faced in procuring most other factors of production (or those items necessary to do business).

The industrial revolution was spawned by tremendous advances in technology, both scientific advances associated with discovering "what is" and the managerial-technological advances associated with ideas of "how to." The managerial advances would have been severely limited had not an ingenious device been invented—the corporation. The corporation is a legal figment: an entity with perpetual life that exists independent of its own creator. The corporation made it possible to accumulate large amounts of financial capital while limiting the maximum risk to individual owners. Bankruptcy of a corporation would not necessarily cause the bankruptcy of each owner. Corporations, even when controlled by a central tycoon, were largely operated by hired managers or executives. The likelihood of the owner hearing the voice of the laborer was reduced by layers of managerial control. While the leading businessmen of the time surely saw themselves as benefactors to society, responsible for the tremendous increases in productivity occurring in America in the late 1800s and early 1900s, labor viewed management as paternalistic at best and uncaring on average.

Labor formed unions so that it might speak with one voice—admittedly a harsh voice in some cases suited to hard conditions frequently observed in American enterprise—to improve the lot of the laborer. Organized labor was treated, first under common law and later under statuatory law, as a "combination in restraint of trade"; that is, the strike threat restrained trade, trade is good, and, therefore, organized labor must be bad. Little parallel was seen between the corporation—an institution created to form combinations of capital—and the union, which combined labor for the ostensible purpose of placing the worker on an equal footing with the employer with respect to bargaining power.

The legacy of a confrontational relationship between labor and management is still in evidence today as "combinations of capital" bargain with "combinations of labor" to determine wages, hours, and conditions of employment.

WHAT IS THE PUBLIC SECTOR?

The public sector is the government sector of the economy. It is distinguished from the non-government, or private, sector, which is roughly more than twice as large as the public sector. The public sector exists at two primary institutional levels, and one of these has been subdivided into two further administrative levels. The legal levels are the federal and the state levels. The Constitution gives these two levels some authority over the lives of citizens. Though the Constitution did not create lower administrative levels, states have seen fit to delegate some of their authority to county and municipal administrative levels. Administrative levels below the state level are encompassed by the term *local government*. Local government may also include agencies that operate below the state level, such as water conservation districts and school districts. Many of these terms will be used interchangeably in the chapters of this book despite technical differences.

The federal government is empowered either to prohibit or to require collective bargaining by its agencies with unions representing federal employees. In fact, the federal government does both. For example, the U.S. Army is prohibited from bargaining with military employees and required to bargain with civilian employees (at least those units in which a majority desire collective bargaining). The requirement to bargain collectively with civil servants was initially levied by executive order and is currently required by the Civil Service Reform Act.[2]

States, similarly, may prohibit or require collective bargaining with some or all state employees. A more detailed discussion of state and federal law is reserved for Chapter 2. The governing laws, orders, and regulations are collectively known as federal public sector law in the first instance and state public sector law in the second.

The federal government may also regulate collective bargaining with some employees in the private sector, specifically those private sector employees engaged in interstate commerce. Collective bargaining in the steel industry, the automobile industry, and the construction industry are all covered by the National Labor Relations Act—the principal statute in federal private sector law. The airline and railroad industries are governed by the Railway Labor Act and are therefore specifically exempted from the National Labor Relations Act.[3]

State governments may also regulate the activities of businesses that operate strictly within their borders (intrastate) and some businesses that operate across state lines (interstate) when the federal government has specifically delegated its jurisdiction to the states to do so (for ex-

Exhibit 1.1
Jurisdictional Sectors

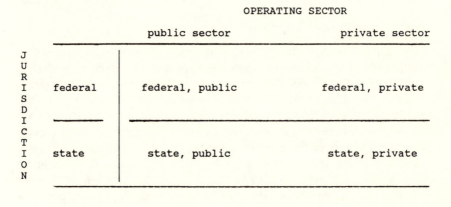

		OPERATING SECTOR	
		public sector	private sector
J U R I S D I C T I O N	federal	federal, public	federal, private
	state	state, public	state, private

ample, Section 14b of the National Labor Relations Act empowers states to prohibit union security arrangements). Such regulation is state private sector law. State regulation is far from homogeneous. Exhibit 1.1 is a tabular representation of the sectors formed by combinations of jurisdiction; Exhibit 1.1 shows that the public sector falls under the jurisdiction of both the federal and state sectors due to the division of the public sector into state and federal levels. The private sector is also under the jurisdiction of both federal and state government. This is attributable to the fact that the U.S. Constitution contains a clause that grants the authority to regulate interstate commerce to the federal government while states retain the right to regulate intrastate commerce.

The focus of this book is on collective bargaining that takes place in the public sector. For reasons to be explained later, emphasis is given to negotiating at the state, county, and local levels.

PHASES OF COLLECTIVE BARGAINING

There are two distinct phases of collective bargaining: contract negotiations and postcontract bargaining. Contract negotiations encompasses all the bargaining that takes place between the employer and employee representatives in order to arrive at a contract that specifies the terms and conditions of employment. Because negotiators cannot anticipate every issue that might arise during the life of a contract, the written contract will be incomplete in some respects. To address those new issues, the employer and employee representatives will continue bargaining during the life of the contract. One example may help to illustrate: A contract may specify that layoffs will be in the inverse order of seniority, thereby giving the most senior the most job security. Should layoffs actually become imminent, the question of implementing the layoff provision, if not addressed by the contract, may surface. The union might contend that seniority is a plant-wide ranking of workers; the company might contend that seniority is a skill-by-skill or a department-by-department ranking. Clearly, additional negotiations are in order.

The focus of this book is on contract negotiations that occur prior to the contract term, rather than contract administration that takes place during the life of the contract. The authors want to emphasize, however, that the principles and laws governing negotiations in the two phases are often virtually identical. The rights, obligations, and options facing the negotiating parties are normally the same regardless of the phase of negotiations.

IMPASSES IN NEGOTIATING

Delivering a contract is a lengthy, arduous, and exciting process; no two deliveries are the same. With some contracts, the difficult times are the first few months while the parties get used to being in negotiations. With some it is later on in the process when negotiations threaten to miscarry. With some the final stages of the process are most difficult. The process often culminates in a delivery only with the observation of outside parties. (Discussion of the art and science of "table bargaining" is presented later in the hope that impasse might be forestalled as a consequence.)

Sometimes the process is more difficult than usual. Outsiders may be called in to assist in the process. In negotiations, these outsiders may be mediators or fact finders. Their role is described in more detail in Chapters 5 through 7. For now it should suffice to describe their role as assisting the parties to deliver their own contract by helping them through the more difficult moments. The material presented later will offer, among other things, practical suggestions so that the parties to collective bargaining may make better use of the available dispute settlement mechanisms.

Sometimes the process stalls completely. More drastic action may be called for to save the contract. One solution is to call on someone skilled and empowered to cut through the difficulties and present the parties with a live contract, termed *interest arbitration*. The arbitrator is called upon to deliver the contract to the parties. Interest arbitration is one of the principal dispute settlement procedures presented in this book and is dealt with at some length in Chapters 7 through 9.

THE PUBLIC SECTOR AND PUBLIC GOODS

It is important to understand the nature of the public sector in order to understand the nature of public sector collective bargaining. The growth of the public sector has been rather steady over the recent history of the United States. One out of every five employed persons in the United States is employed by either federal, state, or local government.[4] Approximately thirty cents of every dollar earned is paid to government through taxes, and a little more than that is paid out by government as wages or payments for goods received. The message in this is: The public sector is a major source of jobs, income, services, and (to a lesser extent) products.

Our system is referred to as a mixed economic system. Even though a mixed system—implying elements of capitalism, socialism, and a command economy—the capitalist orientation generally dominates. This means the dollar is the ballot used to vote for most things. For example, you vote for gasoline instead of diesel fuel by paying your dollars at the unleaded pump. You vote for rye bread instead of whole wheat at your local grocery market. Employers may vote for MBAs instead of Ph.D.'s in the same manner. So why do we have the government getting into the picture?

Programs to redistribute income, "Robin Hood programs," account for a bit less than one-third of government expenditures. Food stamps, social security, and unemployment compensation are examples. Redistribution of income and wealth is not the primary reason for most government spending. The primary reason is to provide goods and services that would not be available in the desired quantities without government action. Those are generally called public goods. Public goods generally cannot be adequately supplied by the private sector since many of these goods generally cannot be restricted for the sole use of those who pay for the goods, hence the free rider concept. Examples of these types of public goods include public health services, national defense, and environmental protection. There are other public goods that can be provided by charging user fees, but the political realities of public opinion frequently bring such goods under the public sector. Police services and fire protection are common examples, though some jurisdictions have privately run fire departments (for example, Scottsdale, Arizona). The highway system is generally tax supported though toll roads demonstrate the feasibility of user fees in some cases. Medical care is provided by both private and public sector hospitals; witness both the Veterans Administration and many church-affiliated hospitals in this country.

Capitalism acting through the private sector does a remarkable job of making sure that store shelves are stocked with the things consumers want to buy. But public goods would not be produced in sufficient quantity in the absence of a government sector. Oft cited examples include city streets, immunizations, national defense, primary schools, mosquito abatement spraying, and police authority. While the private sector may supplement some of these activities, most would not be produced at a socially optimum level without the concerted action of citizenry through government. The government generally tries to get users or potential users of public services to pay their fair share of the cost without attempting to charge by the use. We pay over our lifetime to support public education since we were not charged tuition. We pay tax when we buy gasoline though we may do most of our driving on streets built by someone else's tax dollars. We all share in the cost of national defense as it is difficult to prorate costs by amount of benefit received.

Government generally supports those activities that are in the public welfare and would be underproduced by the private sector. The production of public goods avoids the excessive cost of collecting user fees—imagine every street a toll road! The production of public goods avoids the "free rider syndrome," where nonpayers can receive benefits they have not paid for. The production of public goods gains economies of scale—schools are less expensive than individual tutors.

Because many public goods are not produced in the private sector, public sector collective bargaining experiences some problems that are peculiar to it. Because many public goods are not sold at a profit to users, other problems arise that are peculiar to public sector bargaining. These will be addressed in some detail later.

The requirement to provide public goods requires government. To function properly, government requires employees with various skills. Employees require incomes to maintain themselves and their households. The government then exchanges compensation for services rendered and the taxpayers exchange their tax dollars for the services provided by government. This is a simple flow of goods and services, except that one portion of it involves government and its ability to tax. Of this the American public has always been suspicious because of a perceived lack of motivation in elected officials to control government properly and because of the general apathy of the voting public. Government and its role are therefore highly controversial topics and have been so throughout U.S. history.[5] These components can be thought of as roughly defining the economic environment of public sector collective bargaining. Take the power to tax, add the necessity of providing public goods, and combine with an economic and social history of suspicion of government: This provides the general framework for the economic environment.

Labor unions have not always enjoyed popularity in this country. In fact, today unions are again viewed with a great deal of suspicion from certain quarters much the same as they were in the 1920s, 1890s, and prior to the Civil War. In early U.S. history unions were regarded as criminal conspiracies per se because their objective was to raise wages and improve conditions for the working classes. This was regarded by many, including the courts, as theft because if more was spent on labor then someone would have to pay a higher price for goods and services and workers ought not be allowed to band together for the purposes of theft.[6] In the first of these court cases, shoemakers (private sector employees, not public) were found guilty of a criminal conspiracy because they formed a union to prevent the cutting of their wages. The lot and public image of labor unions improved only slightly over the next 125 years, so this country has a long history of little regard for collective bargaining or unions.[7]

It cannot be any wonder to anyone why labor relations and collective bargaining in the public sector are such controversial topics. The marriage of two extremely controversial and visible institutions could not help but provide for public debate and skepticism. What is perhaps more astounding is that public sector collective bargaining has been as widely adopted and successful as a system of employee-employer relations as it has over the past few decades.

For decades prior to the advent of the widespread unionization of the public sector, traditional organizing attempts frequently met with failure. This was especially true during the 1930s and 1940s, the boom period for industrial unions. Several explanations have been offered for this initial difficulty in organizing public employees. Public employment bestowed benefits not found in the private sector; "merit hiring, broad fringe benefits, almost absolute job security, and an assured income (not dependent on vagaries of weather, availability of risk capital, or the ebb and flow of fads and fashion)" more than offset any of the claimed benefits from unionization.[8] "In truth these were the tradeoffs for private-sector unionism."[9]

As these benefits to public employment declined during the postwar 1950s and the benefits and compensation associated with private sector employment overtook the public sector, public employees became more inclined to organize and collectively bargain. Public employees by the 1970s were far behind private sector employees in compensation and were beginning to find that job security and most of the other amenities associated with public employment had disappeared. Unions were perceived as the only way to prevent further erosion and possibly the reclamation of lost benefits.[10] Add to this difficulty the fact that public services are typically viewed as a nonmarket activity and the public views public services as a right rather than an option and public employees were left politically and economically in an unenviable position.

Public employees were left with relatively poor terms and conditions of employment and a public sufficiently disinterested to correct the problem through the electoral process. Public employees observed the successes of their private sector counterparts through organization and collective bargaining and embraced the private sector approach to correct their perceived problems—that approach being unions and collective bargaining.

This discussion illustrates why employee-employer relations—especially collective bargaining in the public sector—has been so controversial. This sociopolitical environment of public sector collective bargaining provided a significant obstacle to the evolution of mature collective bargaining in this arena. The sociopolitical aspects of the environment are those public opinions developed over the years concerning the role of government and organized labor. The deep-seated beliefs that public sector employees have had it too easy for too long and managers have been too altruistic are important facets of this environment. This discussion also clearly demonstrates that collective bargaining in the public sector is a much newer phenomenon than its counterpart in the private sector. The demands upon the public sector continue to expand. The ability of the public sector to meet those demands as we approach the twenty-first century may hinge on stable, mature collective bargaining relationships. Such is likely only if there are continued increases in the sophistication and competence of the parties to public sector collective bargaining and the neutrals who serve them in their impasse resolution endeavors. The increases in both the efficiency and fairness of government operation—which good labor-management relations has the potential of providing—can improve the lot of all Americans. This is, if not more idealistic, another very good reason to embark on this book.

SUMMARY AND CONCLUSIONS

This book is written for practitioners in the field of public sector labor relations. While the labor law chapter focuses on state collective bargaining laws, the bargaining topics covered and the discussions of the impasse procedures are equally applicable to the federal sector.

The necessity to provide public goods, together with the government's ability to tax, provides much of the economic environment of collective bargaining. The historic suspicion of both government and unions in this country add much to the sociopolitical environment of public sector collective bargaining.

The relatively late organization of unions in the public sector was due primarily to the relatively good working conditions, compensation, and job security of public sector jobs. As these characteristics of public employment eroded, so did public employee resistance to unionization and collective bargaining.

NOTES

1. There are several classic works on U.S. labor history; among the more important of these are John R. Commons, ed., *A Documentary History of American Industrial History*, 11 vols. (Glendale, Calif.: Arthur H. Clark Co., 1910–1911); John R. Commons et al., *History of Labor in the United States*, 2 vols. (New York: Macmillan, 1918); Selig Perlman, *A History of Trade Unionism in the United States* (New York: Macmillan, 1937); and Philip Taft, *Organized Labor in American History* (New York: Harper & Row, 1964).

2. See, for example, Daniel S. Hamermash, ed., *Labor in the Public and Nonprofit Sectors* (Princeton, N.J.: Princeton University Press, 1975); Murray Nesbit, *Labor Relations in the Federal Government Service* (Washington, D.C.: Bureau of National Affairs, 1976); Harry H. Wellinton and Ralph K. Winter, *The Unions and Cities* (Washington, D.C.: The Brookings Institution, 1971); and Sam Zagoria, ed., *Public Workers and Public Unions* (Englewood Cliffs, N.J.: Prentice-Hall, 1972).

3. See Benjamin Taylor and Fred Witney, *Labor Relations Law*, 4th ed. (Englewood Cliffs, N.J.: Prentice-Hall, 1983).

4. Alan E. Bent and T. Zane Reeves, *Collective Bargaining in the Public Sector* (Menlo Park, Calif.: Benjamin/Cummings, 1978), p. 3.

5. See Milton Friedman, *Capitalism & Freedom* (Chicago: University of Chicago Press, 1962) for a reasoned conservative and suspicious view of government.

6. *Commonwealth* v. *Pullis* (1806) reported in John R. Commons, *A Documentary History of American Industrial History*, vol. 3, pp. 59–232.

7. An interesting history of the American labor movement is to be found in Harold C. Livesay, *Samuel Gompers and Organized Labor in America* (Boston: Little, Brown, 1978).

8. Sam Zagoria, ed. *Public Workers and Public Unions* (Englewood Cliffs, N.J.: Prentice-Hall, 1972), p. 1.

9. Ibid.

10. Ibid.

2

Labor Law and Collective Bargaining in the Public Sector

The need for government in these respects arises because absolute freedom is impossible. However attractive anarchy may be as a philosophy, it is not feasible in a world of imperfect men. Men's freedoms can conflict, and when they do, one man's freedom must be limited to preserve another's—as a Supreme Court Justice once put it, "My freedom to move my fist must be limited by the proximity of your chin."

Milton Friedman, *Government in a Free Society*

Labor law has had a profound effect on collective bargaining in the public sector. This chapter describes the development and current character of the legal structure that governs public sector collective bargaining. The labor law governing collective bargaining for state and local governments varies from jurisdiction to jurisdiction in both its scope and requirements. This chapter will examine this body of law.

The ensuing discussions focus on what the law is and how it functions in the public sector collective bargaining environment. This is neither intended to serve as a legal case book nor as a law school text. Rather, it is a practitioners' guide to working within a legal environment.

The authors do make liberal use of examples from the statutory law of jurisdictions across the United States. Numerous comparisons are made with the federal and private sector. But these examples and comparisons are presented only to illustrate points that need to be clearly understood by the reader to practice the craft of labor negotiations.

A rudimentary understanding of the legal environment of collective bargaining is necessary to the understanding of contract negotiations.

That is, in turn, necessary to the understanding of impasse resolution procedures. It is therefore necessary that a basic grasp of what the labor law is and what its functions are be developed before proceeding to a discussion of collective bargaining.

AN INTRODUCTION TO LABOR LAW

Labor law is not necessarily a universally understood segment of law. The term *labor law* has been used to describe the body of statutory and case law that governs the total array of employer-employee relations. In the broadest sense this implies a diverse collection of law with a wide variety of focal points. Such a definition would include such items as the Civil Rights Act of 1964, the Fair Labor Standards Act, various industrial health and safety statutes, the Social Security Act, employment-at-will doctrine, pension laws, and statutes specifically concerning collective bargaining, employees' rights to unionization, and the relation between unions and employers. But this definition is too expansive for our instant needs.

For the present purposes a much narrower definition of labor law is desirable in that the purpose of the present examination is to provide a basis for understanding the legal environment of collective bargaining in state and local government. Labor law, as used in this book, refers only to the last item listed above. The focus is restricted to those statutes that govern the collective bargaining aspects of employer-employee relations in the public sector.

Before we proceed a few remarks are in order, however, concerning those laws that govern such things as wages, hours, discrimination, as well as health and safety. Rights bestowed on employees by statutory regulation or court decision are typically not the subject of collective bargaining. They may not be bargained away by the union, even in return for more valuable employer concessions. For example, the coverage of the Fair Labor Standards Act or an Affirmative Action program cannot be disturbed or displaced by a collective bargaining agreement returning those rights to management. In this manner the range of topics—often called the scope of bargaining—has been limited by legislative, executive, and judicial actions. The labor market is regulated to ensure specific rights for employees, which are, as a rule, in their best interest.

In the public sector, the regulatory environment also retains to management's discretion some rights that may not be bargained away. For example, some states have tenure or due process statutes for specific groups of workers, such as teachers. These statutes require management to keep full authority over evaluating and tenuring public school teachers. Unions are effectively barred by many of these statutes from attempting to wrestle those rights away from management or even substantively limiting those managerial perrogatives.

Whether one accepts the regulatory environment as appropriate or not, the various regulatory laws do affect the nature of public sector collective bargaining. The collective bargaining statutes themselves will frame the respective parties rights and responsibilities. Labor relations statutes typically list mandatory subjects of bargaining and prohibited subjects of bargaining. Many potentially bargainable subjects are not directly addressed in labor legislation. However, the authority or obligation to bargain such subjects may be established by other statutes or by the state's constitution. This additional body of law conclusively demonstrates that collective bargaining does not occur in a vacuum. To understand collective bargaining one must first understand its environment. Labor law is a major aspect of that environment.

THE FEDERAL AND STATE COLLECTIVE BARGAINING STATUTES

Law is a collection of rules that require and/or prohibit certain activities by both labor and management. The labor law of the United States was enacted by Congress in 1935 because of the perceived need to protect workers' rights to form labor unions. It was seen as socially desirable and morally correct that labor be allowed freely, without threat of reprisal, to not only present the workers' views to their employers but to have an effective input into the terms and conditions of employment. This law was seen, understandably, to be pro-union, especially when compared to the status quo of the previous decade.

Over the next dozen years, some prevailing union activities were seen to be inconsistent with the intended public policy of the original statute. That law, the National Labor Relation Act, was amended in 1947 by the pro-management Taft-Hartley Act. The modified federal labor law contained a provision that was extremely important in the history and evolution of the labor law governing state and local government employees in that it exempted public employers from the coverage of the Act.[1] This provision of the Act is Section 2.(2), which states in pertinent part: "The term employer includes any person acting as an agent of an employer, directly or indirectly, but shall not include . . . any State or political subdivision thereof. . . . "

The federal government does not protect the collective bargaining rights of state and municipal employees. In fact, there is considerable controversy whether the federal government could act to protect state and local employee bargaining rights even it choose to do so because of the lack of a delegated power to do so in the U.S. Constitution. States retain all powers not specifically delegated to the federal government within the four corners of the Constitution. Under this theory, unless the interstate commerce clause or some other Constitutional provision is read to grant the Congress legislative power over state and local collective bargaining, then the Congress may be powerless to enact such protective legislation. Section 2.(2) of the Taft-Hartley Act implicitedly recognizes the theory that the Congress may not pass statutes governing state and local employer-employee relations.

The result of this language contained in the Taft-Hartley Act is that there is no law of national scope that governs public sector collective bargaining. The adoption of collective bargaining statutes has been left to the individual jurisdictions. This poses some interesting questions. The public policy of the United States is that there shall not be uniform and consistent treatment of public employers and their employees with regard to collective bargaining. It would appear that some degree of consistency of treatment of all U.S. citizens would be a desirable public policy. In certain states employees have a right to form and join labor organizations, but no right to bargain collectively. In some other states, public employees have the right both to bargain collectively and to strike if a labor agreement is not forthcoming. Such differences have profound implications for public employees, for managers of public agencies, and for taxpayers and the general public. With a highly mobile society and the close proximity of various jurisdictions, this issue has taken on some importance.

It is also interesting to note that there is a disparity between the public and the private sector. Employees in the private sector can expect to have essentially the same collective bargaining rights any place they may choose to work in the United States. This is certainly not true of public employees. Public employees sometimes enjoy collective bargaining rights equivalent to those workers in the private sector, but for the most part they do not. Persons who work in the public sector will find that their rights will vary substantially from one state to another.

There is something to be said for the manner in which Congress decided to handle the public sector with respect to the Taft-Hartley Act. Congress intended that there should be local determination concerning public sector collective bargaining laws. Each state was set free to determine what its own public policy should be with respect to the unionization of and bargaining with public employees. This self-determination and local governance is valued highly by many persons in this country and is not to be taken lightly, even though it certainly creates massive inconsistencies in public employee rights.

There is another side to this self-determination issue. It centers on the relationship of government and worker. Government determines the basic rules that it must abide by in dealing with its employees. This is seen by pro-bargaining advocates as being akin to allowing the offensive team in a football game to determine the rules by which it and the defense must abide. Some claim that this is an inherently unfair system, yet alternatives are hard to come by. In individual states, the system is most often judged by its results. "Good" laws indicate a good system; "bad" laws indicate a bad system—not a very objective method of evaluating. Others emphasize that unfairness is not inherent since the employees work for the executive branch and the rule makers are the legislative branch. This theory is based on the idea that the separation of powers is also effective on the state level.

The lack of consistency in public sector labor law across the United States is in large measure attributable to the public sector's exclusion from Taft-Hartley coverage. This exclusion says much about the perceived role of government and public policy toward public sector negotiations.[2] These issues are controversial and worthy of thought. But the real purpose of this chapter is not to debate the merits of the law but to examine the law; specifically, to examine the law as it pertains to and shapes public sector collective bargaining in this country.

PUBLIC SECTOR STATUTES IN GENERAL

Public sector statutes differ substantially in the types of organizational and bargaining rights bestowed on public employees and their unions. Some states have enacted statutes that are close approximations to the Taft-Hartley Act while others have prohibited public employers from negotiating or entering into collective bargaining agreements with labor organizations.[3] For example, there are three states that prohibit school boards from entering into collective bargaining contracts or labor agreements with teacher representational groups.[4] There are presently thirty-five states that have some form of statute that grants some either organizational and/or bargaining rights to various groups of public employees. These statutes differ substantially in the employee groups they cover and often specify different rights for different groups of employees.[5] Exhibit 2.1 presents information concerning the various state statutes and some of the major provisions contained in those laws. The wide variation in the extent and nature of the coverage of these statutes is striking. The most widely accepted collective bargaining is for public employees in public education, while only eighteen states have omnibus collective bargaining statutes that permit and/or protect collective bargaining rights for all public employees. Exhibit 2.1 presents information on which states protect rights for only state or professional employees and which states protect all public employee bargaining rights. The exhibit further presents data concerning strike rights and the specification of impasse procedures in the law.

Exhibit 2.1 shows the states that protect, by statutory law, the collec-

Exhibit 2.1
Collective Bargaining Laws for Public Employees

State	State Employees	Omnibus	Professional Employees	Strike Protected	Binding Arbitration
Alabama	No	No	No	No	No
Alaska	Yes	No	Yes	No	No
Arizona	No	No	Meet & Confer	No	No
Arkansas	No	No	No	No	No
California	Yes	No	Yes	No	Yes
Colorado	No	No	No	No	No
Connecticut	Yes	No	Yes	No	Yes
Delaware	Yes	No	Yes	No	No
Florida	No	Yes	Yes	No	No
Georgia	No	No	No	No	No
Hawaii	Yes	Yes	Yes	Yes	Yes
Idaho	Yes	No	Yes	No	No
Illinois	Yes	No	Yes	Limited	Yes
Indiana	No	No	Yes	No	No
Iowa	No	Yes	No	No	Yes
Kansas	Yes	No	Yes	No	No
Kentucky	No	No	No	No	No
Louisiana	No	No	No	No	No
Maine	No	Yes	Yes	No	Limited
Maryland	Yes	No	Yes	No	No
Massachusetts	No	Yes	Yes	No	Yes
Michigan	No	Yes	Yes	Limited	Yes
Minnesota	No	Yes	Yes	Limited	Yes
Mississippi	No	No	No	No	No

Exhibit 2.1 (continued)

Missouri	No	Yes	Meet & Confer	No	No
Montana	No	Yes	Yes	Yes	Yes
Nebraska	Yes	No	Yes	No	Yes
Nevada	Yes	No	Yes	No	Yes
New Hampshire	No	Yes	Yes	No	No
New Jersey	No	Yes	Yes	No	Yes
New Mexico	No	Yes	Yes	No	No
New York	No	Yes	Yes	No	Yes
N. Carolina	No	No	No	No	No
N. Dakota	Yes	No	Yes	No	No
Ohio	No	Yes	Yes	Yes	Yes
Oklahoma	Yes	No	Yes	No	No
Oregon	No	Yes	Yes	Yes	Yes
Pennsylvania	No	Yes	Yes	Limited	Yes
Rhode Island	Yes	No	Yes	Limited	Yes
S. Carolina	No	No	No	No	No
S. Dakota	No	Yes	Yes	No	No
Tennessee	Yes	No	Yes	No	No
Texas	No	No	Meet & Confer	No	No
Utah	No	No	No	No	No
Vermont	Yes	No	Yes	No	No
Virginia	No	No	No	No	No
Washington	Yes	No	Yes	No	Yes
West Virginia	No	No	Yes	No	No
Wisconsin	No	Yes	Yes	No	Yes
Wyoming	No	No	No	No	No
TOTAL	15	18	35	9	22

tive bargaining rights of state and school district employees and which
states have omnibus laws (covering all state and local employees).

The right to bargain in other states has come as a result of executive
branch interpretations. Some jurisdictions voluntarily bargained collectively with public employee unions, then an affected party attempted
or succeeded in bringing suit against the state (or local) agency for violation of state law. In one such action, the West Virginia attorney
general's opinion was that state employees could be allowed to bargain
collectively without contravening state law. Such attorney general opinions may gain the weight of law.

The right to bargain in other states has come as a result of judicial
interpretation. Judges in similar cases have sometimes ruled that bargaining with public employees is not in contravention of state law. Unless overruled by a higher court or reversed by subsequent legislation,
judicial interpretations too may gain the weight of law. The most common way for public employees to gain bargaining rights, however, has
been legislative action.

There are several states which have "meet and confer" (MC) legislation
rather than collective bargaining legislation. This distinction is important. Under a collective bargaining law the parties must meet and confer
with the purpose of negotiating a contract. The contract normally in-
corporates those issues on which agreement is reached. A collective
bargaining statute will also generally contain provisions requiring good
faith bargaining, prohibiting unfair labor practices, and often will specify
impasse procedures.

None of these items are typically included in meet and confer laws.
MC laws sometimes contain no provision for an exclusive bargaining
representative. MC laws typically require an employer to inform the
employees (or their representative) of issues relevant to their employment status and then allow the employees an opportunity to comment
on the proposed actions. There is no requirement or provision for bargaining; there is no requirement even that employers give serious consideration to the desires of the employees. These statutes therefore do
not typically provide for an effective input into the range of items generally considered to be terms and conditions of employment as was the
congressional intent in enacting the National Labor Relations Act.

Meet and confer statutes and collective bargaining statutes are very
different laws indeed. It is not inappropriate to view meet and confer
as unilateral decision making by the employer with an opportunity for
employees or their representatives to express their opinions. In contrast,
collective bargaining is a bilateral decision-making process; the employer
and the employees' union together determine wages, hours, and working conditions. As can be readily seen from examination of Exhibit 2.1
collective bargaining has been adopted in most jurisdictions. Only a

relatively few states have opted for meet and confer, and those normally apply only to a select class of public employees.

There are nine states that protect public employee rights to strike in various forms and degrees. There are other states that appear to forbid strikes but levy such minor penalties for strikers that the effect is to condone strike activity (for example, New York).[6] There are twenty-two states that specify that final and binding arbitration is the last step in the impasse procedures. There are additional states that permit the parties to negotiate final and binding arbitration as the last step of the impasse resolution procedure. Of the twenty-two states identified as having final and binding arbitration, some restrict the use of this step to specific issues (for example, Maine and Rhode Island for certain employees for wage issues). Exhibit 2.1 clearly shows that there is a wide variation in the nature of the laws governing collective bargaining for state and local government employees.

ELECTION POLICIES

The responsibility for administering labor legislation is usually levied on agency specifically created to fill that role. Federal labor law is administered principally by the National Labor Relations Board. State agencies similarly created are called PERBs—Public Employment Relations Boards—in this book, though, some state agencies have different names. Thirty-one states presently have such administrative law agencies.[7]

PERBs are normally required to resolve two major issues—unit determination and unit representation—before negotiations can take place. A few remarks on each is in order before moving on to a discussion of the substance and conduct of collective bargaining.

The first function of the PERB is unit determination, that is, determining which employee positions properly belong in the bargaining unit. Employees filling those positions will be represented by a union if the union is later "voted in." A bargaining unit is the group of employees determined according to criteria established in the governing statute. Typical criteria include: (1) similarity of interests, skills, and responsibilities; (2) desires of employees and management; and (3) labor organization and/or bargaining histories. Other criteria often exclude managerial, supervisory, and confidential employees from membership in the bargaining unit because union membership can cause a conflict of interest with performance of assigned employee duties. Some state statutes may include other factors that must be considered but those cited are consistent with the requirements found in Taft-Hartley.

This is an important step because bargaining is done for all in the unit. It might not work well to have a unit composed of both skilled craftsmen and unskilled labor; a unit composed of a majority of one category might place the interests of the majority far ahead of the minority. The generally stated ideal is enough units that all are fairly represented but not so many that the employer's energies are dissipated in bargaining instead of producing public goods and services.

Statutes often prescribe the procedures the PERB is to use in posting a proposed unit determination, in accepting appeals to the proposal, and in finalizing the determination. Once the unit determination is complete, the PERB must perform its second function: representative determination. The PERB determines which organization, if any, should be recognized as the exclusive representative of the bargaining unit members. Thirty-three states provide for employees' rights to exclusive bargaining representatives.[8]

Exclusive bargaining representation is performed by a single union or association that has the sole right and responsibility to represent all employees within the bargaining unit it was certified to represent. The right of representation is typically defined in the bargaining statute. An example of statutory language concerning public employees' rights and exclusive representation from a state statute may prove illustrative. The Minnesota Public Employment Relations Act, for example, states in pertinent part:

Section 179A.06 (2) Public employees have the right to form and join labor or employee organizations, and have the right not to form and join such organizations. Public employees in an appropriate bargaining unit have the right by secret ballot to designate an exclusive representative to negotiate grievances procedures and the terms and conditions of employment with their employer. . . .[9]

For the most part, the policies and procedures developed by the states concerning the certification of exclusive bargaining representatives is similar in most respects to the policies and procedures developed by the National Labor Relations Board (NLRB) for application to the private sector under the Taft-Hartley Act. There are, of course, minor deviations due to specific statutory law in a few of the states. These deviations are not critical to the present discussion. The reader is referred to Bureau of National Affairs' *Labor Relations Reference Manual, State Labor Law* for detailed information and comparisons concerning this topic.[10]

The second function of the PERB is representative determination, that is, to determine which (if any) union is going to represent members of the bargaining unit. The responsibilities of the PERB in this respect are normally enumerated in the bargaining statute. They generally involve three elements. First, as determination is usually made following a vote, the PERB must establish which organizations are candidates for the role of exclusive representative. Statutes frequently specify that "No Union" must be one candidate. Second, the PERB determines who the eligible voters are. Normally all bargaining unit members are the voters, but there may be others. Third, the PERB announces, monitors, and certifies the result of the election, then publishes the result and the effective date of union representation. This function of the PERB is important. It gives reality to the desires of the employees.

Rights and responsibilties of the elected exclusive representative typically include: (1) performing contract negotiations, (2) presenting grievances to management, and (3) fairly representing all unit members. There is some variation on the issues of collective bargaining. Some statutes will provide laundry lists of issues and others will define the issues of collective bargaining as the terms and conditions of employment (this issue will be discussed further in the following sections of this chapter).

EMPLOYEE RIGHTS

Most state collective bargaining statutes will specify certain rights public employees and their unions are granted by the law. This follows the lead set in the federal law for private sector employees under Section 7 of the Taft-Hartley Act. The rights enumerated in these state statutes are probably the most similar sections of all the provisions of the various state collective bargaining statutes. As will be discussed in the following section, the violation of these public employee rights by either the employer or union is an unfair labor practice and may be enjoined and any employee unfairly fired will be ordered reinstated and may be made whole for lost pay and benefits due to the wrongful discharge. These rights are the reason most collective bargaining statutes were enacted—to assure public employees these rights and to provide a mechanism by which these rights could be exercised.

Another illustrative example of statutory language from a specific state may prove useful. The Massachusetts public employee bargaining law contains a typical employees' rights section which states:

Sec. 2. [Right to organize and bargain]—Employees shall have the right of self-organization and the right to form, join, or assist any employee organization for the purpose of bargaining collectively through representatives of their own choosing on questions of wages, hours, and other terms and conditions òf employment, and to engage in lawful, concerted activities for the purpose of collective bargaining or other mutual aid or protection, free from interference, restraint, or coercion. An employee shall have the right to refrain from any or all such activities, except to the extent of making such payment of service fees to an exclusive representative as provided in Sec. 12.[11]

The rights found in this section are individual rights of public employees. Most fundamental among these rights is that of the freedom to join, form, or assist a labor organization or to refrain from such activities. This right, often called concerted activity or self-help, is the keystone to effective labor unionization and collective bargaining. If guarantees of freedom from interference, restraint, or coercion for individual employees were not granted then the remaining provisions would be meaningless.

UNFAIR LABOR PRACTICES

Most state statutes provide for the prohibition and remedy of certain employer and union practices that have been deemed to be destructive of employee or union rights or the collective bargaining process itself and therefore against the public policy of the state. These practices are generally action committed by either the labor organization or management that prevent collective bargaining from functioning or that deny the employees, management, or the union rights guaranteed by the statute.

Prohibited practices—usually called unfair labor practices or ULPs—generally follow the proscriptions contained in the Taft-Hartley Act.[12] There are some state statutes, however, that are notably different. Kansas, for example, makes the interference in any employee organization by a public employer a prohibited practice, even in cases where there is no certified bargaining representative.[13] New York's Taylor Act contains the following unfair labor practice language:

Sec. 209-a. Improper employer practice; improper employee organization practices; application.—1. Improper employer practices. It shall be an improper practice for a public employer or its agents deliberately (a) to interfere with, restrain or coerce public employees in the exercise of their rights guaranteed in section two hundred two for the purpose of depriving them of such rights; (b) to dominate or interfere with the formation or administration of any employee organization for the purpose of depriving them of such rights; (c) to discriminate against any employee for the purpose of encouraging or discouraging membership in, or participation in the activities of, any employee organization; (d) to refuse to negotiate in good faith with the duly recognized or certified representatives of its public employees; or (e) to refuse to continue all the terms of an expired agreement until a new agreement is negotiated, unless the employee organization which is a party to such agreement has, during such negotiations or prior to such resolution of such negotiations, engaged in conduct violative of subdivision one of section two hundred ten of this article [prohibition of strikes].

2. Improper employee organization practices. It shall be an improper practice

for an employee organization or its agents deliberately (a) to interfere with, restrain or coerce public employees in the exercise of the rights granted in section two hundred two, or to cause, or attempt to cause, a public employer to do so; or (b) to refuse to negotiate collectively in good faith with a public employer, provided it is the duly recognized or certified representative of the employees of such employer.

3. Application. In applying this section, fundamental distinctions between private and public employment shall be recognized, and no body of federal or state law applicable wholly or in part to private employment, shall be regarded as binding or controlling precedent.[14]

New York's Taylor Act is somewhat similar, in the unfair labor practices specified, to the Taft-Hartley Act. Paragraph 3 is of some note, this language specifically states that the precedents established under statutes governing private sector labor relations shall not be binding precedents under the Taylor Act. As with the NLRB, the New York Public Employment Relations Board has been specifically limited in the remedies it may impose to correct unfair labor practices.[15] Cease and desist orders and the reinstatement of wrongfully discharged employees (with or without back pay and benefits) is generally all that a PERB may impose as a remedy for an unfair labor practice.

Those activities most detrimental to the formation of labor organizations and the proper operation of negotiations are prohibited by the unfair labor practice provisions of the various state laws. The enforcement of these provisions is only made possible by the creation of an administrative law agency, a PERB. A labor law without ULP provisions or a PERB would be like a street without speed limit or police. The unfair labor practice provisions and their enforcement procedures are what makes the collective bargaining statute work.

SCOPE OF BARGAINING

Scope of bargaining is defined as the range of issues that must be or may be negotiated by the parties. Most statutes divide potential subjects of bargaining into three categories: mandatory, permissive, and prohibited subjects.[16] The most common mandatory subject is wages, although a notable exception is mentioned later. The action that triggers the obligation to bargain is a request by either negotiating party: the employer or employee representative. There are, however, statutes that require that such requests must be made by a specific date or the present contract will continue in force unless reopened by mutual agreement of the parties. Once the request is made, the law mandates the other party to bargain in good faith on that subject.

The second category of potential bargaining subjects is permissive subjects. A common permissive subject is dues checkoff—a contract provision requiring the employer to withhold union dues from employee paychecks, then to pay the withholding to a union account. While different jurisdictions may differ on "how hard" a negotiator may push the request to negotiate a permissive subject, the statutes are unanimous in forbidding "bargaining to an impasse" over permissive subjects. That is, neither bargaining party may refuse to sign a contract that is acceptable in all respects save a dispute over a permissive subject. Impasse resolution is the major substance of Part II of this book.

The third category of potential bargaining issues is prohibited subjects. It is an unfair labor practice to insist on negotiation of a prohibited subject. Subjects may be prohibited by the bargaining statute or another state statute may require that the specific issue should be determined in another forum. Prohibited subjects may include managers' salaries, a requirement of union membership prior to acceptance of employment applications, or promotion based on seniority. This list varies significantly from state to state.

Many states follow a pattern for determining the scope of bargaining that very closely parallels that contained in the Taft-Hartley Act. The California Public Employment Relations Act is a good example. In its pertinent section it states:

Sec. 3504. The scope of representation shall include all matters relating to employment conditions and employer-employee relations, including but not limited to, wages, hours, and other terms and conditions of employment, except, however, that the scope of bargaining shall not include consideration of the merits, necessity, or organization of any service or activity provided by law or executive order.[17]

This California statute is essentially the same as Section 8(d) of the Taft-Hartley Act except that those items required to be fixed under the authority of other statutes or executive orders are not subject to collective bargaining. Various state constitutions or statutes require certain decisions to be retained by the legislative or executive branches of government. This California language is illustrative of the problems encountered in determining the scope of collective bargaining in the public sector: Scope is dependent on other statutes in addition to the collective bargaining legislation. There are, however, other states that have specified laundry lists of issues subject to collective bargaining (for example, Kansas). There are also states that do not differentiate between mandatory or voluntary issues of collective bargaining.

OTHER LEGAL PROVISIONS

There are numerous other provisions that are often contained in collective bargaining statutes. Impasse resolution procedures, for example, are often specified in state collective bargaining laws. These impasse resolution procedures are statutory mechanisms for resolving disputes over the negotiation of a contract. These provisions will be discussed in detail beginning with Chapter 5 of this book and will not be given further attention here except to note that the PERB may be charged with the authority and obligation to administer some or all of the impasse procedures.

Most state collective bargaining laws offer sections defining terms for purposes of the statute. These definitional sections often contain some important substantive provisions. The manner in which a bargaining unit is to be determined and who is eligible for inclusion in such bargaining units are generally found in these definitions. The bargaining unit, as was discussed above, is the group of employees who may vote in a certification election. If the union is certified as exclusive bargaining representative, it is these eligible voters the union must then represent. The nature of this representation and the standards used to make these determinations are also typically included in these definitional sections of state bargaining statutes.

It is not uncommon for a state collective bargaining statute to differentiate between various classes of employees (for example, Ohio differentiates between public safety and other employees; California differentiates between the University of California and California State University in its Higher Education Bargaining Law). Many states (including California, Illinois, and Michigan) differentiate between classes of employees by providing separate bargaining statutes for separate classes of employers and employees. These statutory differentiations often allow certain employees the use of different impasse procedures, may limit or authorize strikes, or even specify that certain issues of bargaining are not protected for certain employees.

Statutory differentiations are due to recognized or perceived inherent differences in various occupations and the role of those occupations in providing public services. Such differences in occupations typically result in differences in bargaining rights as can easily be seen from an examination of Exhibit 2.1. For a counterexample, police, firefighters, sanitation workers, and public school teachers are covered by the same law in Ohio; the Ohio situation is not uncommon. The message is that state treatment of public employee collective bargaining varies tremendously in the details. Nevertheless, there is a great similarity in the essentials, and that provides the core of this book.

Union security arrangements are often limited by state collective bargaining laws. Nevada, for example, provides for collective bargaining rights for public employees but prohibits union security arrangements. The most common union security arrangements are union shop and/or agency shop. Union shop provisions require employees to join the union after a specified period of employment. In lieu of mandating union membership, agency shop provisions require the unit employee to tender a service fee equal to the dues and fees charged a union member. These provisions are negotiated between the union and the employer and are designed to give the union some degree of financial security.

In some cases, the state public employment collective bargaining law will reference another statute, commonly called a right-to-work law, that prohibits such union security arrangements for all bargaining relations in the state regardless of whether in the private or public sector. Approximately twenty-two states prohibit or limit union security arrangements for public employee unions.[18] Most of these states are southern and/or agrarian. Virtually none of the northern and/or industrial states have such prohibitions of union security arrangements.

THE EFFECT OF THE LEGAL ENVIRONMENT ON COLLECTIVE BARGAINING

As should now be obvious to even the most casual reader there are substantial constraints placed on the parties as well as several rights guaranteed to the respective parties by the various state labor laws. In the extreme, those states that prohibit public employee collective bargaining impose upon public employees a system of labor-management relations that is inconsistent with the treatment of the majority of public employees in the United States and most of the employees in the private sector, that is, unilateral determination of the terms and conditions of employment by management or the legislative branch of government.

Thirty-five states have chosen various forms of bilateral determination of various issues, including the terms and conditions of employment at least in part if not in total. In the thirty-five states with bargaining statutes most provide the bare necessities for an orderly collective bargaining system. Only four of these thirty-five states do not have a Public Employment Relations Board charged with responsibilities of administering the state law.[19]

This leaves approximately twelve states that have not taken legislative action on the subject of public sector collective bargaining. A few of these states permit collective bargaining either in a de facto manner or because of an attorney general's opinion or court case. In these twelve states there are no unfair labor practices, administrative law agencies, or definitions of the scope of bargaining that can serve as a guide to assure peaceful and mutually acceptable collective bargaining. These states have adopted a public policy that assumes that the parties will respect each other's rights and the institution of bargaining or, worse, assume that without statutory protections unions will be ineffective.

Industrial warfare—strikes by unions and lockouts by employers—is sometimes allowed and sometimes prohibited. If industrial warfare is permitted both parties are free to test their relative bargaining power and resolve. In those states where the strike and lockout are prohibited to the parties, substitute impasse resolution procedures are generally provided. Voluntary and mandatory impasse procedures have the potential of influencing the behavior of negotiators and have the general effect of insulating the public from the inconveniences associated with a work stoppage.

The issues that must be and may be negotiated are typically defined in detail in the statute. The issues included within the scope of bargaining will help to shape the final product as well as the course of negotiations. In jurisdictions with limited bargaining scopes, there are fewer substantive issues that may be negotiated to impasse.

The rights guaranteed public employees within these statutes may influence the scope of bargaining as well as its conduct. A law providing specific rights, such as due process if discharged, mitigates the need to negotiate due process provisions into the contract. This reduces the likely scope of bargaining and the probability of impasse. If a statute fails to provide assurances from failures to bargain in good faith, then there is an obvious and predictable effect on the conduct of negotiations. Employee rights guaranteed under the state statutes, where they exist, are nearly uniform and are (for the most part) consistent with those rights guaranteed private sector employees.

The significant differences between states and between public and private employees occur with respect to the scope of mandatory subjects, the right to strike, and the presence of mandatory impasse resolution procedures in the absence of a right to strike. The nature of the collective bargaining will vary, state by state, with the requirements of law.[20] It is therefore important that the reader bear in mind the presence of substantial differences in the legal environments of the various states.

SUMMARY AND CONCLUSIONS

The public sector—federal, state, and local government—is not governed by the Taft-Hartley Act. The legal environment for public sector employees and employers is the enabling labor legislation in combination with other controlling legislation. Several states (thirty-five) have enacted some form of labor law supportive of public sector collective bargaining. A few states (three) have prohibited public employee collective bargaining.

There is wide variation in the details of the various public sector collective bargaining laws. Some jurisdictions have enacted omnibus statutes that protect the bargaining rights of all employees. Professional teaching employees have the widest coverage of collective bargaining statutes. The majority of states prohibit strikes by public employees and almost half of the states provide for the final and binding arbitration of contract disputes. Some states such as Ohio and Illinois allow strikes under certain circumstances but also provide for procedures to resolve contract disputes.

The majority of state collective bargaining laws guarantee public employees the right to form, join, and assist labor organizations for the purpose of collective bargaining. Most of these statutes provide for rights that are very similar to those rights granted private sector employees under the Taft-Hartley Act and are fairly consistent from jurisdiction to jurisdiction. The violation of these public employee rights are generally proscribed as unfair labor practices.

Most state statutes provide for an administrative law agency whose function it is to determine appropriate bargaining units, conduct certification elections, and administer the unfair labor practice provisions of the law. Most state statutes provide for certain employer and union activities to be against the public policy and allow the administrative law agency (for example, PERB) to remedy the prohibited practice through injunctions or reinstatment orders for wrongfully discharged employees. The unfair labor practice provisions and election policies and procedures under most state statutes are relatively uniform across jurisdictions and are generally similar to those found in the Taft-Hartley Act, but there are notable exceptions (for example, New York and Kansas), but even these exceptions do not deviate far from the Taft-Hartley example.

The scope of collective bargaining refers to those issues subject to collective bargaining. Many state statutes provide that the terms and conditions of employment are mandatory issues of bargaining. Some state statutes provide laundry lists of items that are mandatorily negotiable and some even provide for definitions of voluntary issues of bargaining. The various states are not consistent in their handling of the scope of bargaining and wide variations can be found.

As should be obvious with the amount of variation present in the various state statutes the legal environment may differ significantly from state to state. It is likely that the conduct of negotiations and their results will be affected by these differing legal environments. This should be expected to result in different bargaining relations between states and provide for a lack of consistency in the collective bargaining observed across state and local government.

NOTES

1. Labor Management Relations Act of 1947, cited as National Labor Relations Act, as amended (commonly called Taft-Hartley Act after its authors) 61 Stat. 136.

2. For further discussion see Charles O. Gregory and Harold A. Katz, *Labor and the Law*, 3d ed. (New York: Norton, 1979), pp. 599–606.

3. Benjamin J. Taylor and Fred Witney, *Labor Relations Law*, 4th ed. (Englewood Cliffs, N.J.: Prentice-Hall, 1983), p. 647.

4. These states are Texas, North Carolina, and Virginia.

5. Indiana, for example, has a statute protecting collective bargaining rights for teachers but prohibits collective bargaining for state employees.

6. This topic will be discussed in greater detail in Chapter 11.

7. Bureau of National Affairs, Labor Relations Reference Manual, State Labor Laws.

8. Ibid.

9. Chapter 179A of Minnesota Statutes, as amended, effective May 21, 1985.

10. The manual is usually available in the reference section of a major university's labor relations, industrial relations, or business school library. It is also available on a subscription basis directly from BNA.

11. Chapter 150E, Section 2, Massachusetts Laws 1986.

12. Bureau of National Affairs, Labor Relations Reference Manual, State Labor Laws.

13. Kansas Statutes Annotated 75–4333 (b) (1), Kansas Public Employer-Employee Relations Act.

14. Sections 200 to 214 of the Civil Service Law of New York, commonly known as the Taylor Act, last amended June 30, 1985.

15. *Board of Supervisors* v. *PERB*, NY Ct App (1975), 89 LRRM 2713.

16. *NLRB* v. *Wooster Division of Borg-Warner Corporation*, 356 U.S. 342 (1958).

17. Sections 3500 through 3510 of the California Government Code, last amended October 16, 1981.

18. Bureau of National Affairs, Labor Relations Reference Manual, State Labor Laws.

19. Ibid.

20. See Thomas A. Kochan, *Collective Bargaining and Industrial Relations* (Homewood, Ill.: Richard D. Irwin, 1980), Chapter 4, for further discussion.

3

Contract Negotiations and the Birth of Impasses

> In discourse thou must attend to what is said, and in every movement thou must observe what is doing. And in the one thou shouldst see immediately to what end it refers, but in the other watch carefully what is the thing signified.
>
> The Meditations of Marcus Aurelius

This chapter will introduce the concept of collective bargaining, examine various theories of negotiations, examine insights these theories provide for the practicing negotiator, and explain how impasses can result. While some theoretical development is necessary, this chapter will focus on the practical aspects of negotiations in the public sector.

Collective bargaining is best viewed as three overlapping activities: organization, contract negotiations, and contract administration. This division of activities into distinct categories is somewhat artificial since there is frequently significant overlap, but the distinction is, however, useful for our present purposes.

Union organizational activities are primarily the organization and formation of the union local, certification of the labor organization as exclusive representative, and the establishment of the bargaining relation. Management organizational activities center on establishing an industrial relations section. For large organizations, industrial relations is often a subsidiary function of the personnel branch. For smaller organizations, it often involves identification of a management team whose primary duties lie outside labor relations.

Contract negotiations are concerned with the creation of an agreement outlining the rights and responsibilities of the respective parties. Negotiations are the more visible and dramatic portion of the collective bargaining institution. Negotiations include the preparation for and the actual face-to-face table bargaining.

Contract administration is the exercise and enforcement of the negotiated rights and responsibilities. Besides the day-to-day decision making of management, the grievance procedure is generally the focal point of contract administration activities. The overlap between contract negotiation and administration is easily identified since a well-written contract will specify procedures to be followed by each of the parties in that exercise.

With a reminder that organizing, negotiating, and administering are overlapping activities, it is now appropriate to begin the examination of collective bargaining in the public sector. This book has as its central focus one aspect of collective bargaining: contract negotiations. Contract negotiations is the birthplace of impasses and must be understood before impasse resolution can be fully examined and understood. This is not to minimize organizational and contract administration activities but these latter topics are adequately treated elsewhere (see note 1 in Chapter 1) and space in the present work is limited.

COLLECTIVE BARGAINING DEFINED

Collective bargaining is a system of labor-management relations under which labor and management mutually determine the terms and conditions of employment (or those issues specified by statute as the proper scope of bargaining).[1] Mutual determination means, in this sense, the representatives of employees (not necessarily the employees themselves) and the representatives of the employer (generally not the taxpayers or governing body themselves) meet to decide what the terms and conditions of employment shall be. Before continuing the discussion of collective bargaining, two alternative labor-management systems are described: codetermination and meet and confer.

In West Germany and a few other industrial nations a system of codetermination is used. Under a codetermination system, there is no institutionalized bargaining relation between an exclusive representative of labor and management as such. Decision making for the organization is placed in the hands of a team composed of management, union, and government officials with roughly equal representation. The system of codetermination erodes private property rights and sovereignty. It is ideologically inconsistent with the normal conduct of affairs in both the public and the private sectors in this country.

The meet and confer system of labor relations has gained some popularity in this country, particularly in the public sector. There are no mandatory issues of bargaining. There is no requirement to bargain a contract. Management must keep the labor organization informed of various problems as they arise. Management must discuss actions it is planning to take. Also, management must allow the union an opportunity to comment. Indiana, for example, uses the meet and confer system with state employees. The discussion now returns to the traditional model of collective bargaining observed in the United States.

The "wages, hours, terms, and conditions" of employment is one common definition of "scope" of mandatory bargaining. The scope of bargaining may be thought of as that collection of issues that are the legal subjects of negotiations. The use of the language "terms and conditions of employment" is taken from the Taft-Hartley Act. Other jurisdictions, as well, have adopted this definition of the scope of bargaining.[2] As noted in Chapter 2, some states have opted to forgo such a general statement and have instead provided "laundry lists" of bargainable issues. Some issues that are not terms and conditions of employment may be added to the list of negotiable items, while many issues that are terms and conditions of employment may be excluded from bargaining; the latter being the most common.

Bargaining "in good faith" is a general requirement of all federal and most state statutes. Bargaining in good faith typically means that the parties have a mutual obligation to meet at reasonable times and reasonable places for the purpose of negotiating an agreement concerning those issues that are proper subjects of negotiations. This definition of bargaining in good faith has variants across jurisidictions but means that more is required than simply getting together with the other side. It does not mean that either or both sides must make concessions. It does not mean that the parties must draft a contract when no agreement can be reached. It does mean that an earnest effort must be made by both parties to reach a mutually agreeable settlement on those issues on the bargaining table. Unfortunately, good faith and bad faith are not directly observable. Fortunately, they can sometimes be inferred from behavior. While it is a tough standard to enforce, it is an easy standard for the parties to live up to.

Having explained the terms *collective bargaining, scope of bargaining,* and *bargaining in good faith,* attention can now be turned to the various theories of negotiations. Following the theories, we move to the practice of negotiating.

A PREFACE TO TWO THEORIES OF NEGOTIATIONS

Theories (or models of behavior) are no better than their ability to explain events in the real world. Two particular theories were selected because they lend the greatest insight into the internal workings of collective bargaining and are readily accessible to the practitioners for

whom this book was written. One is from the class of deductive bargaining models; one from the inductive class. The deductive model chosen was developed by Sir John R. Hicks; it is commonly called the
"resistance-concession model."[3] The inductive model chosen is based
on the work of Richard E. Walton and Robert B. McKersie; it is called
the "behavioral theory of negotiations."[4]

Deductive bargaining models typically proceed from a restrictive set
of assumptions concerning some aspect of human behavior. Deductive
reasoning is utilized to develop generalizations or principles concerning
whether bargaining will produce a negotiated settlement.[5] These models
are most often associated with the study of economics.

Inductive models rely on observation of real-world phenomena to
discover cause-and-effect relationships rather than logical and rigorous
theoretical constructs. Sociologists and psychologists most frequently
employ this type of investigation to develop useful theories of how
negotiations produce settlements or impasses.[6]

As is true of most endeavors, "two heads are better than one." Developing an understanding collective bargaining is no exception. Both
the inductive and deductive approaches lend useful insights to the practitioner attempting to master the subject of negotiations. Understanding
either the economics or psychology of bargaining without the other
would be insufficient preparation to master the art and science of collective bargaining. The greater the negotiator's mastery of both elements,
the more successful that negotiator will be.

There are other theories of collective bargaining not presented here.
Political scientists, sociologists, and others have worked through the
problems associated with collective bargaining and developed their own
theories. Many of these other theories have not found their way into
common acceptance or widespread usage in this field. It is the considered
opinion of the authors that the two basic models presented in this chapter
reflect the current state of the art in collective bargaining in both the
private and public sector. Once the general framework (both economic
and psychological or behavioral models) of bargaining is understood,
then the reader can focus attention on the finer points of developing
serviceable and appropriate strategies and tactics for collective bargaining. The strategic and tactical aspects of negotiating are the subjects of
Chapter 4.

THE ECONOMICS OF BARGAINING

Sir John Hicks developed a model whose message is relatively simple
but extremely powerful. Hicks believed that bargaining was simply a
matter of the relative costs and benefits that each party faced in negotiating. In other words, the possession of and willingness to use bar-

gaining power was critical to negotiations outcomes. Even as simple as this sounds, there are complications. The first assumption necessary for this model to have any predictive power is that the negotiating parties have a coincidence of wants. A coincidence of wants means that each party has something the other wants. In police negotiations this coincidence of wants is relatively clear. The city wants police services, and the police officers want a paycheck. The city's ability to pay comes from its power to tax; the police officers have the ability and the time to provide the police protection for the taxpayers.

The second assumption of the Hicks resistance-concession model—that of perfect information—is less realistic. The assumption is that each party has perfect information regarding not only its own position but also the position of the opponent. The conceptual model fails to operate without this assumption. This provides a very valuable lesson for negotiators. Real-life negotiations often fail due to insufficient or inaccurate information regarding one's own bargaining position and that of the opponent. Information is how bargaining power is recognized and brought to bear to produce negotiated settlements.

Preparing for negotiations—including information gathering—is vital to the success of any contract negotiation. Without proper preparation, a party cannot know its bargaining power or the bargaining power of the other party. With insufficient information, there are two possible scenarios. First, if one party underestimates its own bargaining power and overestimates the power of the other party, many unnecessary concessions may be made to the detriment of those represented. Second, if the party overestimates its own power and underestimates the power of the other party, then it is likely that the bargaining will come to an impasse—parties will be attempting to gain concessions that the opposing parties are either unwilling or unable to make. This restrictive assumption does little violence to the conceptual value of the model, but may limit its direct applicability for predictability purposes.

The remaining critical assumption is that the bargaining parties will act in their own best interest. In other words, the parties are economically rational. This assumption has been attacked as being unrealistic, but on closer examination is more realistic than its critics would propose. Most humans are rational and do behave in their own best interest. Unions and businesses both value dollars. But there are other interests that are not readily quantifiable that hold value for bargaining parties. Successful bargaining requires an appreciation of this fact by both parties when expecting rationality from the other. The real problem is identifying what it is the opposing party and one's own constituents value.

Recently, a business student was determined to demonstrate to his professor the fallacy in this assumption of rational behavior. The student, convinced that he had discovered the unrefutable example, said "If economic rationality is a realistic assumption how does one explain St. Francis and the order he founded?" St. Francis took vows, among which were poverty. To choose poverty when alternatives are available and in his case, without measurable opportunity costs, demonstrates irrationality to the student. The professor agreed the student had found a most enlightening example, but the student had made a fatal logical error. The student had ascribed to Francis a value system with which he was familiar—his own (those of a business student). The business student's values focused on economic security and the accumulation of wealth in this world. Francis did not value material well-being foremost, believing that life in this world was but a test of short duration and that God's will must be served if the test was to be successfully completed and much greater rewards were to be reaped in the world to follow. One must be certain of the relevant value system before judgments can be made concerning the rationality of any bargaining agent.

Hicks focused his analysis on strike duration. The model developed by Hicks to explain the duration of strikes relies on the interaction of the union's resistance curve and the employer's concession curve. The intersection of these two curves determines the length of the strike and the wage rate that will be negotiated. The union's resistance curve is the schedule of wage rates and expected strike durations that are equally costly to the labor organization; it takes a greater wage gain to justify a longer strike. The employer's concession curve is the schedule of wage rates and expected strike lengths that are equally costly to the employer; a longer strike is acceptable only when wage concessions can be kept to a minimum. The union's resistance curve is downward sloping, which indicates that as the costs associated with strike activity increases the union will settle for a smaller wage. The employer's concession curve is upward sloping, which suggests that as the costs of strike activity increase the employer will settle for a higher wage. The exact point of intersection of the resistance and concession curve is determined by the relative bargaining power possessed by the union and the employer. Exhibit 3.1 depicts the Hicksian resistance-concession model in graphical form.

If the union possessed all the bargaining power in the depicted bargaining situation, then the wage would be set at W_u and the strike would be of zero duration. If, on the other hand, the employer possessed all the bargaining power, then the wage would be set at W_e and the strike would be of zero duration. It is rare that either party would be able to dictate to the other the wage (or other terms of a settlement). The more common situation is that each party has some bargaining power. The intersection of the resistance and concession curves demonstrates that with the bargaining power associated with the respective shape and position of the two curves that a strike would be of an expected duration

Exhibit 3.1

Concession-Resistance Curve

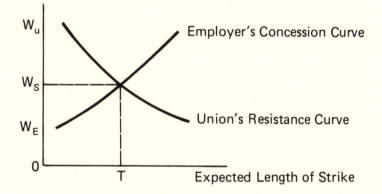

of *OT*. This result suggests that the union would accept a wage between W_s and W_u rather than bear the cost of a work stoppage. The employer would accept a wage between W_s and W_e rather than bear the burden of a strike.

The model implies that the negotiator's primary functions are to determine the shape and position of the opponent's curve and to gain as much of the wage as possible. Information concerning the relative bargaining power possessed by the opponent is therefore the modus operandi of collective bargaining in this model. This information, as suggested by the upward slope of the concession curve and the downward slope of the resistance curve, is obtained by learning. The learning in this model is the trial and error of proposal and counterproposal by the respective parties. In other words, the negotiators attempt to determine the opponent's bottom line while not revealing their own.

Public sector differences complicate this analysis somewhat. In most jurisdictions the strike is illegal, making the model less descriptive because of its reliance on the strike as the sole measure of the cost of disagreement. This problem is, however, easily overcome. The impasse procedures employed in most public sector collective bargaining laws also impose costs on the parties.

Mediation is not a cost-free process. The parties must devote time and effort in meeting with the mediator. There is generally widespread media coverage of the fact that outside intervention was necessary to settle the contract. Such outside intervention may erode public support for the labor organization, for the jurisdiction's governing body, or for the individual negotiators.

Fact finding has generally higher costs than mediation. Most impasse procedures provide for the parties to share the fee for the fact finder's services, requiring direct monetary expenditures by the parties. Furthermore, the fact-finding process in the public sector is more formal than mediation and is often open to the public and the media. Generally, fact-finding reports and recommendations can be made public by the parties, thereby creating the possibility of generating public support for one position and eroding public support for other positions. The uncertainty of public response is often seen as an undesirable risk, hence a cost of proceeding to this step.

Should fact finding fail to help the parties resolve their dispute, then an even more costly process is employed: interest arbitration. Direct monetary costs are again imposed on the parties for the services of the arbitrator, but these are not the most significant costs of interest arbitration. The real cost is the loss of self-determination. Rather than recommendations for resolution, the arbitrator issues a final and binding award. The arbitrator's award is enforceable through the courts if either party fails to honor its provisions.

The impasse procedures specified in most public sector collective bargaining laws do impose costs and are, therefore, a close approximation of the strike for purposes of the Hicksian model. The escalating cost, greater publicity, and loss of mutual control by the parties are costs just as the effects of a work stoppage impose costs. The costs are different under impasse procedures and strikes, but they are real costs capable of driving the model. This analysis lends some insight into what actually constitutes bargaining power.

Bargaining power in the private sector and in those jurisdictions allowing public employees to strike is simply the ability to withstand a strike and impose costs on the opponent. In the public sector the issue of bargaining power becomes somewhat more complicated when the strike is proscribed by statute and impasse procedures are substituted. There are those that claim that a statutory prohibition of the strike simply reduces union bargaining power unless the unions are willing to strike in the face of the prohibition. Naturally those unions willing to strike in the face of such prohibitions are likely to garner considerable bargaining power if the public supports their position. This has been demonstrated time and again in such states as Illinois and Michigan. The Professional Air Traffic Controllers Organization strike in the early years of the Reagan administration showed that such strike activity is a risky business—strikers were warned, then fired, and their union decertified.

Bargaining power can be amassed by the unions even if unwilling to engage illegal strike activity. Bargaining power can be gained through public support for union positions. The fact-finding process and the typically open nature of bargaining in the public sector provide easy access to the media and can be used to gain the necessary public support for union positions. Management can similarly avail itself of the same access to media to influence or consolidate public opinion.

Governing bodies such as school boards and city commissions are elected bodies. The political fortunes of candidates can be influenced by their stands on issues such as taxes and quality public service. Bargaining parties often use the available forums to shape perceptions of the electorate concerning labor-management relations and their effects on the efficiency and quality of operations. Quite often, neither the union nor management is very adept at these public relations activities. Neither may be able to bring the requisite bargaining power to bear to resolve impasses.

BEHAVIORAL THEORY OF NEGOTIATIONS

There have been, in recent years, numerous popular treatments of the topic of negotiations.[7] Most of these focus on the behavioral theory of negotiations or some mixture of the behavioral theory and sociological models.

In some specific cases other interesting, but untested, theories are presented concerning such issues as body language. Mastery of the behavioral theory is prerequisite to becoming an effective negotiator. Gimmicks, more associated with poker rather than negotiations, may prove useful but are not generally the foundations of successful negotiations and are therefore not reviewed in this book. Some of the more successful of the poker-type techniques are discussed in Fisher and Ury's book, *Getting to Yes*, and the reader is referred to that work for such techniques.[8]

The basics of the behavioral approach are presented now. The insights from the Hicks model, together with the behavioral theory, form the fundamentals of successful negotiations. Once the basics are presented and summarized in this chapter, the more sophisticated activity of formulating strategies and tactics is presented in the following chapter.

The behavioral theory of negotiations can be subdivided into four interrelated bargaining activities, each of which has a somewhat ponderous sounding label. The four are normally called (1) distributive bargaining, (2) integrative bargaining, (3) attitudinal structuring, and (4) intraorganizational bargaining. Each of these component activities is examined before presenting a synthesis.

Distributive Bargaining

Distributive bargaining is the activity that is most closely associated with collective bargaining. This activity involves assignment of rights

Exhibit 3.2
Matrix of Bargaining Positions—Salaries

	Desired	Worst Acceptable
Union position	$12,000	$11,200
Management position	$11,000	$11,700

under a collective bargaining agreement or the allocation of tax revenues among competing activities. For example, the bargaining over rights may concern the scheduling of vacation time for firemen; the union may prefer seniority to govern, while management wants to retain full discretion. Bargaining over allocation of revenue may concern distribution of dollars between improved teacher salaries and improved school buses. Distributive bargaining is that bargaining activity to resolve pure conflicts of interest. Distributive bargaining is that part of the bargaining process that is pictured as fixed sum; that is, one party's gain comes only at the other party's expense. This activity is unfortunately overemphasized at the expense of the other activities that are critically important to successful negotiations.

Distributive bargaining focuses on issues. In this sense an issue is an area of common interest over which the parties are in conflict. This conflict need not be dysfunctional—damaging to the bargaining relationship—but has the potential for dysfunctional results if not well managed by the negotiating parties.

In distributive bargaining, the negotiating parties will typically each determine the desired level (upper limit) and the minimum acceptable level (lower limit) for each issue. During the early negotiations, each party tries to determine the other party's limits while attempting to hide their own. As each of the parties begins to get a feel for the other's position, the trading on issues begins. A significant miscalculation of the opponent's lower limit and sending an erroneous a signal as to one's own position are the most common sources of impasses under this bargaining model. For example, see Exhibit 3.2 and the discussion that follows.

If management perceives that the union will accept a wage level of $11,000 or perhaps less, management is likely to be inflexible despite entering negotiations with a willingness to go above that figure. Similarly, if management sent the union a false signal that its worst acceptable salary was $11,000, this misperception is likely to result in impasse. Thus, the idea is to hide one's own position without hiding it too much.

Integrative Bargaining

Integrative bargaining is in some ways the antithesis of distributive bargaining. In integrative bargaining the focus of negotiations is on objectives that are not in fundamental conflict with the opponent's. The primary purpose of the integrative bargaining process is to make both parties better off than they could be without the negotiations. This process is most closely associated with labor-management cooperation and increasing or varying-sum games.

Integrative bargaining is frequently given lip service by both labor and management and rarely receives the attention it deserves by negotiators. The basic idea is either (a) to combine forces or share responsibilities to further either some shared goal or (b) to find and exploit, to mutual advantage, some area in which both parties can be made better off. The concept is appealing to most negotiators but, because of the openness and trust necessary to make this model produce the desired results, negotiators find this too risky to try unless they find themselves seriously threatened by a common set of problems. The automobile industry's and United Auto Workers' joint attempt to limit Japanese imports is a very good example of such reactive forms of integrative bargaining.

Attitudinal Structuring

Contract negotiations serve to cement or to alter the relationship of union and management representatives as well as the relationship of the organizations they represent. Whereas distributive and integrative bargaining are both based on economics and the respective rights of the parties, attitudinal structuring has the goal of developing the relationship between negotiators (and/or their organizations) in a particular direction.

A union may feel that it is acceptable to have the relationship become more adversarial if it can achieve some goals that it has been unable to achieve in contract negotiations in previous years or it may feel that maintaining a good working relationship is more important that any issues at hand.

City management may feel that a serious confrontation with union negotiators is unacceptable in the face of upcoming elections and so instruct the city's negotiators. Similar reelection concerns could dominate the bargaining strategy of a union local.

. Reputation may be the driving concern in negotiations. A school district may feel that its reputation for bargaining only mandatory issues— refusing to bargain on any other issues—is more important that the dollar cost of the negotiated contract or having a good relationship with the teachers' union. A negotiator may be focused on maintaining a "hardball player" reputation rather than the best possible contract for the union or town represented.

The perception to outsiders of a good relationship may dominate bargaining strategy. A chamber of commerce may have passed the word to city hall that the only way the city can attract major businesses to the area is to "clean up" labor relations with city utilities employees because prospective firms don't want any threat of interrupted services.

The previous examples should highlight the fact that attitude-structuring activities of negotiators will depend on (a) organizational attitude presently in evidence, (b) political realities and vested interests of organizational leaders, (c) "outside" socioeconomic influences, and (d) goals the negotiator wishes to accomplish. The desired relationship between individual negotiators or organizations may be prerequisite to the accomplishment of particular goals within the distributive or integrative bargaining models. It is also possible that the personal or organizational costs of negotiations require that attitudes be structured to achieve an accommodation. Achieving change can require a change of negotiators to emphasize sincerity of intent.

Intraorganizational Bargaining

Not all the bargaining that occurs during contract negotiations takes place between union and management representatives. When there is a lack of unanimity in either organization—as regards goals or means—intraorganizational bargaining must take place. It is the bargaining within a union or within the corporate structure that takes place to elicit support for a position to be taken at the negotiating table.

These activities generally occur at both the planning and the implementation stage of negotiations. At the planning stage, negotiators attempt to garner sufficient information to formulate bargaining goals and tactics that will produce results acceptable to those represented by the negotiator. At the implementation stage the goals have been set and the negotiator must attempt to gain and maintain solidarity among the individuals that comprise the organization.

Intraorganizational bargaining is essential if the organization is to be effectively represented by any negotiator. If an opponent sees internal conflicts over particular goals, these conflicts can be used to undermine a negotiator in such a manner as to render the negotiator ineffective.

Behavioral effects of intraorganizational bargaining can also be evident in the tactics employed. In public sector negotiations, the issue of whether the strike ought to be threatened in jurisdictions where such activity is illegal is a good example. In conservative unions where strikes are simply not considered by union members, a negotiator suggesting such a bargaining tactic would find a lack of support for this tactic, which could become a general lack of confidence in the negotiator's capability to be a good bargaining representative.

Behavioral Theory: A Synthesis

The behavioral theory of negotiations presents a useful, comprehensive statement of the different types of bargaining that occur in conjunction with contract negotiations. While each of the four activities described bargaining, none alone could describe the totality of the negotiations process. The successful negotiator will view the four as overlapping processes that reflect the multifaceted character of contract negotiations. A successful negotiator must master a whole array of demanding activities. Distributive bargaining and integrative bargaining focus on the creation and allocation of resources and rights. Neither distributive bargaining nor integrative bargaining occur without elements of both attitudinal structuring or intraorganizational bargaining. In fact, the success of distributive or integrative bargaining may critically depend on the success of the negotiator's efforts in the attitudinal structuring and intraorganizational bargaining arenas.[9] The successful negotiator has learned to operate simultaneously on several plains. The development of intraorganizational support, the search for mutual concerns to apply integrative approaches to bargaining, the structuring of attitudes, and the more familiar ground of distributive bargaining all require practiced skills and anticipated tactics. A successful bargaining strategy must also identify the bargaining activity most appropriate to the accomplishment of certain goals.

The overlapping activities present a challenge to the novice negotiator. The isolation and examination of a particular aspect of bargaining can lead to an unbalanced, hence unrealistic view, of negotiations.[10] To focus purely on labor-management cooperation ignores the fact that labor and management have a range of goals that, by definition, are in conflict. This conflict of goals is easily missed by those who are familiar only with the integrative model while ignoring the distributive model of negotiations. There are numerous examples of such failures in both the real world and the academic literature.[11] By understanding that negotiations is a system of varied processes such mistakes should be minimized. The economic as well as the behavioral aspects of negotiations are components of a whole; no portion of the whole can be ignored and expect the system to function properly.

Impasses can easily result from the failure of any of these activities, as well as from enviromental causes. Diligent attention to the entire bargaining process greatly reduces the likelihood of avoidable impasses. Impasses and their birth are the subject of the following section.

IMPASSES AND THEIR BIRTH

Contract negotiation is the birthplace of the majority of impasses. To understand the nature of an impasse, one must understand how and why impasses occur. It is equally true that if impasses are to be successfully resolved their nature must be understood. Appropriate bargaining techniques can often be identified to minimize impasses, but unless the underlying causes are examined only the symptom is known. Impasses may be classified into three categories by their underlying cause: (1) miscalculation, (2) lack of appropriate negotiations activity, and (3) intended or calculated impasse.

Miscalculation may be the most common source of impasses. The discussion of distributive bargaining included a matrix of salaries that were acceptable and desirable to the negotiating parties. The effect of holding out for a concession the other party cannot afford to make is impasse. A miscalculation of the other party's position led to this impasse. Similarly, leading the other party to miscalculate your position seriously can result in an impasse as they await your concession that is not forthcoming. Thus, miscalculation of either your own or your opponent's positions can and generally does result in an avoidable impasse. This is not to say that all of one's cards should be placed on the table during the first negotiations session, but there are appropriate signals and times for those signals during negotiations that can serve to prevent your opponent from miscalculating. An experienced negotiator should also be able to determine from available information what solutions to the bargaining problem will result in a negotiated settlement.

Miscalculation may be in the estimation of the costs associated with holding a known position. If a union correctly perceives that the employer can afford another $900 per year per employee, bargaining for the entire $900 could involve a miscalculation. The real cost to the employer of such a raise may be significantly higher due to additional tax, insurance, and retirement payments based on the $900 increase. Such hidden costs must be taken into consideration by both parties to bargaining. It is not uncommon to believe that an opponent's lower limit is much lower than what the opponent is actually willing to accept. Though miscalculations in the distributive bargaining sense may be more common, those of greater importance may be miscalculations in the Hicksian sense—miscalculations of cost or bargaining power.

Another miscalculation of cost is due to the tendency to think of cost only in an accounting sense of dollars and cents. Quite often the concept of economic cost or opportunity cost is more appropriate. Hospital employees may be bargaining for a cost of living adjustment they consider fully appropriate. The hospital may concur that such a raise is warranted but may view other expenditure areas as being of a higher priority. The hospital may be planning to shut down temporarily the old wing of the hospital to remove asbestos insulation, a known health hazard. But the hospital may not feel free to advertise its hazard until it can advertise its solution. The problem for the hospital is compounded by the reduced revenues during the period of renovation since the wing is not available for patients. Miscalculation of costs presents the risks of impasse. In this situation, employee terminations or walkouts due to not getting a cost of living adjustment may solve the employer's problem of what to do with "excess" staff during a period of reduced operations.

A lack of appropriate negotiations activity within the behavioral theory context may occur at several points. If attitudes toward certain bargaining tactics have not been structured in the opponent so that they are acceptable, resorting to such bargaining tactics may shut off lines of communications that will ultimately result in impasses. An automobile driver accustomed to heavy traffic uses his horn to say "I'm here." A driver accustomed only to rural traffic interprets it as "Get out of my way!" Bargaining tactics—such as throwing papers in the air or walking out of negotiations—may be similarly misinterpreted unless appropriate attitudinal structuring has taken place.

Impasse can occur when intraorganizational support for positions has not been established prior to sitting down to the negotiating table. When a negotiator detects a failure of intraorganizational bargaining, it may result in a successful power play: divide and conquer at the bargaining table. Or the attempt to exploit friction between "teammates" may result in open dispute. If the dispute within the other negotiating team becomes too severe, impasse may result because of their inability to reach an accord with each other.

Frequently a lack of appropriate bargaining activity is exhibited by one party or the other failing to formulate a realistic bargaining strategy or to adequately prepare for negotiations. In such cases objective, rational bargaining will be difficult and the negotiations may degenerate into a test of personalities. This increases the probability that an impasse will occur. There are dozens of such examples of where either the failure to understand the bargaining process or failure to implement properly some aspect of the bargaining process generated impasses. These impasse situations are easily prevented through education of the negotiators and proper preparation for negotiations.

The most difficult set of impasses to resolve through most statutory impasses procedures are those where one party or the other intentionally sets impasse as their bargaining goal. This calculated type of impasse can occur for several reasons. A city commission or school board may be ideologically opposed to collective bargaining and wishes to demonstrate that they are the ultimate decision-making authority and have no intention of sharing that authority with their employees or the union. A union may wish to demonstrate to management that it has sufficient support within the bargaining unit to impose a strike on the jurisdiction, independently of what management may offer at the bargaining table. There are also a wide array of irrational bargaining tactics that are also consistent with the intentional creation of impasses, most of which center on the creation of public support for particular positions.

While intentional creation of an impasse does occur, in all probability it is fairly rare. When such an impasse is observed, it should be recognized for what it is: an element of a bargaining strategy designed to accomplish some goal. The avoidance of an impasse is typically desirable, but only within the context of the respective bargaining strategies. If one party perceives that its opponent will attempt to avoid an impasse at any cost, then there is no reason to continue a bargaining relation because the impasse adverse party has lost any bargaining power it may have had.

The resolve to bargain to an impasse when necessary is an important component of successful bargaining. On the other hand, the prevention of unnecessary impasses resulting from miscalculation or the lack of bargaining activity is generally more desirable to both parties. Generally, neither party looks forward to resorting to statutory impasse procedures or strike activity. Naturally, there are cases where there is no choice but to take the impasse to the mediator or arbitrator. In such cases, the negotiator must be adequately prepared to effectively utilize the impasse procedures. Fortunately, there are often some therapeutic aspects of the impasse procedures. The impasse procedure experience could be one that will produce a better bargaining relation and situation for both parties in the future. This effective use of the impasse procedures depends on the understanding the parties have of their own negotiations, the source of their impasse, and what the impasse procedure can and cannot accomplish.

SUMMARY AND CONCLUSIONS

There are several elements that comprise collective bargaining. The oganization of labor, the negotiation of a labor contract, and administration of that contract define the range of bargaining activities. Only contract negotiations was examined here.

Collective bargaining is not the only system of labor management relations. Codetermination is widely used outside of the United States, and a system of pure "meet and confer" is used in some bargaining relations in the United States. But collective bargaining so dominates the labor relations arena that it is the only system explored here.

Contract negotiations are often examined from the naive view that one conceptual model can explain the complex process of bargaining. The process of bargaining is a system of economic and behavioral activities. The economics of bargaining demonstrates that negotiations critically depend on bargaining power and the will to use it to impose costs on an opponent while withstanding those costs the opponent can bring to bear on your organization. While the economic model proposed by Hicks is a conceptually powerful explanation of negotiations, the authors find the behavioral theory a necessary complement.

The behavioral theory of negotiations adds four activities to the economics of bargaining. Distributive and integrative bargaining, attitudinal structuring, and intraorganizational bargaining complete a conceptual tool kit preparatory to the understanding of contract negotiations. The skillful and successful negotiator will have a practical understanding of the concepts embodied in these models as well as the strategic and tactical implications of these processes.

Impasses are born in contract negotiations. For impasse procedures to be successfully utilized by the parties the sources of these impasses must be recognized. There are three basic categories of impasses: (1) miscalculations, (2) lack of bargaining activity, and (3) intentional impasses. Each of these categories has specific implications for the impasse procedures as well as future bargaining tactics and strategies.

NOTES

1. David A. Dilts and Clarence R. Deitsch, *Labor Relations* (New York: Macmillan, 1983), pp. 5–7.

2. Section 8(d) 61 Stat. 136 as amended by 73 Stat. 519, commonly called the Taft-Hartley Act.

3. John R. Hicks, *The Theory of Wages* (New York: Macmillan, 1968), Chapter 7.

4. Richard E. McKersie and Robert B. McKersie, *A Behavioral Theory of Labor Negotiations* (New York: McGraw-Hill, 1965).

5. For an example of this type of reasoning see H. C. Cross, "A Theory of the Bargaining Process," *American Economic Review* 55 (March 1965), pp. 67–94.

6. For an example of this type of reasoning see J. A. Ruben and B. R. Brown, *The Social Psychology of Bargaining and Negotiation* (New York: Academic Press, 1975).

7. For example, see Roger Fisher and William Ury, *Getting to Yes* (Boston: Houghton Mifflin, 1981).

8. See Part III for a discussion of these topics.

9. For example see, Kenneth E. Boulding, *Conflict and Defense: A General Theory* (New York: Harper & Row, 1962).

10. Richard E. Walton and Robert B. McKersie, *A Behavioral Theory of Labor Negotiations* (New York: McGraw-Hill, 1965), p. 8.

11. Sidney Garfield and W. F. Whyte, "The Collective Bargaining Process: A Human Relations Analysis," *Human Organization*, part I, vol. 9 (Summer 1950), pp. 5–10; part II (Fall 1950), pp. 10–16; part III, (Winter 1950), pp. 25–29; and part IV, vol. 10 (Spring 1951), pp. 28–32.

4

Negotiations Strategies
and Tactics

If a man would pursue Philosophy, his first task is to throw away conceit. For it is impossible for a man to begin to learn what he has a conceit that he already knows.

The Golden Sayings of Epictetus

The purpose of this chapter is to examine the formulation of bargaining strategies and their implementation through bargaining tactics. The chapter begins with formation of a strategic planning team—those who will develop the bargaining strategy. It continues with formulation of the bargaining strategy; the emphasis is on short-run and long-run goals. Then it concludes with bargaining tactics; the emphasis is on how to achieve those goals.

Reasonable familiarity with the material presented in the preceding negotiations chapter is presumed. If it has been a while since the reader has thought about that information, the authors recommend a quick or comprehensive review (whichever seems more appropriate) before continuing with the present subject matter.

Bargaining strategies are a lot like house plans. A house can be built without a plan, but the resulting structure will not be a comfortable home well suited to the needs of the occupants. Similarly, a labor contract can be negotiated without a bargaining plan. But the resulting contract will fail to meet the needs of at least one of the parties, most likely both. It will not be a comfortable one with which to live. The bargaining strategy is the master plan of contract negotiations. It describes the goals of labor and management and the general approach to achieving them.

Bargaining tactics are the activities necessary to implement a sound bargaining strategy. The tactics that will be most effective depend on several things, principally: the strategy adopted, the general bargaining relationship, and the maturity and expertise of the respective negotiators. This is like saying that the best way to get from here to there is dependent on where you're going, how good the roads are, and how good you and the other drivers are. Tactics are akin to the electrical diagrams and plumbing diagrams for a house; they show the detail work required to be successful.

DEVELOPING A STRATEGY FOR COLLECTIVE BARGAINING: AN OVERVIEW

Eminent historian Sir B. H. Liddell Hart differentiated between grand strategy and strategy.[1] The labor relations equivalent to grand strategy is practiced by only the largest unions and employers. The essence of a grand strategy is that the overall well-being of the national union (or state agency) takes precedence over the well-being of the individual local (or district office). As this is the exception rather than the rule in public sector negotiations, grand strategy is mentioned in passing because of one important implication for local bargaining. Local bargaining teams may be led or assisted by a professional on loan from a parent state or national organization. Both sides should know and understand that an outsider may be less averse to bargaining to impasse (because of grand strategy considerations) than local labor and management who bear the brunt of the impasse.

Most strategic planning does not involve grand strategy. It does involve using an organized approach to achieve objectives. As this book is intended primarily as a practitioners' guide, the authors present instructions for the forming of a strategic planning team followed by a five-step approach to strategic planning.

FORMING A STRATEGIC PLANNING TEAM

The strategic planning team should include at least one member of the senior leadership of the union (or government agency) such as the union vice president (or the director of personnel). This presence lends the team authority.

The planning team should include at least one member of the negotiating team that will conduct the table bargaining for the union or agency. The senior negotiator should be involved with the planning since that person will have to make the plan work.

The team should reflect the diversity of interests of the union or agency. A union representing craftsmen, semiskilled, and unskilled workers should have a team that reflects that mix. An agency representing all local utilities should have representation from water, gas, and electric divisions.

The team should reflect all strata of leadership. For the union that means from the shop steward to the local officers. For the agency that means from the foreman to the directorate.

The team should be composed of individuals with varying skills and expertise. Someone needs an understanding of the mechanics of collective bargaining. Someone needs to be able to advise on public relations aspects of bargaining. Another should be familiar with political processes relevant to the bargaining relationship and bargaining issues. Quite often, local expertise is supplemented by individuals from parent organizations with which the union or agency is affiliated. In teacher contract negotiations for example, state teachers associations often help the local union, and school board associations often help the local school board. The use of a "hired gun" is also common. Attorneys are often hired because of their familiarity with extensive state laws restricting and mandating certaining bargaining activities.

With all these "shoulds" in mind, it is important to select a team appropriate in size to the task at hand. When bargaining is immature, more subjects will normally be at issue and the planning team will have to be larger. Immature bargaining relationship is a descriptive term in labor relations; it is not a judgmental term or a derisive term. Immaturity is not descriptive of the behavior of individuals but of the relative stability of the bargaining relationship. First-time bargainers can hardly be expected to have an established relationship. A bargaining relationship often takes a decade or more of contract negotiations and contract administration to become relatively settled. Even in enduring relations, a significant change in leadership will have an unsettling effect on the bargaining relationship, which is only reestablished over time. The less mature the bargaining relationship and the more inexperienced the planning team, the greater is the need for managerial control of the planning document formulation process.

A sidelight on maturity of the bargaining relationship is in order before returning to the issue of maintaining managerial control of the planning process. As the knowledge of team members increases and the bargaining relation matures wider rein can be given, but it must be remembered that the timing of many elements may be crucial. For example, it is meaningless to negotiate a grievance procedure with an employer that is simply not going to bargain in good faith; it is equally meaningless to negotiate a management rights clause containing those management rights that are placed with the employer by statute or the state's constitution. If, however, either of these elements of the environment change then the strategy should be adapted to account for the environmental change.[2]

If there are many issues to be considered, the bargaining team will have to be split into committees. One might handle all wage and fringe benefit issues such as group insurance. Another might handle working conditions issues such as hours and vacation schedules. A third might handle contract administration issues such as the grievance resolution apparatus. If possible, the senior leadership should be represented on each working committee.

As the number of committees increases, managerial control becomes more difficult. Others will be required to help formulate the planning document who may not be involved in the table bargaining sessions directly. The tasks reflected in the planning document must be clear enough so that representatives who did not develop them can clearly understand them. Others who will have to implement the tasks (if adopted in collective bargaining) during contract administration should be consulted to ensure that the provisions are efficient and effective. All of this necessitates the delegation of authority to the planning committees.

When delegation occurs, managerial control requires additional emphasis. The decision makers must monitor planning progress and focus the efforts of those assigned specific planning tasks. This is easier said than done. The "Rule of P's" applies: prior planning prevents poor performance. Beginning the planning process well before the negotiating sessions is the best insurance that senior leadership will be able to maintain managerial control. All too often only poor planning performance is recognized while good planning performance goes unnoticed. This is simply due to the fact that when an effective job of planning has been done there are fewer problems in the bargaining process and when planning is absent problems arise.

STRATEGIC PLANNING—A FIVE-STEP APPROACH

The five steps in strategic planning are introduced in quick succession. Then each one is again examined at a more leisurely pace. The first step is identifying goals: developing a "wish list" of what the organization hopes to achieve in the arena of labor relations. The second step is to categorize goals as (1) distributive, (2) integrative, (3) attitudinal, or (4) intraorganizational. As the reader will observe, these goals mirror the elements identified in the behavioral theory of negotiations in the preceding chapter. The third step is to assign priorities to the goals. The result may be a rank ordering of the wish list or a categorization of issues into high, middle, and low priority items. The fourth step is evaluating the likelihood of achieving the goal. This is a rough estimation since tactics have not been considered yet. The fifth step is scheduling the goals—developing a calendar showing when each goal might be

Exhibit 4.1

Step 1—Listing of Union Goals (Tentative)

```
pay increases  —  8% this contract

               —  3% per year

               —  more money

               —  cost of living adjustments

               —  match national average

               —  60¢ hourly across the board

retirement issues  —  begin at age 60

                   —  begin at age 70

                   —  partial after 25 years service
```

---

achieved. This too is a rough estimation. When scheduling each goal, the planning team should identify the likely implementor(s)—the one(s) who will make it happen. If the goal requires legislation, the state or national organization to which the local unit is affiliated is the likely implementor. If the goal is a contract change, the bargaining team is the implementor.

Identifying Goals

The authors recommend that the senior leadership seek input from as large a base as possible. Ideally, the union may be able to query all bargaining unit members and the employer may be able to query all management level employees. A demonstrated interest in members' views can increase the members' identification with the union or agency objectives—normally a prime intraorganizational goal.

Initially, all recommended goals should be listed without comment or evaluation. The military Air Command and Staff College refers to this as the "brainstorming phase" of strategic planning. Evaluation occurs at a later step. Like recommendations can be grouped as in Exhibits 4.1 and 4.2.

Note that not all the listed items will be compatible. Some union members wanted a percentage pay increase while others wanted an across-the-board increase. As should be obvious, different managerial and union bargaining unit positions may view the pay issues quite differently.

Exhibit 4.2

Step 1—Listing of Employer Goals (Tentative)

---

    pay issues — 9 month freeze on hourly wages

                — tie annual increases to productivity

                — cap increases to reflect tax base changes

                — higher pay to aid recruiting applicants

    retirement issues — forced early retirement option

                — require 10 years for vesting

                — based on consecutive years employed

To allow evaluation of the different proposed goals, many need to be "fleshed out," or in other words, rephrased to remove ambiguity. "More money" is the most obvious example. Others might originally read "more authority" or "more say."

Other recommendations may need to be costed out to allow a comparison. Both sides would want to know how a percentage wage proposal compares to cents-per-hour proposals. Costing out will be reconsidered under bargaining tactics. Once each of the recommended proposals has been clarified, the planning team is ready to move to the second step.

Categorizing Goals

Each goal should be identified at being distributive, integrative, attitudinal, or intraorganizational. The method of handling each, especially when it comes time to select tactics, will differ based on the categorization. Goals categorized as distributive, such as most wage issues, will normally require extensive preparation for table negotiations.

Integrative issues may similarly require significant preparation so that both parties are convinced of a mutual gain. For example, an employee early retirement option may well be one topic that offers room for gain to both parties.

Some attitudinal issues may offer no current possibility of compromise, but introduction of a sensitive subject may begin a year's long process of attitudinal restructuring. Some subjects once unthinkable have become commonplace in the last quarter of this century. Examples of such issues are abundant. Some issues such as reserved parking slots for union officials may involve status concerns that transcend cost concerns. Some issues—perhaps joint sponsorship of Labor Day activities adjacent to the workplace—may have been proposed because there is so much room for cooperation. Attitudinal issues may be identified for proposal or action either at or away from the table negotiations depending on their topical proximity to the work environment.

Intraorganizational issues are not normally presented at the bargaining table because they are primarily internal to the union or agency. However, some issues may be presented at the bargaining table only to satisfy a vocal minority within the organization that the senior leadership did try to get what they asked for. The primary benefits of classification will be evident in the discussion of choosing appropriate tactics.

Assigning Priorities to Goals

Once step three has begun, it is essential that both management and organized labor emphasize security. The planning document must be protected from purposeful or inadvertent disclosure to the other parties. If the task is too large for one group, each committee should be allowed to work only its own assigned issues. Only the senior leadership and bargaining team should have access to the full document.

The senior leadership, with the advice of assigned committees, must evaluate the proposed goals for the union or agency, discard the unacceptable, and assign priorities to the remaining. The priority should reflect the expected benefit to the union or agency if the goal is attained. To some extent, the leadership is asked to make value judgments as to the relative importance of "apples and oranges," but such are the responsibilities of leadership. At this point the priority is based on "wants," not on reality, just as a teen might want a Corvette more than a stereo.

Evaluating Probability of Success

With this step the dream is forced to accommodate realities. Proposed goals that are deemed individually unachievable (or only achievable at too high a cost) should be moved to the bottom of the listing and labeled "trading points." If most of the remaining goals are in a single category, such as distributive issues, then it is unlikely that most can be achieved. Senior leadership should consider moving some to the list of trading points. The list now contains goals that are individually achievable. They are not likely to be simultaneously achievable, however. The practitioner should note a strong bias toward overly optimistic estimates of success by planning teams. Without worrying about that, the planning team should move to the next step.

Scheduling Goals and Assigning Implementors

Effective strategic planning for collective bargaining requires explicit consideration of the time dimension. For convenience, goals targeted for the upcoming contract negotiations are called short-run goals; those targeted for the more distant future, long-run goals. The short-run dimension of strategy culminates with a general plan and framework describing what the current negotiations should produce. The long-run dimension of strategy is the plan and framework for the remaining goals. Before discussing how this is applied to the priority listing, some remarks are in order to put the long run and short run in perspective for the novice negotiator.

The preceding and subsequent discussions are based on the concept of the strategic management of negotiations. The natural starting place is the long-run dimension of strategy. In the absence of a long-run dimension to strategy, negotiations simply meander year after year. The reason for this is a lack of organization and coherent framework that accomplishes bargaining goals.

There are, however, two explanations for the fact that the long run is sometimes ignored. First, volatile economic conditions—such as those experienced in recent years—often make constituents impatient for immediate gains. Second, novice negotiators reflect the experience and training of the lay population in that they are more familiar with the short-run goals of bargaining than the long run. The familiarity and the impatience tend to make both practitioners and those they represent shortsighted.

That tendency is understandable. Indeed, millionaire economist John Maynard Keynes is credited with uttering, "In the long-run we are all dead." This is unfortunate because the overall success of negotiations critically depends on the formulation and appropriate implementation of long-run planning much as an athletic team's success is dependent on recruiting, scouting, coaching, and practice. The authors reiterate that the long-run dimension of strategy is of central importance to continuing successful negotiation of short-run goals. The following remarks are aimed at providing the student and practitioner alike with an understanding and appreciation of long-run strategic planning.

Quite often, parties are able to obtain in the long run, through legislative lobbying, what they are unable to obtain in the short run through repeated negotiations. Some states have retirement program rules for public employees that are more generous than unions might have been able to negotiate with individual state or municipal agencies. Some agencies have succeeded in having public employee strikes made illegal when the agencies may have been unable to secure "no strike" pledges as part of a collective bargaining agreement. Legislative action typically requires a long-run effort. That effort is often the result of many unions or agencies at the state level. The coordination of efforts is typically by a parent organization to which the union or agency is affiliated voluntarily or by statute.

The bargaining unit's desires and needs are reflected in the union's long-run strategy. Constant contact and readily available channels of communications must be maintained with the bargaining unit so that this type of information can be accurately gathered and frequently updated. Public employers must do the same sort of things with the voters, patrons, and taxpayers. Our republican form of democracy requires decision makers to ascertain what the public desires and act accordingly. Of course, with either the union or employer, there are many issues about which their respective constituents need to be informed. Education of their constituents is one of the long-term responsibilities of the senior union or agency leadership.

Formulating the initial short-run strategy is relatively simple once the preparations have been completed. The primary short-run strategic objectives are the high priority items with a high probability of being achieved. Secondary strategic objectives are high priority items with only a moderate or low probability of being achieved. Also secondary strategic objectives are those with a moderate or low priority and a high probability of being achieved. Tertiary strategic objectives are those with moderate to low priority and probability of being achieved.

Once the bargaining issues are so identified they can be scheduled for negotiations. Care should be exercised to assure that this list is accurate and realistic. If negotiators are bargaining one-year contracts, it is doubtful that more than a dozen high priority items can be successfully bargained. If there are forty or fifty issues on the agenda, then senior leadership needs to reevaluate the short-run goals. Probably a dozen high priority issues, with 8 or 9 issues of opportunity (discussed below), and 6 or 7 trading points is about all one can realistically expect to handle in any single one-year contract bargaining session—remember, the opponent is going to have demands too. Further, only the most experienced and skilled negotiators are going to meet with any degree of success with such a multitude of issues. Those negotiators with less developed skills and limited experience may be able to handle only three or four high priority issues and a couple of issues of opportunity. It is therefore obvious that patience is a virtue without substitute in the long-run planning of a labor contract. One important aside should be mentioned at this point. Too frequently both labor and management have a tendency to change negotiators. Unions are operated on democratic principles and union leadership attains its position through elections. This can and often results in frequent changes in the negotiating and planning committees and has the potential for causing difficulties in obtaining bar-

Exhibit 4.3
Strategic Plan for Collective Bargaining

[sample page]

Activity (Priority/Term)	CFCT Goal	Implementor
****** DISTRIBUTIVE GOALS ******		
Negotiation of salaries	USD XXX to be in	Bargaining
(TOP PRIORITY-short term)	upper 25% of USDs	Team
	of like size in US	
Paid sabbatical leaves	75% of annual	Bargaining
(LOW PRIORITY-long term)	salary	Team
****** INTRAORGANIZATIONAL GOALS ******		
Membership in Union	Bargaining unit have	Local Union
(MID PRIORITY-long term)	87.5% dues paying	President &
	members	Treasurer
****** ATTITUDINAL STRUCTURING ******		
Binding arbitration of	Included as last	SFCT/AFL-CIO
contract impasses	step of impasse	lobby State
(LOW PRIORITY-long term)	procedures	Legislature

gaining goals. Smooth transitions and cooperation between factions in the union are necessary if damage is to be prevented. Management often faces the same constraint. There is also a tendency in some agencies to change negotiators and labor relations personnel simply to give a broader range of managers an opportunity to gain negotiations experience. These changes are typically unwarranted and risk damage to the planning process as well as the maturity of the bargaining relation.

A SAMPLE STRATEGIC PLAN

Exhibit 4.3 presents a very simple form of strategic plan. Naturally, the issues are minimized, the goals are not complex, and the implementors are limited to one specific group. Some of these characteristics are not very realistic but ease presentation. Further, Exhibit 4.3 does not contain contingencies for those goals that become recognized as unattainable. A good strategic plan will detail first level contingencies as a minimum. This plan is for a hypothetical City Federation of Classroom Teachers (CFCT) local about to enter negotiations.

This document shows the activity, the terms, the relative priority, the category of activity, the goal, and the implementor. Some planning documents go a step further and detail the anticipated tactics for the implementor to accomplish the assigned mission.

The control that is exerted by the chief negotiator or decision-making authority can vary significantly across issues. The implementors assigned to accomplish some goals are delegated "upstream" of the union. The SFCT, State Federation of Classroom Teachers (with which the CFCT is affiliated), perhaps with the assistance of the state branch of the AFL-CIO, is expected to lobby for pro-teacher legislation. The local depicted in Exhibit 4.3 is unlikely to have much direct control over what the state organizations do. Requests, offers of assistance, and support can be shown, but not much more of substance can be accomplished on legislative issues at the local level.

Other tasks depicted were assigned to the bargaining team. Still others, to officers of the union local. Such specific assignments are necessary for accountability and assist the bargaining team in maintaining control. Without specific persons being assigned to each task, the process of control breaks down from a lack of accountability.

The compromise most experienced negotiating teams rely on to maintain intraorganizational support is to include every issue supported by a major constituency. However, the less popular goals will have a lower priority and be planned for further in the future than most goals.

Once the strategy has been established, it is important that the planning team take a look at the overall planning document. Does it seem comprehensive? Is it consistent with previous union or agency positions? The long-run strategy should serve to make sense out of what has gone before and to key on what elements can be accomplished during the forthcoming negotiations. Long-run strategies should be reevaluated after every two or three years (in the case of annual negotiations and no more than every three contracts in the case of longer-term agreements) to ensure that a planning document remains realistic and appropriate to the present bargaining climate.

A FEW SUMMARY AND CONCLUDING THOUGHTS ON STRATEGY

A strategy with long-run and short-run goals is generally formulated early in a bargaining relation. Some bargainers, satisfied with the outcome of initial negotiations, then misplace, ignore, or set aside strategy as too much trouble. This is self-defeating.

Short-run and long-run goals should be revised as soon after the contract is signed as possible. Many employers and unions give the negotiators a week to reflect on the negotiations and then require a draft of next year's stategy within forty-eight hours of their return to work.

After each contract is negotiated, those items obtained should be noted and new priorities assigned to those items remaining. The addition of new items should then be considered with appropriate priorities and implementors assigned to them. The long-run strategy should be zero based and totally reconstructed roughly every three contracts. The new strategy should then be compared with the old strategy and possible revisions considered.

No later than two months before renegotiations commence, the negotiating team should reassemble for the purpose of reviewing the draft of short-run strategic goals. The strategy should be reevaluated then revised based on what new information is at that time available.[3]

The strategic planning process cannot be minimized in its relative importance to the success of negotiations. The parties will find that strategy formulation is hard work but the payoffs (in both tangible issues negotiated and the proper attitudinal structuring process) are well worth it.

Strategy is the plan to achieve goals. Tactics are the immediate means used to implement that plan.

TABLE TACTICS—A FOCUS ON ISSUE-ORIENTED METHODS

Tactics to be described here include trading points, objectives of opportunity, flexibility, reducing predictability, and predicting opponent positions.

Trading points should be identified during the strategic planning stage. Trading points are those issues of a low enough priority to your own constituents that they are not goals of the current negotiations. They are particularly valuable in tactical bargaining when it is determined that these issues are of a higher priority to the other party. It really helps to have someone on the negotiating team who is adept at "reading" feelings; it aids immeasurably the early identification of the other team's priorities. The tactical objective is to concede a trading point to the other party in return for a concession on an issue that is an identified goal.

Objectives of opportunity may be identified during the table negotiations. The opponent may consider them to be trading points. But if they have some value to the bargaining team, they should be given consideration. The message is: don't disregard a concession merely because you haven't planned for it.

Strategy is probabilistic; it is based on the likelihood (rather than certainty) of events occurring. Tactics—and occassionally the short-run goals of the strategy itself—may have to be modified based information received during the course of the negotiations that alters the estimated probabilities. Tactics can be planned, but they should not be inflexible. The negotiating team needs to be able to react quickly to new information and opportunities. There must be strong leadership on the negotiating team to react quickly. This is often difficult to agree upon ahead of time if the negotiating team represents a fractionalized constituency.

If the current negotiations is not the first time at the table for the parties, once the initial short-run strategic goals are established, the negotiating team should endeavor to identify those tactics that have been the most successful in attaining the desired results in past negotiations. This emphasizes the absolute need for accurate prior negotiations data. A little creativity and sharing of information between negotiators can be of great assistance at this juncture. If agreements can be reached on data and facts then the actual work of coming to conceptual agreements is facilitated.

If tactics become too predictable after a history of bargaining, they may telegraph your resistance or trading points. Tactics should be varied. Try to use one or two new tactics at each subsequent negotiating sessions. Such changing of tactics helps to conceal the team's real position until the appropriate time in the negotiations. It doesn't hurt to be a little creative or to borrow from other school boards, cities' commissions, or unions.

Preparation for future negotiations during the current contract can give a negotiating team a "leg up" on the other party. It may be possible to predict the issues and priorities of the other by looking at the data accumulated on grievance filings, turnover rates and reasons, public statements, and other such items.

It is also important to bear in mind that at some time in the negotiations process you may wish the opponent to have a good idea of the priorities you have assigned to issues. Without a short-run strategy, a party's positions and the signals it communicates concerning those positions will become difficult for the other party to ascertain and negotiations could fail as a result.

Timing is a tactical adjunct to assigning strategic priorities to bargaining goals. The negotiating team will formulate bargaining calendars. The calendars indicate the planned timing of demands so that they will be appropriately introduced and the foundation laid for their acceptance by the other party. A team proposing off-premises continuation training for employees would introduce this idea prior to recommending that meal costs for off-premises work be absorbed by the employer or employees. These calendars will reflect the priority of the goal, the present thinking in the bargaining environment, and likelihood of accomplishing the goal.

The great majority of negotiations take place at the bargaining table—

the daily, weekly, or monthly meetings of the negotiating teams. Preparation for table bargaining makes up the major portion, but not all, of tactical planning.

MOVING THE BARGAINING AWAY FROM THE BARGAINING TABLE

Sometimes a negotiating team feels the need to get outside public support for a particular negotiating position. This involves a shift to a public forum, away from the private forum of the negotiating table. The objective is generally to garner public support for the negotiating position. The focus may be on issues or on the lack of agreement to date. The risks of such tactics are also mentioned.

One tactic is to shift the focus of the negotiations from the bargaining table to the constituencies. Large-scale media coverage, press conferences and releases, and information leaks on highly volatile issues can cause public pressure to build. A negotiating team may be swayed by public sentiment to yield on some issues by the skillful publication of those issues and the parties' respective positions in a public forum.

Another tactic is to force media attention on overall disagreement rather than on individual issues. Public officials facing reappointment or reelection may be particularly susceptible to this type of pressure. Realize, however, the immediate gain may come at the cost of a deteriorating relationship. Similarly, an agency may be able to take advantage of known fractionalism in the union environment by skillful portrayal of union advocates or leadership as ineffectual or inflexible. Again, such tactics are confrontational and may bear larger long-term costs than are immediately evident, especially if the tactics are unsuccessful.

Even if these tactics are seen as unproductive, each party should plan for the eventuality that its opponent may shift to the public arena for debate. There are a multitude of responses that range from public silence to "fighting fire with fire." It is important to plan ahead for such contingencies. Prepared press releases and a schedule of possible speaking engagements are two methods of preparation for the eventuality.

BARGAINING TACTICS—A FOCUS ON STYLE INSTEAD OF ISSUES

Bargaining tactics can be classified into several categories, including (1) aggressive, (2) nonaggressive, (3) debate, and (4) irrational tactics. Each of these categories of tactics will be examined, in turn, in the following paragraphs.

Aggressive Tactics

Aggressive tactics, sometimes referred to as commitment tactics, are active, directed actions to accomplish a particular goal and are most frequently associated with distributive bargaining.[4] Certain of these bargaining tactics, such as threats and coercion of bargaining unit members or negotiators, are generally prohibited practices. Other of these tactics, such as truthfully contending that specific proposals are likely to result in adverse conditions for the bargaining unit, are lawful and widely used. Veiled threats and coercion may or may not be unfair labor practices. Such statements as "if we can't get rid of the early retirement program the public will become suspicious of further budget allocations to firemen," while a veiled threat may be a proper consideration for bargaining.

Aggressive tactics are generally the least sophisticated and frequently the most effective bargaining tools in the negotiators' arsenal. The greatest care must be exercised in utilizing these methods to assure that one does not go beyond the limits established by law or that permanent harm is not done to the collective bargaining relation.[5]

Probably the most effective and common of the threat-type bargaining tactics is the expressed intention to do one's opponent harm if the opponent does not agree to your position. Unions frequently threaten to work to change the composition of a board, council, or commission through lawful political actions if the decision-making body does not meet its demands. These are common lawful threats and often very effective if there is a favorable political environment within the jurisdiction.

Another arena of collective bargaining that often generates aggressive tactics are the negotiations required after a fact finder has issued the report in an impasse. The threat to use the report to one's own advantage in the press and other public relations activities may be effective, depending on what is to be found in the report and how sensitive one's opponent is to such activities. The fact-finding report is often the source of such bargaining tactics even though the fact finder or the opponent may not wish to have the report so used. In many bargaining relations in the public sector the parties will routinely agree not to make the specific language of the fact finder's report or an arbitrator's opinion public unless the entire report or award is made public or jointly released. This prevents the isolation of sentences or phrases and the use of innocent language, out of context, to paint unintended pictures of the other party. Joint release of the report or award also lessens suspicions that the public may have about one specific party's goals and actions. Often, joint release of a report or award can be the first step in developing, at least, the image of labor-management cooperation and can have positive long-run implications for collective bargaining.

There are of course other such aggressive tactics but these are dangerous from several perspectives. There are other more sophisticated tactics that create greater benefits in several arenas and these will be now examined.

Nonaggressive Tactics

Nonaggressive tactics can be subclassified as (a) conciliatory, (b) reward, or (c) appearance tactics. Conciliatory tactics are often used to elicit certain behavior from an opponent. This category of tactics is on the behavioral level rather than on the tangible or economic plane. The reward tactic cuts across both planes (behavorial and tangible). The basic idea is to reward an opponent to reap or continue to gain one's own rewards. The classic example of such a tactic is to praise one's opponent in public for their wisdom and foresight in agreeing to a compromise position, which you had demanded. The appearance tactic is designed to have an impact on the behavioral plane and to modify an opponent's view of your strengths or weaknesses or to disguise certain attributes or activities. Each of these categories of tactics will be examined further in the following sections. These tactics are most often associated with integrative bargaining and attitudinal structuring models of bargaining.[6]

Conciliatory Tactics. A frequently used categorization of bargaining strategies is that of the hard bargainer or the soft bargainer. The aggressive tactics outlined above are most commonly associated with hard bargaining, while conciliatory tactics are most often, but incorrectly, ascribed to soft bargaining. Often a bargaining relation will run upon rough times. Human relations breakdowns are often the source of impasses. The conciliatory bargaining tactic is designed to develop trust, cooperation, or even understanding from one's opponent. For example, a concession may be made for the outward purpose of saving a certain critical area of the public service, but there may have been equally effective methods to accomplish the same result but at a great amount of embarrassment or hardship to one's opponent. If the concession "gets the opponent off the hook" without harming your own position, go for it, but make sure your opponent understands you are doing him a favor.

There are numerous such conciliatory bargaining tactics: opening the books, defining and addressing common problems, making concessions for which no immediate repayment is necessary, failing to retaliate, signaling shifts in bargaining tactics, and exhibiting patience with an opponent. Each of these tactics is designed to be conciliatory and can be potent bargaining tools if applied to the proper situation. With the recent interest in labor-management cooperation schemes these conciliatory tactics have been more frequently employed by negotiators. It is important to remember that labor-management cooperation can be a very productive arrangement, but both unions and managers must represent their own respective constituents.

Reward Tactics. Reward tactics are activities designed to elicit continued preferable opponent actions. If the opponent makes a reasonable compromise, reciprocate; by so doing the opponent is rewarded for his actions. Such rewards will often be viewed favorably and frequently continued.

Similarly, withholding rewards can be used to signal dissatisfaction with the opponent's behavior. If a reward is withheld, the other party must be signalled that a reward has been held back and why. Again, make sure that you identify the cause of the withholding of an acceptance of a compromise or your failure to offer a compromise on one of your positions. If such signals are not sent then the opponent will not be able to predict your behavior and this could short circuit the bargaining process.

Examples of applied reward tactics are agreeing to trading points on the opponent's terms, pointing out where the opponent is being too tough, displaying trust in the opponent, enabling the opponent to revise certain commitments (on a one-time basis), confering status of the opponent, defending one's opponent in the press, and providing the opponent with an obvious line of retreat from hot issues.[7]

This category of bargaining tactics is based on what behaviorists often call the "hot stove rule." If a person gets burned for doing something they will avoid it. If a person is rewarded for doing something they will continue and often strengthen their efforts to accomplish the desired results. The key is to make sure the opponent readily connects the behavior with the punishment or the tactic will not be effective.

Appearance Tactics. As in military endeavors it is best to hide one's weaknesses and display one's strengths. The creation of such appearances is equally important to the collective bargaining process. An employer will often cite public support for a particular stance when in fact the public, if polled, would overwhelming object to such a position. Unions do the same thing with relation to both the public and the bargaining unit. This range of activities is an important, if not a critical, adjunct to intraorganizational bargaining. The creation of support through appearances could be as effective as actually doing it through intraorganizational bargaining. There is a danger. If the use of these tactics is to buy time to gain support that is certain to come then there is no problem, but a bluff can't be maintained forever!

Debate Tactics

There are three basic categories of debate tactics, these are (a) structural debate (b) joint problem solving, and (c) competitive debate. Structural debate focuses on interpersonal relationships and issues together. Joint problem-solving debates are concerned with facilitating integrative bargaining. Competitive debate is the model that most public sector negotiators are the most familiar with and is associated with distributive bargaining. Debate tactics are, however, frequently used in each of the models of labor negotiations. Each of the categories of tactics will be discussed in turn in the following sections.

Structural Debate. Structural debate is concerned with institutional issues and their fit with people. One of the most common examples of structural debate is the age-old question in many public sector bargaining relations, "Do you as chief negotiator have the authority to speak for ...?" Here the discussion focuses on the role of a particular person within the institution he or she purports to represent.

There are several common variations of this same theme to be found in labor-management relations. Agreements to establish channels of communications, caucus rights, the establishment of bargaining rules, inquiries as to the relationship between the negotiation team and its constituents, and bargaining agendas are all tactics that if properly handled can give an advantage. Maybe the best example of this is the bargaining agenda. The shrewd negotiator will get his high priority issues toward the top of the bargaining agenda in cases where there are a multitude of issues to be dealt with and only a short period of time in which to conduct negotiations. By doing so the negotiator is assured that his issue will receive attention and that negotiations on other issues will have to be truncated or bargained toward the top of the agenda if they are to make it to the table in a meaningful way.

Joint Problem Solving. Joint problem solving tactics are closely associated with the integrative bargaining model. These tactics are focused on the identification of and resolution of problems in which the parties share a common interest. By identifying and working out mutually acceptable solutions to these problems both parties benefit without necessarily costing the other party. In general trust and cooperation are necessary prerequisities to these tactics being successful. There are, of course, other tactics used to set the table for these tactics.

The most common of the joint problem solving collective bargaining tactics are thinking out loud, role reversal, trial balloons, and heuristic searches for solutions. These tactics are most successful in mature bargaining relations with sophisticated negotiators. Often in crisis bargaining situations (for example, Chrysler and the UAW in 1983) the joint problem solving tactics are forced on the parties by an outside problem of major magnitude. The joint problem solving technique is then adopted as a self-preservation tactic for both labor and management. The adoption of joint problem solving, however, is not necessarily founded on outside sources of harm. There are many integrative bargaining issues that readily lend themselves to the use of category of bargaining tactics.

Competitive Debate. Competitive debate is the category of bargaining tactics with which the majority public sector negotiators are the most familiar. These tactics are most commonly associated with distributive bargaining. Competitive debate focuses on the use of logic and evidence to persuade one's opponent of the propriety of one's own position.

If collective bargaining were conducted in a near perfect world, that is, good faith bargaining was defined in its narrowest possible sense, personalities and emotions were held in abeyance, and logic and rationality prevailed in all circumstances, there would be no need for other bargaining tactics. Yet this idealized world does not exist. Distributive bargaining still occurs in this imperfect world and competitive debate is one of the most important weapons in this arena as well as others.

Competitive debate focuses on the presentation of evidence in a logical manner in the hopes of persuading an opponent that your suggested course of action is the proper direction. The tactics most frequently employed from this category are baiting one's opponent into errors of logic and fact, negotiating with the least-schooled bargaining team member on the opponent's team, insistence on rational and objective standards, and persuasion. These tactics are used for the simple purpose of convincing an opponent, with proof, that you are, in fact, right.

Too often a negotiator will rely solely on the tactics found in this category. There is a real danger in this approach. If your tactics become predictable so, too, do your resistance points. Further, there may be other tactics better suited to your purposes and situation. An appropriate mix of tactics is necessary if your strategies are to bear fruit. Sole reliance on competitive debate can and frequently will bring disaster.[8]

Irrational Tactics

Irrational bargaining tactics are those that seem to lack reason or sense. For the most part these tactics are to be avoided, but there are rare occasions where these tactics can prove useful. Mutual assured (nuclear) destruction has been a successful international political bargaining tactic. Though categorized as irrational, this tactic has forestalled world war for more than forty years. Irrational bargaining tactics can be used with success if the parties recognize the circumstance where they are of value, mostly where greater costs can be imposed on an opponent than what you will suffer for implementing the tactic.

The tactics that fall under this category are self-destructive proposals, demonstrated incompetence, irrational acts, and maintenance of unacceptably high costs. These tactics can often bring public attention to unreasonable working conditions and even unreasonable negotiators. For example, the acceptance of zero raises while building a new basketball arena will generally gain for teachers more public support than could be mustered by fighting in the press.

As absurd as it may sound on its face these tactics are often successfully used. These tactics often have an important role to play in getting an opponent's or the public's attention. The irrational tactic to be successful must be utilized sparingly and great care taken so as not to appear to be unreasonable or irresponsible. Only the most sophisticated and technically competent negotiators should attempt such tactics and generally only in situations where no good alternatives are available.

PUTTING TACTICS AND STRATEGIES TOGETHER

There are few generalizations that can be offered in this section. The bargaining history, bargaining relationship, demands on the table, and the economic environment will in large measure dictate what tactics can and should be used to accomplish the goals outlined in the bargaining strategy. One word of advice can be offered: Homework and anticipation can do a lot for a negotiator in selecting the proper tactics to implement a strategy, but there is simply no substitute for good old-fashioned common sense.

Strategies are simply an outline and plan for what goals are to be accomplished and what tactics are likely to be successful in accomplishing those goals. It is always wise to list those tactics that will be initially tried in the first round of strategy formulation. If the tactics are successful a note should be made reflecting the success, but if unsuccessful the opponent's response should be recorded and any other observations as to why that tactic failed. This information will be invaluable in revising future strategies and in revising the current bargaining strategies. Frequently, negotiators learn more from their failures than their successes and the use and selection of tactics is where this adage is most true.

SUMMARY AND CONCLUSIONS

Bargaining strategies are the blueprints for contracts. The strategic plan that must be formulated with a balanced view of the long-run and the short-run dimensions of strategy. The purpose of the long-run goals is to focus effort to the ideal contract over several negotiations, while the short-run goals guide negotiations in any one specific year. The short-run plans should reflect a comprehensive long-run plan. Each in turn gives rise to the tactics that are most appropriate to achieving the goals.

Tactics are both table and nontable bargaining techniques used to implement bargaining strategies. While discussed at some length in this chapter, they will be considered again when focusing on specific issues which lead to impasse. The tactics used to resolve impasse are often ones that could have been used to avoid impasse in the first place.

In table bargaining there are four basic style categories of tactics, these are aggressive, nonaggressive, debate, and irrational. These tactics should be appropriately mixed to avoid predictability and selected for the best chance of success in the attainment of goals given the climate of negotiations, bargaining history, and bargaining relation.

Tactics and strategies are dependent concepts. Without the tactic there is no way to implement a strategy, and without a strategy the tactic is simply a random event. The coordination of tactics with the formulated strategy is therefore important to the overall success of negotiations, yet there is little guidance that can be given here for that purpose, other than to use good common sense and do your homework.

NOTES

1. Sir Basil Henry Liddell Hart, *Strategy*, 2d rev. ed. (New York: Frederick A. Praeger, 1967), chapter 22.

2. See A. Douglas, *Industrial Peacemaking* (New York: Columbia University Press, 1962), for further discussion.

3. See Richard B. Freeman and James L. Medoff, *What Do Unions Do?* (New York: Basic Books, 1984), for further discussion.

4. See Richard E. Walton and Robert B. McKersie, *A Behavioral Theory of Labor Negotiations* (New York; McGraw-Hill, 1965), pp. 82–125, for further discussion of what they call "commitment tactics."

5. T. C. Schelling, "An Essay on Bargaining," *American Economic Review* vol. 46 (June 1956), pp. 283–285.

6. See Roger Fisher and William Ury, *Getting to Yes* (Boston: Houghton Mifflin, 1981), chapters 2–4, for further discussion.

7. See Thomas Kochan, *Collective Bargaining and Industrial Relations* (Homewood, Ill.: Irwin, 1980), for further discussion.

8. See Walton and McKersie, *A Behavioral Theory*, for further discussion.

PART II

PUBLIC SECTOR IMPASSE RESOLUTION PROCEDURES

5

Impasse Procedures

He that wrestles with us strengthens our nerves and sharpens our skill. Our antagonist is our helper.

Edmund Burke, *Reflections on the Revolution in France*

The purpose of this chapter is to introduce impasse resolution procedures and discuss some practical ways to reduce the likelihood of a bargaining impasse. A brief discussion will be offered concerning the prevention of impasses before proceeding to examine the mechanisms provided for their resolution. The nature of impasse procedures will be examined, including their general structures and their purposes. Once the impasse resolution procedures have been identified, attention will be turned to the neutrals that make the processes work. An examination is presented of how the mediators, fact finders, and arbitrators become professional neutrals and what their qualifications are for such work.

INTRODUCING PUBLIC SECTOR IMPASSES

Impasse resolution procedures have been legislatively promulgated in most states to provide a mechanism for labor and management to resolve their contract negotiations disputes. This is because of the general prohibition of public sector employee strikes and employer lockouts that exists in most states. The diversity of legislated impasse resolution mechanisms has made the public sector the proving grounds for impasse procedures. The test of economic strength inherent in the strike or lockout serves to help resolve most contract disputes in the private sector. But to resort to these types of economic warfare is considered by most policymakers as inconsistent with the role of government. As bargaining and economic warfare were once considered flip sides of the same coin, for many years collective bargaining in the public sector was also regarded as inconsistent with effective government. As attitudes slowly changed, so did public policy. Public employees in most jurisdictions now enjoy statutorily protected rights to unionization and collective bargaining. The problem then becomes one of how can the process of collective bargaining be made to work if the strike, the traditional means of settling industrial disputes, is not to be permitted. A substitute for the strike was judged needed (in many jurisdictions) to make the collective bargaining process work in the public sector. That substitute is still needed to provide for the continued delivery of essential public services. The substitute is statutory impasse procedures.

The alternative to the strike, in the absence of impasse procedures, is management's (or the legislature's) unilateral authority to set wages and other terms and conditions of employment. In either case, the public employee is left without negotiating power over the terms and conditions of employment. Having seen public employees gain bargaining power in some of the larger, more industrial states, public employees in other states have over the past few decades become increasingly insistent on gaining the same or similar rights. The result is that there is wide adoption of collective bargaining laws throughout the United States. States as diverse as New York, Michigan, Iowa, and Kansas provide for public sector collective bargaining even though each have very different economies, traditions, and social attitudes.

IMPASSE PREVENTION

Maybe the most effective method of impasse resolution is to prevent them from arising. Negotiators, mediators, fact finders, arbitrators, and academics have all examined the causes and nature of impasses. They have suggested numerous ways in which impasse activity can be minimized. If impasses can be prevented, then reliance on statutory or negotiated procedures to resolve those conflicts will become less the focal point of public sector collective bargaining. As will be discussed in the chapter concerning experimental impasse procedures, this goal of reducing impasses seems to be consistent with most experimental procedures. The fact that some states now allow public employees to strike suggests a basic dissatisfaction, by some, with the importance that impasse procedures have gained in the public sector.

There have been many suggestions on how to reform collective bargaining in both the private and public sector so as to minimize conflict. One important point should be kept in mind: by its nature, distributive bargaining always generates some conflict; and where there is conflict, there is a potential for impasse. Furthermore, and maybe more importantly, collective bargaining is an institution operated by human beings. As such, collective bargaining is subject to the many whims, vagaries, and frailties of human beings.

The tactics and strategies discussed in the previous chapter provide a starting point for a discussion of impasse minimization techniques. The first and maybe most powerful minimization techniques involves the development of an appropriate philosophy of collective bargaining. This philosophical technique will affect the strategic plan developed for collective bargaining and, therefore, the tactics utilized. The adoption of a philosophy consistent with fair but firm collective bargaining principles is suggested by many authors.[1] This philosophy—known as the developing communication philosophy—recommends that both labor and management should establish a practice of fair and firm administration of existing contracts and should carry over this same method of operation to contract negotiations. A negotiator with the motivation and ability to see things from the other side's perspective will frequently be able to inspire trust and confidence from opponents. This, however, is a long and frequently difficult process. Such trust and confidence is the product of several years of experience and cannot be fostered over a period of days and weeks.

Developing such an approach to collective bargaining may not be easy. Years of open conflict and mistrust may have to be overcome, but this is the prime application of attitudinal structuring. It is much easier to bargain with someone who you have confidence in and who has confidence in you than to bargain with cutthoats. Negotiators must resist the temptations to play both ends against the middle and engage in shortsighted tactics designed to accomplish short-run goals at the expense of the longer-term bargaining relation. Two basic rules will go a long way in accomplishing this task. The first is always bargain at least one contract ahead. That is, don't get too greedy; establish the ground work for demands and bargain in such a manner that no single goal is worth destroying progress toward a cooperative bargaining relation. The second is absolute honesty. Never commit yourself or organization to things you cannot deliver, and be open and candid as to why certain things may not be delivered this year. Never attempt to hide the blame for rejection of bargaining proposals, and always give honest, supportable reasons for positions. This does not mean you have to "give away the family farm"; firmness is as important an element of this philosophy as fairness.

There are also several suggestions for negotiations tactics that can be used in the short term to minimize the chances of reaching a negotiated impasse. Among these suggestions are three that are most frequently suggested by the federal mediators and experienced negotiators: (1)

never box in an opponent; (2) present counterproposals as revisions of an opponent's demand; and (3) suggest various compromise alternatives so that the opponent always has an array from which to choose.

Never boxing in an opponent sounds so simple, but it is a real art form in practice. The least successful bargaining technique known to man is "take it or leave it." The bottom line settlement point should never be used as a bargaining proposal. In the majority of cases, leading with the bottom line is assuring an impasse. Search for acceptable compromise alternatives that will leave your opponent with a graceful way out. Never be unwilling to modify your positions, even if the modification is purely symbolic and without substance. A shrewd negotiator will attempt to bargain a contract and not a position. The approach of bargaining a contract allows for trading points. Trading points may be needed to get yourself and your opponent out of corners.

One of the best tactical rules is: Never reject an opponent's proposal outright if there is any merit to it. If a proposal can be reshaped to make it acceptable, it should be revised. It's often more a matter of form than substance to submit a revision rather than a counterproposal to one's opponent. It is not unwise to assume always that an opponent has some pride of authorship in every bargaining proposal. With such an assumption it is always better to suggest wording changes and even conceptual changes to the opponent's proposal than to suggest new language of your own. This approach has an added benefit; opponents already understand their own proposal, so they do not have to be reeducated when a counterproposal is offered as a revision of their own proposal, as is often the case if totally new language is substituted.

Suggesting several alternatives is often an effective method of putting packages on the table or presenting one's own initial demands. Choices from an array of alternatives allows not only for the perception of flexibility in your own positions but also allows an opponent to have some freedom of movement on those issues that may be of the highest priority to your own organization. Room for movement may be the best assurance against impasse—movement in your own position, but also room provided for the opponent to move.

There are also several other human relations aspects of bargaining that can result in impasses that should be avoided if at all possible. Personality attacks are inappropriate to the bargaining process. Losing one's temper will generally cause losing one's respect in the eyes of others; breaks and caucuses are excellent ways to allow tempers to subside. Dishonesty in any form will always damage the bargaining relation. Arrogance or a condescending attitude is a sure way to human relations failures. Direct confrontation should be avoided, where possible; questions are generally preferable to challenges. Most of these human relations tips are merely common sense, but common sense is sometimes not common enough at the bargaining table.

The one final aspect of preventing impasses is to be well trained and versed in labor relations. Education in the labor relations business is too often in short supply. Never assume that you know all you need to know or that your opponent is equally competent. Often one will find that an opponent may not be competent in collective bargaining matters. It is unwise to challenge another's bargaining ability, but an uneducated opponent can cause significant hardship. The best way to handle such problems is to suggest the establishment of joint training programs or seminar attendance. Most jurisdictions have, within their borders, several opportunities per year to learn about various aspects of collective bargaining. It is often a good idea to attend as many of these as possible or to establish some relationship with a state agency or university so that training can be developed for your specific needs and brought to your organization. Unfortunately, most people pride themselves in being expert negotiators when in reality there is always more to learn no matter how long one has been involved in collective bargaining.

If impasses cannot be prevented, then the parties must rely on the impasse resolution procedures if conflict should arise. The remainder of this chapter will be devoted to introducing the impasse resolution procedures most commonly used throughout the United States.

IMPASSE PROCEDURES: VOLUNTARY OR COMPULSORY

Most of the states with public sector collective bargaining laws have also enacted compulsory impasse procedures. Compulsory impasse procedures are those that must be followed in the case of a declared impasse. The declaration may be an individual or joint statement of the parties that an impasse exists, or the declaration may be automatic if the parties have failed to achieve a negotiated contract by some specified point in the calendar. The parties have no choice as to whether the impasse resolution procedures will be implemented in the case of compulsory procedures. As a matter of practice, parties are often allowed to extend a statutory deadline if they jointly state that negotiations have not reached an impasse. This is often the case when state funding of local agencies is delayed past the normal date for the beginning of negotiations or where there are numerous issues on the bargaining table, such as initial contract negotiations.

Some jurisdictions allow the parties to negotiate mutually acceptable or voluntary impasse resolution procedures to be used as a substitute for the compulsory procedures. The Ohio General Assembly enacted the Public Sector Labor Act in 1983.[2] This law contains several alternative impasse resolution procedures. Under Chapter 4117.13 of the statute, public safety employees, the employees of state school for the deaf, the state school for the blind, and similar employees are denied the right to strike and must utilize the impasse procedures contained in the statute. All other employees may strike or submit the issues to the statutory impasse procedures for settlement.

It is also interesting to note that the Ohio Act provides for numerous alternatives in the dispute settlement arena. This may be referred to as an arsenal of weapons approach to impasse resolution. The Act specifies that:

Sec. 4117.13 (C) In the event the parties are unable to reach an agreement, they may submit, at any time prior to forty-five days before the expiration date of the collective bargaining agreement, the issues in dispute to any mutually agreed upon dispute settlement procedure which supersedes the procedures contained in this section.
(1) The procedures may include:
    (a) Conventional arbitration of all unsettled issues;
    (b) Arbitration confined to a choice of the last offer of each party to the agreement as a single package;
    (c) Arbitration confined to a choice of the last offer of each party to the agreement on each issue submitted;
    (d) The procedures described in division (C)(1)(a), (b), or (c) of this subsection and including among the choices for the arbitrator, the recommendations of the fact finder, if there are recommendations, either as a single package or on each issue submitted;
    (e) Settlement by a citizens' conciliation council composed of three residents within the jurisdiction of the public employer. The public employer shall select one member and the exclusive representative shall select one member. The two members selected shall select the third member who shall chair the council. If the two members cannot agree upon a third member within five days after their appointments, the Board shall appoint the third member. Once appointed, the council shall make a final settlement of the issues submitted to it pursuant to division (G) of this section.
    (f) Any other dispute settlement procedure mutually agreed to by the parties.

The Ohio Act also specifies the more traditional three-step process of mediation, fact finding, and interest arbitration should the parties fail to make a selection under the provisions Sec. 4117.13(C)(1). This array of impasse resolution procedures is significantly larger than that contained in most state statutes and allows considerable flexibility to the parties in selecting the approach best suited to their mutual needs.

The voluntary or compulsory nature of the impasse resolution procedures used in the public sector is of some significance. State legislatures cannot possibly anticipate the various needs of all the public employers and unions within their jurisdiction. To specify one uniform impasse resolution system that all unions and employers must follow is to assume away the possibility that unique impasse procedures may be more servicable for specific bargaining relations. Ohio, California, and Iowa are three of the states that allow the parties some discretion in selecting the impasse resolution mechanism to be utilized. This recognizes that there are individual differences among the many bargaining relations and environments within their states. The result of these arsenal approaches to impasse resolution should be more useful and effective impasse resolution procedures.

IMPASSE RESOLUTION PROCEDURES:
THE TYPICAL STRUCTURES

There is no uniformly structured impasse procedure. States vary substantially in the steps and the form of procedures utilized. As described above, Ohio allows some classes of public employees to strike while mandating that others use either a negotiated procedure or the multistep procedure provided for by the General Assembly. Oregon takes a slightly different approach providing for compulsory arbitration of contract disputes but limiting interest arbitration to employees who do not have the right to strike.[3] Michigan is among the states that provide for a mediation-arbitration process where the arbitrator is to act as mediator in carrying out his role, but then if an arbitration award becomes necessary the arbitrator is to select from the final offers of the parties.[4]

The majority of states with impasse procedures make fact finding the final step in the statutory impasse procedures.[5] Indiana and Kansas are examples of this statutory system. Several of these states (fourteen) also allow the parties to submit their impasse to arbitration if fact finding fails to resolve the impasse.[6] In Rhode Island fact finding is the final step of the mandated impasse procedures for wage disputes; other issues remain subject to final and binding arbitration. Connecticut employees covered under the Municipal Employee Relations Act of 1965 also have fact finding as their final impasse step.[7] As should be obvious there are almost as many forms of impasse procedures as there are states.

There are, however, two basic forms or classes of impasse procedures—closed ended and open ended—with variations on each theme. A closed-ended impasse procedure is typically a multiple-step procedure, but the distinctive feature is a definite cloture—hence the term *closed ended*. Closed ended impasse procedures typically begin with mediation. They typically end either with final and binding arbitration or with the right to resort to economic warfare (strike or lockout).

Open ended impasse procedures are more common than closed-end procedures. Open ended also typically begin with mediation; but open ended do not have cloture to the process. Fact finding is the common last step to an open-ended procedure. If the parties are unable to resolve the impasse on the basis of the fact-finding report, several alternatives are possible. In Kansas for example, if the parties are unable to resolve their dispute after receipt of the fact finding report, the public employer is free to determine unilaterally the terms and conditions of employment. The public employer is required to take the interests of the public, the agency, and the public employees into consideration in issuing this "unilateral contract."

Mediation is almost always the starting point for statutory impasse procedures. Mediation is that form of dispute resolution that is the least intrusive. A mediator is an expert in negotiations and is neutral. The mediator's role is simply that of assisting the parties in reaching a privately negotiated settlement through skills as an intermediary or even bargaining consultant.

Fact finding typically follows mediation in most impasse procedures. Fact finding is a quasi-judicial form of impasse settlement. The fact finder conducts a hearing, gathers the relevant facts, and listens to the parties' contentions. After the parties have presented their evidence and made their contentions, the fact finder adjourns and prepares a written report. Most fact-finding reports contain recommendations for resolving the dispute. Each recommendation is supported by a written opinion explaining why the recommendations are fair and should be acceptable to the parties. The fact-finding report is purely advisory and is effective only if the parties choose to accept the fact finder's recommendations. Acceptability is the key to effective fact finding. The fact finder's recommendations are little more than formalized mediation, without any binding authority save persuasion.

Interest arbitration is typically the final step in closed-ended impasse procedures. Interest arbitration is also a quasi-judicial form of dispute resolution. It is very similar to fact finding in that a hearing is typically conducted and the arbitrator provides each party with an opportunity to present their evidence and contentions. The main difference between fact finding and interest arbitration is that the arbitrator prepares a written award. The award contains the final and binding resolution of the issues at impasse. Unlike the fact-finding recommendations, which are advisory, the interest arbitration award is binding on the parties. This award settles the impasse by the "brute force" of a final decision much as a jury award settles civil disputes. The interest arbitrator's award, if ignored by one or the other of the parties, can typically be enforced in a court of law.

Each of these methods of dispute resolution will be examined in detail in the chapters that follow. Attention will now be turned to those responsible for the effectiveness of each of the impasse procedures.

THE NEUTRALS

One of the most often asked questions of a professional arbitrator or mediator is, "How did you become an arbitrator (mediator)?" This is also one of the hardest questions for most neutrals to answer. Many professional arbitrators are really unsure of the path that brought them to their present profession. There is an interesting colloquy between two professional arbitrators that indicates some of the depth and breadth of an appropriate answer to this question. Unfortunately, that colloquy is an entire chapter of a labor relations text and cannot be duplicated in this work; the best that can be offered is a citation and a suggestion that those seriously interested in the answer read it.[8]

Mediators are typically full-time employees of either the Office of Mediation Services of the Federal Mediation and Conciliation Service (FMCS) or some similar state agency. Mediators employed by FMCS are required to complete a one-year training program successfully, which involves substantial classroom instruction and on-the-job training under the guidance of an experienced mediator.

Most mediators are selected from a competitive screening of applicants. The successful applicant will have either a significant academic background in law, economics, or labor relations or several years of experience as a labor relations practitioner or negotiator. Most federal mediators have both types of background. State mediators are generally subjected to substantial training similar to (and in many cases conducted by) the FMCS to supplement a substantial background in labor relations and/or an appropriate academic background.

The mediator must also have well-above-average communications skills and be neutral. The techniques necessary to mediate a labor dispute successfully are often based on personal qualities that simply cannot be taught. Integrity, neutrality, and a demeanor that is consistent with inspiring trust and confidence are personal characteristics that are very difficult, if not impossible, to impart through a training program. There has been a continuing debate about whether a good mediator is born or trained. In fact, most good mediators are born with certain essential personal characteristics and then trained to make the most of what they have. That training teaches the sound mediation techniques that experience has shown to be most useful in a labor relations setting is probably closest to the truth of the matter.

Arbitrators and fact finders are a different group than mediators. In some cases, however, the state agency responsible for mediation requests a professional arbitrator or fact finder to serve in the capacity of mediator. It is not uncommon for the parties themselves to ask a fact finder or arbitrator, in whom they have mutual confidence, to act as mediator. Most arbitrators and fact finders do not specialize in interest disputes. It is common for a fact finder or arbitrator to hear an interest arbitration case one day and later in the week hear a grievance arbitration in the private sector; yet the processes and their purposes are significantly different. Grievances and contract disputes embody different subject matter and the decision-making processes are quite different.

A grievance arbitrator has the guidance of a written labor agreement and the practices and customs that have developed between the parties for guidance. The interest arbitrator has only those standards specified by statute or, in the absence of statutory standards, those commonly employed by the parties in negotiating their contracts and those traditionally utilized by interest arbitrators in similar disputes. The grievance arbitrator is typically confronted with issues concerning what the contract requires, while the interest arbitrator is asked to determine what the contract should require.

In addition, the types of evidence entered into the record will frequently differ between rights and interests disputes. In grievance cases the evidence is generally documents concerning events or incidents and the testimony of witnesses. Interest cases, more typically, focus on statistical evidence designed to show comparisons and bargaining history. The evidence and its weighting is therefore somewhat different between the two types of procedures.

There are relatively large numbers of grievance arbitrators who have not gained party acceptability as interest arbitrators, and vice versa; while there are also many arbitrators who have gained substantial acceptance as both. This illustrates the relatively wide variation in the background, experience, and abilities of those who serve as neutrals in labor disputes.

There are two basic elements to becoming a fact finder or arbitrator. The first of these elements is panel acceptability, and the second is party acceptability. An arbitrator can never get started in the business unless he or she is selected by the parties. Most parties select an arbitrator from a list provided by some administrative agency such as the American Arbitration Association, the Office of Arbitration Services of the Federal Mediation and Conciliation Service, or some state agency. These administrative agencies maintain panels of professional arbitrators and fact finders for the parties to select from. All of these administrative agencies have certain standards that must be met by the aspiring arbitrator before their names are added to panel of professional neutrals.

The requirements to be added to a particular state agency's panel vary substantially. In New York, for example, the State PERB requires substantial experience as an arbitrator in public sector cases and generally admission to the Federal Mediation and Conciliation Service's panel is a good start. Other states, such as Kansas, have specified training programs required of any would-be fact finder before listing on that panel normally occurs.

The standards for admission to the American Arbitration Association's labor arbitrator panel is a minimum of occupying a position of neutrality—that is, not representing either labor or management—and some significant labor relations experience. Normally the AAA will ask for references from representatives of both labor and management to assure that such qualifications as neutrality and expertise are met.

The Federal Mediation and Conciliation Service has several general requirements for admission to its arbitrator roster. Neutrality and adherence to the code of ethics (contained in Appendix C of this manuscript) are prerequisites to admission. Normally the FMCS will require reference letters from several representatives of both labor and management who are familiar with the applicant's ability as a neutral in labor relations matters and at least five arbitration awards where the applicant was the arbitrator of record. If this evidence suggests that the applicant is competent and is likely to gain party acceptability, then the applicant will be added to the FMCS's roster of arbitrators.

The requirements discussed above for admission to the AAA, FMCS, and state agency panels are intended to reflect the experience of professional arbitrators known to the authors (who are themselves arbitrators) and are not intended as official statements of policy for the appointing agencies. As is the case with any such judgments, the appointing agencies have other criteria that may be applied in special circumstances. The basic message is that each of these agencies takes great care to assure that the quality of those admitted to their rosters of professional labor arbitrators are fit and qualified to give proper service in that capacity. Party acceptability is the real test of whether someone will become a professional labor arbitrator.

There are basically two types of selection processes: ad hoc and permanent umpireships. In ad hoc arbitration, an arbitrator is selected from a list of qualified professionals either by mutual agreement or the alternate striking of names from the odd number of arbitrators until only one name remains. The ad hoc arbitrator is generally selected to hear one specific case. This is the primary difference between ad hoc arbitrators and permanent umpireships.

In permanent umpireships the parties select one or more arbitrators—depending on the number of cases and the number of arbitrators to hear each case—to hear all of the cases that arise between the parties. The same umpire(s) may hear both interest cases (to determine terms of the contract) and rights cases (to determine implementation of the contract terms).

Arbitrators selected to serve on permanent umpireships are arbitrators familiar to the parties and who have earned confidence in their neutrality and professional abilities. The reason for this is that most permanent umpireships are for the life of the contract. In most cases the lengths of the relationship will be for several years at a minimum. To fire a permanent arbitrator normally requires mutual agreement of the parties, therefore great care must be taken to appoint only those persons who will maintain neutrality and who are known to be very good at their profession.

The selection process should give a clue as to why party acceptability is the biggest hurdle to establishing a career as a professional labor arbitrator. Arbitrators may not advertise or seek appointments. Arbitrators must therefore rely on their track records and professional reputations to gain work. This generally means that the most professionally active and recognized professionals are selected to be arbitrators because they are the most visible. There is an implicit "catch 22" in party acceptability. An acceptable arbitrator must be accepted to be acceptable. The trick is to be accepted. The first years in the arbitration business are almost always slow years waiting weeks or even months for cases. As the cases come and the arbitrator writes awards, the parties become more aware of the arbitrator's abilities and talents. The best of these arbitrators will find that their case load accelerates over time, and the less able or lucky will find that they wait weeks or months between cases until finally, losing interest in the area.

The marketplace seems to work well in the area of labor arbitration. Parties learn which arbitrators are competent and which arbitrators are less so. Those who withstand the test of time and cases will establish a reputation and will quickly find themselves overworked and wondering why the parties have not tried more novice arbitrators. Arbitration is a rewarding field, especially for those who strongly believe in the peaceful resolution of conflict, but it is also a trying field. This may be no more evident than in the area of gaining party acceptability.

SELECTING A NEUTRAL

For most public sector impasses, the parties have little or no say in the choice of mediator. If the FMCS is used, that agency will choose and assign a mediator. A minority of state agencies will allow the parties some latitude in selection of a mediator if the agency maintains a panel of several mediators.

The first impasse procedure step at which the parties generally have some ability to select a neutral is with fact finding or interest arbitration. The selection of a fact finder or interest arbitrator can be a tricky and sometimes an expensive proposition. The parties will sometimes spend a great deal of time and effort in examining past recommendations and awards, articles written by the neutral, and inquiring of parties whom the neutral has served about the neutral's background and abilities. Such activities are not without merit, but some reliance in the appointing agencies' ability to screen neutrals may save a lot of time and headaches. The idea of examining past recommendations and awards is somewhat dangerous. Without a knowledge of the facts in the case the parties seeking to appoint a neutral run the real danger of not having sufficient information to make a judgment concerning the nature of the recommendation or award. Often the parties will get a better idea of the neutral's values and decision-making abilities by reading the articles and books that neutral has written on the subject of collective bargaining and impasse resolution.

Another often relied upon technique of selecting neutrals is to use only those fact finders and arbitrators who are members of the National Academy of Arbitrators. The National Academy of Arbitrators is a professional organization with approximately 700 members. The membership is selected from those neutrals who have demonstrated wide party acceptability (a minimum of 50 cases over the past five years, and the average for number of cases for entering members over the last three years has been over 120 cases each). Neutrals who are accepted into Academy membership will have established a wide reputation as neutrals and will have pledged to strictly adhere to the code of ethics (see Appendix C). This may not be a poor method of selecting an arbitrator or fact finder, but these 700 arbitrators are the busiest neutrals in their respective geographic areas and there could be significant delays in scheduling hearings. The use of nonmember neutrals may be a bargain in both time and money.

SUMMARY AND CONCLUSIONS

Impasse resolution procedures are substitutes for the strike and lockout, which are generally prohibited in the public sector. Impasse procedures can be classified in several ways. There are compulsory and voluntary impasse procedures, the former being specified by statute and the latter left to the parties to negotiate a mutual acceptable mechanism. Impasse procedures can also be classified as open ended or closed ended. Open-ended impasse procedures do not provide cloture to the bargaining process and typically end with fact finding. If the fact-finding recommendations do not provide an acceptable solution then generally the public employer may take unilateral action of some sort. Closed-ended impasse procedures generally provide some cloture to the procedures. The cloture is generally either final and binding interest arbitration or in some cases permitting the union to strike and the public employer to lock out.

The typical impasse procedure provides for mediation and should this fail fact finding. The majority of impasse procedures do not require final and binding arbitration nor do they permit the strike or lockout.

Mediators are generally full-time employees of either the Federal Mediation and Conciliation Service or some counterpart in state government. Mediators are selected for personal characteristics, professional background, and aptitude. Most mediators are then subjected to an extensive training program. Arbitrators and fact finders have two hurdles to clear. The first is panel acceptability and the second and more rigorous is party acceptability. Arbitrators are selected either on an ad hoc basis or as permanent umpires for the life of a contract or some other specified time period. The real test of whether one is going to make it as a professional arbitrator or fact finder is whether the person can establish a reputation with the parties for excellence.

NOTES

1. See David A. Dilts and Clarence R. Deitsch, *Labor Relations* (New York: Macmillan, 1983), chapter 11, and Roger Fisher and William Ury, *Getting to Yes* (Boston: Houghton Mifflin, 1981).

2. Chapter 4117 of the Revised Code of Ohio.

3. See Ben Taylor and Fred Witney, *Labor Relations Law*, 4th ed. (Englewood Cliffs, N.J.: Prentice-Hall, 1983), chapter 21, for further discussion.

4. Ibid.

5. Paul D. Standohar, "Constitutionality of Compulsory Arbitration Statutes in Public Employment," *Labor Law Journal*, vol. 27, no. 11 (November 1976), p. 675.

6. Robert E. Dunham, "Interest Arbitration in Non-federal Public Employment," *Arbitration Journal*, vol. 31, no. 1 (March 1976), pp. 45–46.

7. Ibid.

8. Paul Prasow and Edward Peters, *Arbitration and Collective Bargaining: Conflict Resolution in Labor Relations*, 2d ed. (New York: McGraw-Hill, 1983), chapter 17.

6

Mediation of Impasses

The sublime and the ridiculous are often so nearly related, that it is difficult to class them separately. One step above the sublime makes the ridiculous, and one step above ridiculous makes the sublime again.

Thomas Paine, *Age of Reason*

The impasse procedures utilized in most jurisdictions specify multiple steps for third party intervention in the case a bargaining impasse is reached. Mediation is typically the first of these procedures; should mediation fail then fact finding may be requested, and should fact finding fail then many jurisdictions require final and binding arbitration of the dispute. Mediation is the subject of this chapter, while fact finding and arbitration will be discussed in the following chapters.

THIRD PARTY INTERVENTION

Third party intervention in any labor dispute is based on the assumption that the parties have been unable to resolve their differences without some sort of assistance. Third party intervention can take one of several forms. The form of least substantive impact on the collective bargaining process is mediation, while interest arbitration is of the greatest substantive impact. Fact finding occupies a middle ground between these two forms of third party intervention.

Mediation is generally the first method of intervention employed in the public sector because it allows for the parties to exercise the most discretion in resolving their own impasse. In effect mediation can be thought of as a "jump start" to collective bargaining. Fact finding and interest arbitration are both quasi-judicial processes that differ in form and in some sense serve as a substitute for collective bargaining between the parties. Mediation takes place in the same forum and is simply an adjunct to the parties' own negotiations. The mediator's role in large measure and effectiveness critically depends on the parties and their negotiating skills. It is impossible for a mediator to assist parties who simply have no conception of their own roles or who are determined not to bargain in good faith to settle their dispute.

WHO ARE THE MEDIATORS

In the previous chapter a discussion of who the neutrals are and how they became neutrals was offered. It is worthwhile to review briefly who mediators are before proceeding to the discussion of the mediation process.

In the majority of jurisdictions, the mediators are provided to the parties by the Office of Mediation Services of the Federal and Conciliation Service. The FMCS is a government agency created under the Taft-Hartley Act for the purpose of assisting parties in resolving labor disputes. The FMCS provides two basic services. The Office of Mediation Services employs full-time mediators who are assigned to cases solely for the purpose of mediating. The FMCS's Office of Arbitration Services maintains a panel of professional labor arbitrators for rights (contract and discipline) disputes. There are several corollary functions of the FMCS including education, training and developing arbitrators and mediators, and fact finding for the health care industry under the 1974 amendments to Taft-Hartley. There are jurisdictions, however, that maintain their own mediator staffs, Iowa being most notable among these. The state of Iowa relied on the FMCS to provide much of the training for its state mediators. So even in the case where FMCS is not used directly to provide mediator services, it is generally relied upon for the training of mediators who will replace the FMCS mediation function.

Mediators are chosen for their expertise and experience in labor relations matters. Many FMCS mediators have served as chief negotiators for labor and/or management and are themselves wily old negotiators. Many FMCS mediators are attorneys who specialized in labor relations and bring substantial academic credentials to their mediation roles. In either event, FMCS puts their mediators through a rather rigorous training program including classroom study and on-the-job training. Mediators are, like arbitrators, neutrals whose sole function and interest in cases is to assist the parties in negotiating a settlement to their impasse.

THE MEDIATION PROCESS

The driving force of mediation is compromise. The mediator's role is to assist the parties in voluntarily negotiating a resolution to their impasse. There are different views concerning the mediation process, how it functions, and what successful mediators do to resolve impasses. According to Professors Bent and Reeves: "The mediator's objective is to progressively narrow the differences between the parties, relying on his abilities to persuade and cajole the parties to compromise."[1] Similarly, Staudohar sees mediation standing or falling as a dispute resolution process on the basis of the mediator's personality traits: "The mediator's stock-in-trade is persuasion applied through the use of pressure in order to modify attitudes and behavior."[2] Carl M. Stevens, on the other hand, believes that concentration upon the personality traits of mediators as an explanation for the success or failure of mediation is likely to be misleading: "While these qualities may be a necessary condition for successful performance, they are not also a sufficient condition, a successful mediator must have the specialized skills of conflict resolution."[3] In other words, the mediator must have some understanding of the negotiation process—why agreement takes place or an impasse develops. The mediator must be able to guide and assist the parties in the strategic and tactical pitfalls of negotiations while steering a course of personal neutrality.

A distinction that is currently in style is that between "crisis mediation" (that is, the traditional mediation concept) and "preventative mediation." William E. Simkin defines the former as "assistance in dispute settlement when a stalemate develops just prior to a strike deadline or after a strike starts" and the later as "assistance in the development of ways and means to avoid a crisis or make productive the crisis elements that must remain."[4] Preventative mediation techniques run the gamut from the "more activist" (that is, earlier intervention during negotiations) mediator approach to the "more traditional" approach (that is, intervention after an impasse but before a job action). The timing of the intervention depends critically on the nature of the bargaining relationship and the issues under consideration. There are several criticisms of the active mediation process that point out the risks in intervening in negotiations prior to impasse. Mediators must maintain their neutrality and therefore have the trust of the parties if they are to be effective. If mediation is injected into the process in the early more tactical stages of negotiations, it is not unlikely that the mediator could find himself directly involved in the tactical operations of the parties. This could result in reduced faith in the mediator by one party or the other, thus preventing the mediator from gaining the requisite information to be of assistance to the parties. It is also quite difficult to project whether specific negotiations will result in impasses that would normally require mediation. Preventative mediation is a risky business and is not normally employed in the public sector.

The more traditional model of mediation, that of crisis mediation, focuses on resolving impasses rather than the prevention of impasses. This is the type of mediation most frequently utilized in both the public and the private sector in the United States. The mediator's role is to resolve the impasse that has already surfaced. The mediator will normally spend the initial hours with the parties gathering sufficient information to ascertain the nature and causes of the bargaining impasse and the respective positions of the parties. Once the requisite information is gathered, the mediator enters the parties' negotiations to assist in resolving the matters remaining on the table.

MEDIATION TECHNIQUES

Mediation techniques may be generalized into several basic categories (presented in Exhibit 6.1). Before such generalizations are proposed and explained, a word of caution is in order. Each collective bargaining relation and impasse is in some respect unique. While many relations and impasses are generic in their causes and effects, there are often specific circumstances and complications that require the tailoring of any mediation technique to the specific situation or impasse to which it is to be applied.

It should be noted that the mediation techniques presented herein are very similar to the conflict avoidance techniques suggested in the previous chapter. There is a very good reason for this similarity. Mediation is designed to help the parties settle their own impasse. Frequently the mediator can facilitate a settlement by the simple application of conflict avoidance techniques to correct failures in the negotiating parties tactics or to point out miscalculations in strategies. There is also the possibility that the parties may have experienced other sources of conflict requiring more than corrections of bargaining tactics. It is not uncommon for communications or human relations difficulties to short circuit the collective bargaining process. A mediator can assist the parties in establishing open lines of communications and often help mitigate human relations problems. Environmental bargaining problems are more difficult for mediators but these too can be identified to the parties, often helping to prevent further impasse difficulties from such environmental sources.

Exhibit 6.1 presents an outline of the more commonly used mediation techniques.[5] As can be easily seen there are several techniques available to the mediator and most are directly related to effective bargaining

Exhibit 6.1
Mediator Skills and Techniques

FACE SAVING:

Mediator serves as scapegoat permitting one or both parties
to abandon untenable positions without loss of face.

RATIONALIZATION:

Mediator convinces one or both parties that specific demand
is not essential to to achievement of high priority goal
during negotiations.

ALTERNATE SOLUTION:

Mediator recognizes that parties are in latent agreement and
suggests a specific (i.e., alternate) provision that meets
the parties' needs and brings the parties to the realization
that they are in agreement. For example, a maintenance-of-
membership clause may meet a union's requirement for security
and at the same time be consistent with the employer's
principled opposition to a union shop clause.

SEPARATION OF PARTIES:

Mediator wins the trust of the parties and utilizes separate
caucuses as forums for eliciting the confidential information
critical to successful implementation of the other mediation
techniques noted herein. If the mediator's neutrality is
suspect, caucuses become pointless, and mediation breaks down.

PROMINENT SOLUTION:

Mediator recognizes that any one of many potential solutions
is preferred by both parties to an impasse and brings both
parties to converge on one of the potential outcomes by
highlighting it as the natural (i.e., prominent) solution.

REAL SOLUTION:

Mediator recognizes that, although the final-offer positions
of the parties diverge, their real positions, ascertained
during the caucusing process, coincide and simply advises the
parties that they are in agreement.

Source: David A. Dilts and Clarence R. Deitsch, *Labor Relations* (New York: Macmillan, 1983), p. 293.

techniques. These will be discussed in turn to assist the reader in understanding the strategies employed by most federal mediators.

Face Saving

In the course of negotiations there are often problems that develop in both the tactics and strategies employed by the parties. Some of these failures can be anticipated and avoided but when they cannot then one party may find itself painted into a corner from which there is no graceful way out. An astute opponent will sometimes recognize what is happening and will provide the party a way out. As with all human endeavors the opponent may not wish a way out or may even fail to recognize that he is in the corner. Mediators, who are generally pretty astute and have not been involved in the negotiations, are in a natural position to recognize when one or the other party is backed into such a corner and can provide the parties with a solution for which the neutral can be blamed if it is not what one or the other party wants. The mediator is not bound to the contract and is not charged with its administration or facing the party's constituents—he simply walks away after the negotiations. It is a part of the mediator's territory to take the heat for unwanted compromises and the astute negotiator will place the blame for mediator suggested compromises with the mediator thereby getting out of the corner. Here's one case where honesty is not only the best policy but also the most expeditious way out of a bind.

Rationalization

Much of the negotiation process is based on perceptions—perceptions of the other party's position and perceptions of your own position. Bargaining strategies are formulated and implemented on these perceptions. It is therefore not surprising that as negotiations proceed parties may become "wedded" to positions based on perceptions that may not be accurate. One of the primary roles of a mediator is to examine the parties' positions, arguments, strategies, and determine whether their perceptions of the events at the negotiating table are consistent with reality. Often one or both parties have come to focus on issues that do not accomplish much for their constituents. The mediator's role is to bring each party back to a rational position on the specific issue or issues. In so doing, it is relatively common that the revised position is acceptable to the party's opponent. Convergence of positions is what the mediator is really interested in, however, albeit uncommon, by rationalization a party might come to realize that its position, when revised, is even further from the opponent's. Even in these cases the rationalization of positions is important because the parties have a more predictable (rational) position on the table that allows for more meaningful discussions and is more likely to be discussed in light of objective criteria rather than emotional or subjective terms. While a short-term setback, the result is typically that the parties have a better chance of settlement even though more work lies before them.

Alternate Solutions

One of the most important bargaining techniques is to ease the decision-making costs of the other party. Proposals that give alternatives are often effective in giving an opponent an opportunity to decide to accept your position. Mediators have essentially the same tool in their kit as well. Agreements in principle are often difficult to put into language. Mediators who have seen hundreds of labor contracts negotiated have a wide range of experience in the solutions that other parties have negotiated to like problems and can often suggest draft language to help resolve such problems.

Mediators are often able to identify compromises where there is not an agreement in principle but the parties' positions are very close. Alternatives, even compromise alternatives, are extremely important to the process of negotiations and the mediator's fresh view of your negotiations and experience with other parties' negotiations frequently allows for such suggested alternatives.

Separation of the Parties

The separation of the parties can serve two useful functions. Occasionally tensions build in the negotiations process where a forced break in the face-to-face bargaining allows the parties to recover their wits and consider what is happening. This cooling-off function is, however, a byproduct. The mediator hopes that by separating the parties and caucusing with each individually he will be able to acquire sufficient information to determine three things: whether mediation may be useful to the parties and is warranted, what methods of mediation may be the most appropriate, and the data necessary to successfully implement the appropriate mediation technique.[6]

For a mediator to be effective (in all but the facing saving and prominent solution situations) the parties must have faith in the mediator's expertise and trust in his neutrality. Without these elements of trust and confidence the mediator's fact-finding functions will typically be compromised to such an extent as to short circuit most of the basic mediation techniques available to him or her. Further, if the parties are not honest and open with the mediator the effect is the same as the mediator not being trusted.

Prominent Solution

Often the mediator, through his or her fact-finding efforts, will discover that there is an acceptable middle ground to the parties. This middle ground may be a considerable area, especially in situations where the parties may be faced with proceeding to the next step of the impasse procedure where the costs of disagreement may be considerably higher. Fact finding is much more public, often takes months, and results in a set of recommendations rather than the flexibility of mediation, and final and binding arbitration generally takes the process out of the direct control of the respective parties. Faced with such alternatives, the parties may prefer compromise to risk. Advancing to the next stage of impasse procedures risks "bad" results and their attendant costs. Compromise, in the language of economic game theory, reduces the worst possible outcome to a tolerable one; it minimizes the maximum "bad" that can occur. Compromise also reduces the maximum "good" that might be attained however. The parties' attitudes toward risk come into strong play during mediation.

In an effort to sell a compromise proposition to the parties, the mediator may point out what the alternatives to resolving the impasse means to the respective parties. Many mediators hesitate to engage in this type of arm twisting without sufficient reason to believe that the parties will be receptive; it's a mediation technique used when experience indicates probable success. The parties should recognize what the mediator is doing and reevaluate their own and their opponent's positions to determine whether such a compromise would be in their best interest. Most often if a mediator suggests such an approach it is in the parties' mutual best interest. Recall that a prominent solution is a position that was acceptable to both parties when they developed their goals, strategies, and tactics; they had each hoped, naturally enough, to improve on their minimum acceptable positions.

Prominent solution techniques are, however, not dependent on a multiple-step impasse resolution procedure. It is sometimes the case that the parties may have a middle ground over which compromise is possible and they simply have failed to recognize it. In many situations, packages of issues may be put together in such a manner as to be mutually acceptable to the parties and the parties have simply failed to see how certain package offers could produce settlement. The mediator can often identify these situations and guide the parties to the middle ground and hence settlement. Prominent solution techniques are closely related to the next technique to be discussed, that being real solution. In practice it is often difficult to separate the two techniques.

Real Solution

In the negotiations chapter there was a discussion of resistance points. A resistance point is the minimum that a party has decided is acceptable. It is a "must have" on the issue. This bottom line is generally hidden from the opponent to avoid having to settle for the minimum or go to impasse over every issue.

It is not uncommon for a mediator to discover that the resistance points of the parties open a wide range for settlement. In one school case, the mediator was called in only to find the parties widely separated on the single issue at impasse—salaries. The union was demanding a 9.7 percent increase; the board was offering 5.9 percent. The mediator separated the parties. He found that the union would accept as little as 7.5 percent, but only if it could retain its present contract year of 180 days; the board proposed a three-day extension. The board was willing to grant up to an 8 percent increase and drop the demand for the three-day extension of the contract year, but only if the union dropped its demand for a reduction in force clause in the contract. The union viewed the reduction in force as a trading point for this year but wanted the board to start thinking about the inclusion of such language in a future contract. Here the mediator's job was easy. The parties had an agreement and didn't realize it because of the fear to drop trading point demands. The parties, oddly enough, settled the contract with no changes in current language and a 7.75 percent increase in the salary schedule.

Real solutions are one of the mediator's most commonly used tools in jurisdictions where annual negotiations are the rule due to the short time frame in which the negotiations must be completed. This technique only works when the parties trust the mediator and share with him what their bottom line really is, otherwise the technique is obviously of little or no value.

PARTIES' RESPONSIBILITIES TO THE MEDIATOR

There is a considerable body of academic and professional literature concerning the responsibilities of neutrals, much of which will be examined in the following chapter. But little has been written or said about what the parties owe the neutrals, especially mediators. The mediator enters the parties' negotiations for the sole purpose of assisting them in reaching a negotiated settlement. The mediator's mission is simply not going to be accomplished unless the parties are willing to do a few basic things, some of which are even required by law. The prerequisite to mediation being successful is that the parties meet and confer in good faith. Mediation, as an adjunct to the bargaining process, cannot accomplish anything unless the parties collectively bargain in good faith. There are an array of other obligations for the parties to observe if mediation is going to be successful in resolving impasses, most of which stem from good collective bargaining practices and common sense.

The parties must understand that the mediator is coming to their negotiations "cold." The mediator will generally know very little, if anything, about the status of negotiations and the nature of the issues at impasse. In most cases, the mediator will have virtually no background concerning the parties' bargaining history. The parties should seek to inform the mediator of the relevant facts succinctly and accurately. Some mediators are more perceptive than others and some prefer different sorts of information. It would be more than worth the parties' effort to offer to stipulate the requisite background information, including past agreements, budgets, and/or issues that have been resolved.

The mediator will also need to hear what the parties' positions are and what contentions and evidence they have in support of those positions. You will find that most mediators will want to hear your responses to your opponent's position including the evidence and contentions you have used to refute the opponent's positions. In fact, here is one of the strongest arguments for preventative mediation. The parties have been present during the negotiations sessions and have knowledge of what has happened; the mediator does not. The mediator needs much of the same information that the parties have been gathering for weeks and maybe months but only has days or hours in which to gather the needed information. The clearer the picture painted for the mediator the better mediation services you will receive.

Complete honesty is necessary if the mediator is going to be successful. Mediators do not (in the vast preponderance of cases) play one side against the other. If you can't trust the mediator and honestly present your positions to him then the mediation process is probably not going to work. The mediator is a little like the family doctor. If you don't tell the physician what your symptoms are (all of your symptoms) in an accurate manner how could you expect an accurate diagnosis? You can't! So be honest and candid with the mediator, even though it may be a little frightening at first, the mediator will not carry tales to the other side that will endanger your position.

Set reasonable times and places for mediator-assisted negotiations sessions. If you have to move your schedule around, so be it. The mediators serving most jurisdictions are few and they have a lot of territory to cover, both geographically and in terms of the industries and sectors served. If one party boxes the mediator in with time constraints' then he or she is probably not going to be able to do much for the parties. The parties should be as flexible as possible to allow the mediator to render the best possible service.

Try to avoid turning the mediation sessions into public forums for your positions. Mediators are not very useful at the posturing stage of bargaining where most of that activity should have occurred. You can't play to the press or your constituents and the mediator at the same time. The mediator is there to help you resolve an impasse, not as a tool for the formulation of public opinion.

Mediation can be and is frequently a successful form of third party intervention. The FMCS mediators generally put a great deal of effort into trying to make the process work. It is grossly unfair to the mediator for the parties to sit back and adopt an attitude of "O.K. Mr. Mediator let's see if you can straighten this mess out." The parties must put forth even greater effort at this stage of negotiations than they generally have at the other stages because there are now three actors, not just two. Active and willing participation is necessary in many cases if mediation is going to be successful.[7]

These are but a few of the more obvious obligations that the parties have to the mediator. In most cases trying to put yourself in the mediator's shoes and the use of common sense is going to take care of the rest of the things the parties owe the mediator; but we will list a few of them just to make sure everyone is operating on the same plane. When a tentative agreement is reached it should be reduced to writing, initialed, and left out of future bargaining efforts. If the mediator is told something don't keep uping the demands; tell the mediator what you want and what your bottom line is. Don't let personalities influence your interaction with the mediator.[8] Some mediators inspire confidence and trust from the beginning; others are not so inspiring from first impressions. The FMCS wouldn't be using a mediator who is dishonest or incapable of assisting the parties. Don't waste the mediator's time with side shows and personality conflicts. Act like responsible, professional negotiators; mediators are more familiar with these people than with cry babies and con artists. Finally, remember that your goal is to bargain a contract, don't get sidetracked on legal issues, personalities, or other corollaries. If these few and basic rules can be followed mediation can be successful.

MEDIATION IS A USEFUL TOOL

The success rate of the FMCS in resolving labor disputes is surprisingly high. The target settlement rate is 80 percent and the FMCS does, in fact, settle roughly 80 percent of all impasses it is asked to mediate.[9] This should inspire some confidence not only in the mediation process and the FMCS but in the parties' own abilities. In most states the settlement rate is very close to this FMCS average, which indicates that the parties are doing a relatively good job at this stage of most public sector impasse procedures.[10]

For an impasse resolution technique without teeth, mediation is extremely effective. This record of success not only speaks well of the skills and efforts of the mediators but also says much for the parties to collective bargaining. The success rates experienced would simply not be possible without good faith bargaining and skillful negotiators representing a very large number of managements and unions. While this evidence is indicative of maturing bargaining relations there is always room for improvement.

SUMMARY AND CONCLUSIONS

Mediation is the first step in the impasse resolution procedures in most public sector collective bargaining statutes as well as in the private sector. Mediation is a relatively successful method of third party intervention and is the least substantively different from the actual negotiations process. Many of the techniques employed by mediators are similar to those techniques employed by the negotiators themselves. To be successful the mediation process requires honest and active participation by the parties, which for the most part is in evidence in the public sector.

Mediation, while the first step in the impasse procedure, can also provide the parties with useful and direct feedback concerning their bargaining tactics and strategies. In the interaction between the mediator and the parties many suggestions and criticisms are often offered in a constructive manner that can provide valuable insights into the strengths and weaknesses of the parties' bargaining activities as well as the environment in which the parties negotiate. The mediation process should be looked upon not only as an opportunity to resolve an impasse but also as a learning experience.

Mediation may be viewed as a transition between negotiations and fact finding. While the mediation process is similar to negotiations, it is also similar to fact finding in many important respects. Fact finding has often been called "formalized mediation" and, in the manner in which it has an impact on the parties' negotiations, this is accurate. The procedures used in fact finding and mediation differ substantially. While officially many state labor relations agencies (PERBs, PERCs, and so on) discourage their fact finders and arbitrators from attempting to mediate, there are occasions where the parties and the fact finders or arbitrators will attempt to mediate certain issues or even the entire case. This is the general rule under the Taylor Act in New York, but this is an exceptional situation. These cases are rather infrequent outside of New York and fact finders or arbitrators will generally not propose mediation unless both parties agree that this is the way they wish to proceed.

NOTES

1. Alan E. Bent and T. Zane Reeves, *Collective Bargaining in the Public Sector* (Menlo Park, Calif.: Benjamin/Cummings, 1978), p. 244.

2. Paul D. Staudohar, "Some Implications of Mediation for Resolution of Bargaining Impasses in Public Employment," *Public Personnel Management* (July/August 1973), p. 300.

3. Carl M. Stevens, "Mediation and the Role of the Neutral," in *Frontiers of Collective Bargaining*, ed. John Dunlop and Neil W. Chamberlain (New York: Harper & Row, 1967), p. 272.

4. William E. Simkin, quoted in E. Wright Bakke, Clark Kerr, and Charles Anrod, eds., *Unions, Management, and the Public* (Chicago: Harcourt, Brace, Jovanovich, 1967), p. 320.

5. For a further discussion see William E. Simkin, *Mediation and the Dynamics of Collective Bargaining* (Washington, D.C.: Bureau of National Affairs, 1971).

6. For a further discussion see Arnold M. Zack, "Improving Mediation and Fact-Finding in the Public Sector," *Labor Law Journal*, 21(5) (1970), pp. 259–273.

7. For a further discussion see David A. Dilts and Clarence R. Deitsch, *Labor Relations* (New York: Macmillan, 1983), particularly chapters 14 and 15.

8. Ibid.

9. See various annual reports of the Federal Mediation and Conciliation Service. Naturally, these settlement rates do differ somewhat from year to year.

10. Ibid.

7

Preparation and Procedures in Interest Arbitration and Fact Finding

> Few are open to conviction, but the majority of men to persuasion.
> Johann Wolfgang von Goethe

This chapter will focus on two major facets of fact finding and interest arbitration. They are case preparation and case presentation (hearing) procedures. Negotiator control differs greatly between the two facets. Case preparation lies totally within the control of the negotiators. However, hearing procedures used in fact finding and arbitration hearings are determined primarily by statute and the neutral, so they are not normally within the control of the negotiators. This chapter describes commonly adopted methods of preparing for and conducting fact-finding and interest arbitration hearings.

Knowledge and astute application of both facets provide for successful impasse fact finding (or interest arbitration). The preparation is similar to the hours of practice of a dedicated sports team. Practice does not guarantee a victory, but it certainly does improve the odds. Impasse is analogous to a tie score at the end of regulation time in the contest. The hearing procedures are akin to the tie-breaker rules of the sport. Since tie-breaker procedures often differ in some respects to the rules applicable in the earlier quarters, halves, or periods, the team needs to be prepared for this eventuality. A good understanding of the fact-finding and interest arbitration procedures is similarly important to a negotiations team having experienced impasse. Preparation and procedures are now considered in turn.

PREPARATION FOR FACT FINDING AND
INTEREST ARBITRATION

Recall the Rule of P's—prior planning prevents poor performance. Preparation for a hearing determines the likelihood of success of a party's case. Unfortunately, solid preparation requires a lot of hard work that all too often goes unrecognized. Preparation is so critical to the success of any arbitration case that case preparation is addressed before examining the controlling procedures.

The first element of preparation is identification of the objective. The objective in table negotiations was to convince the opposing side to accept your position. Note that it was not to convince them that your position was nicer—nor better, nor more reasonable, nor more just, nor more convenient. While the position might be modified during the negotiations, the objective was always acceptance by the other party. The objective in mediation was unchanged. While modifications to the position may have continued, the focus on acceptance of the position continued. The objective does change with impasse and resort to the resolution steps of fact finding and interest arbitration.

The objective in fact finding is acceptance of your position by the fact finder. While many impasses are settled during fact finding, the expectation is that fact finding will be completed before the impasse is resolved. Therefore, the case presentation is directed to the fact finder. Again, the objective is acceptance of your position by the fact finder.

Why is the objective different in fact finding than it is in mediation? The objective in mediation is not to convince the mediator. The answer lies in the role of the neutral. The role of the mediator is to find contract terms that the parties consider acceptable (though perhaps not optimal). The role of the fact finder is to find the contract terms the fact finder considers most appropriate. The hope is that once you have gained the fact finder's support for your position, you can convince the other party to accept your position.

The hope remains that your opponent is convinced to accept your position during fact finding so that the impasse is resolved earlier rather than later. Nevertheless, the case presentation during fact finding is focused on the role of the fact finder. When choosing among tactics in fact finding, it is best to choose the one that is most likely to persuade the fact finder. The arguments best designed to sway the opponent should have already been presented prior to the impasse. Though the arguments may differ, it is important to remember that the manner of presentation is likely to alter or maintain the good, fair, or bad relationship existing between negotiating parties. Review the successful tactics for negotiation; they still apply.

Even if there is a difference in objective, why should that cause the case presentation to differ between fact finding and mediation? The answer lies in the tactics deemed best. A tactic that is unsuccessful with the opponent might be successful with a fact finder.

For example, a union may have argued that the agency could afford to give a pay raise. The sanitation workers' union may have even presented evidence that the agency has sufficient funds in its budget to be able to finance that raise. The agency could have agreed that the budget might be sufficient but responded that the proper issue is what ought to be paid, not what could be afforded. The agency may have focused on wage issues other than the ability to pay. In negotiations, there is little reason to emphasize a point already "won" such as ability to pay. However, the fact finder may weigh the ability to pay considerations more heavily than the agency considers appropriate if the union pursues the tactic of emphasizing the issue and supporting it with convincing evidence. An argument unconvincing to an opponent may be convincing to a neutral because the neutral may weigh the issue differently.

This aspect of tactics, the preparation of evidence, is considered further below as a part of case preparation. So far the message has been that (1) preparation for impasse procedures is important, (2) the objective of case presentation during fact finding and interest arbitration differs substantially from that of table negotiations and mediation, and (3) the difference in objectives calls for different tactics.

The second element in preparation is identification of the issue and its scope. Normally only specific issues at impasse are presented to the fact finder or interest arbitrator. Issues on which agreement has already been reached are considered resolved. It is the responsibility of the parties to identify the issues at impasse. One such issue may be the salary schedule. Salary schedules typically show the job title, the job level, the years of experience, and other creditable quality considerations that determine salary. For a school teacher the title might be "classroom teacher." Job levels may be K, 1–6, 7–8, and 9–12 for the different grades taught, though that is not a salary factor in many school districts. Years of experience may be total years, years in the state, or years in the district. Other considerations may be degree levels (associate, bachelor, master, doctorate), specialty (for example, special education), or extracurricular activities (for example, coaching).

Determining the scope may narrow the subject at impasse. For example, a teachers' union and school district may agree on premiums for advanced degrees, experience, specialties, and extracurricular activities. They may agree to use the same schedule for all grade levels. Then the scope of their impasse is limited to the base salary that will determine all the salaries on the schedule.

The third element of preparation is determination of the issues relevant to the issue at impasse. Salary issues, other dollar issues, and

Exhibit 7.1
Issues Related to Impasse

RELATED SALARY ISSUES

   salaries paid private school teachers

   salaries paid other teachers in the state

   salaries paid teachers in other states

   salaries paid non-bargaining unit principals, etc.

   salaries paid other public employees

OTHER RELATED DOLLAR ISSUES

   level of the cost of living

   changes in the cost of living

   school district budget

   state support of school district finances

   school district tax base

   other school district expenditure considerations

   school district tax base level/changes

   other revenue considerations

RELATED NON-DOLLAR ISSUES

   enrollments

   student-teacher ratios

   average daily attendance

   curricular and extracurricular programs

   quality of education issues

---

nondollar issues related to an impasse over teacher base salary are shown in Exhibit 7.1. This listing of related issues is extensive but not all encompassing. It is presented to emphasize that the task of identifying issues, gathering evidence, and organizing its presentation is not one to be accomplished in a short period of time. Preparation is clearly the key to being ready for pre- and postimpasse arguments of one's position.

The fourth element of preparation is collection of information or evidence for the issues identified. Sources include state and federal publications, state library reference services, professional consultants, state university or college departments and faculty, and professional publications. Analysis of data and organization of the information usually falls to the professional staff of the agency or union and their negotiating teams. College students may be willing to lend assistance if the information is then available for them to use for college credit research projects. Be innovative in your search for assistance during the preparation phase.

The preparation that occurs before the first negotiations session or even the notice of issues for negotiations is also critical to the preparation for the final step in the impasse procedures. Negotiators do not have the time to do this amount of research if they wait to begin after an impasse has been reached. This preparation should have been completed prior to the first day of table negotiations. The bargaining strategies, tactics, and evidence gathered to support demands at the bargaining table are the same key elements that are necessary if one is to prevail in fact finding or arbitration.[1] The only difference is in the tactical use made of the evidence.

The fifth element of preparation is of the presentation of evidence. It is important to educate the neutral as to the nature of statistics provided in evidence. Those with a statistical background may be well familiar with the terms *average, median, mode,* and *standard deviation* when used to describe data. But this is not true of every neutral. Diagrams, bar graphs, and pie graphs sometimes are helpful. Data needs to make a picture in the neutral's mind; and the picture is given credence by the supporting numbers. Each point the negotiating team is trying to make should be summarized in no more than three sentences. If that can't be done, the point will probably not be made clearly.

The elements of preparation form a cohesive whole and a step-by-step approach to impasse avoidance/resolution. As described they are: (1) identification of the objective, (2) identification of the issue and its scope, (3) determination of related issues, (4) collection of information/ evidence, and (5) preparation of the presentation of information/ evidence.

The strategy is the guide to tactics and the issues to be negotiated. The goals established through this plan determine what preparations are necessary. If the parties have effectively planned then the preparatory gathering of evidence necessary to effective bargaining will provide the data sources necessary for effective advocacy in interest arbitration. One measure of the success of a negotiator is to weigh the relative efforts before an interest arbitration. If the advocate spends more time gathering evidence than organizing the evidence for presentation then the negotiator has probably done a poor job at the bargaining table. If organization for presentation represents greater effort than the discovery of evidence, this indicates that the negotiator gathered the evidence necessary to convince the opposing party of the merits of the party's demands and the negotiator probably did an adequate job.[2]

The evidence to be gathered depends on the issues and the standards established for negotiating those issues. Each case and each issue will require specific types of evidence and the types and sources of the evidence necessary to prove a case will be examined in the chapters concerning the decisional standards employed by interest arbitrators and fact finders. It is important to note, before proceeding, that the evidence gathered and presented must be credible. Sources of the data must be cited, methods of gathering empirical data shown, and witnesses' testimony corroborated if the evidence is going to be deemed credible by the neutral. Shortcuts in gathering and preparing evidence are taken only at great risk. It is true that most impasse procedures are informal, but that does not provide the advocate with license to do a poor job in the discovery and presentation of evidence.

PROCEDURE IN INTEREST ARBITRATION AND FACT FINDING

The fact-finding or interest arbitration procedures required or utilized will vary substantially from one jurisdiction to another. The Kansas Professional Negotiations Act does not contain a specific procedure to be utilized.[3] This, in theory, leaves Kansas fact finders free to employ any reasonable methods to gather the relevant facts upon which to base their recommendations. However, the Kansas Public Employment Relations Board has established some rather restrictive regulations that force the fact finders to adhere to procedures not unlike those discussed in this chapter. A thorough preparation brings such facts to light.

The Ohio statute, on the other hand, explicitly requires fact finders and arbitrators to follow "prescribed guidelines" promulgated by the State Employment Relations Board.[4] The guidelines established by the Board also closely follow those procedures presented below. The reader should remember that jurisdictions differ in their legal environment and in many other aspects. The procedures used in fact finding and interest arbitration cases may naturally reflect some of these differences. Despite individual differences, the majority of procedures employed in public sector fact finding and interest arbitration bear a striking resemblance to those outlined in this chapter.

An alternative definition of fact finding is advisory interest arbitration. This definition emphasizes that the procedure used in fact finding is very similar to that used in labor arbitration.

Because of this similarity, the authors make no attempt to differentiate

Exhibit 7.2
Typical Fact-Finding or Interest Arbitration Hearing

    A. pre-hearing conference.

    B. pre-hearing stipulations and motions.

    C. opening arguments.

    D. presentation of respective parties' cases.

    E. closing arguments.

    F. post-hearing stipulations and motions.

between the procedures utilized in these two processes, except where there is a clear need for such differentiation. Any differentiation with respect to procedural issues would be, for the most part, artificial; it does little violence to reality to view the procedural issues as virtually the same between the two forms of dispute resolution. There are, however, differences in how interest arbitrators and fact finders will decide various issues and weigh certain evidence, but those differences will be examined in the following chapters.

Exhibit 7.2 offers an outline of a typical fact-finding or interest arbitration hearing. It will serve as a reference point for further discussions.

This outline depicts the general sequence of procedures observed in impasse resolution hearings. Arbitrators are not bound to it, so some would deviate slightly to suit the circumstances. This outline does contain the elements most frequently found in interest arbitration cases.[5]

The procedural elements are discussed sequentially below, though the sequence in individual cases may differ. For example, it is not uncommon that a pre-hearing conference or posthearing stipulations and motions would be waived with simple, single-issue cases. Neither is it uncommon for a pre-hearing conference to take several hours in complicated matters. The outline of the "typical" case is offered as the array of possibilities, but is not the only manner in which a fact-finding or interest arbitration case can proceed.

Pre-hearing Conference

The pre-hearing conference is the vehicle by which the arbitrator ascertains several important pieces of information: What issues are at impasse (or even how many issues are at impasse); whether the parties intend to call witnesses and, if so, whether the witnesses should be sworn or sequestered; and whether the parties have any stipulated (agreed upon) facts or evidence they wish to have entered into the record as joint exhibits. The arbitrator will typically take a few minutes to explain how he or she is going to conduct the hearing; sometimes more than a few minutes are used if the parties are new to the process.

This pre-hearing conference may sound as though it is nothing more than a warm-up exercise preceding the real contest, but it is more important than that. In several cases, parties have been able to reach tentative settlement on some of the issues previously at impasse. In some instances, a contract has even been settled during the pre-hearing conference. As the parties sift through the evidence in an attempt to identify points that may be stipulated, the parties have sometimes discovered that they were not far from agreement. With a little assistance from the arbitrator, mutually acceptable terms can sometimes be negotiated. These instances are certainly the rare exception rather than the rule, occurring more with relatively inexperienced bargaining parties.

The importance of the pre-hearing conference comes more from getting stipulations agreed to and into the record than from possible agreements through mediation. This saves valuable hearing time for both the arbitrator and the parties. The prehearing conference also establishes the fact that the arbitrator is there to conduct the hearing, establishes who is in charge, and gives notice to the parties of the procedures that will be in effect. It serves the parties well to have all this established during the stress of impasse proceedings.

Arbitrators are paid a per diem fee. The parties are generally obligated to pay this fee. In some states, however, the fee is paid from the budget of the Public Employment Relations Board. Regardless, it is incumbent on the arbitrator and the parties to assure a hearing that is both equitable and efficient. One efficiency-enhancing device sometimes used to supplement the pre-hearing conference is the pre-hearing brief. While pre-hearing briefs are almost never used in grievance arbitration, they do serve a useful function in interest disputes. (Recall that interest arbitration resolves the dispute over what the contract language will be; grievance arbitration resolves disputes occurring after the contract is in effect.)

Normally there are several unresolved issues in interest arbitration cases. The pre-hearing brief serves to inform the arbitrator in advance of the hearing what issues are at impasse, what the parties' arguments will be, and what documentary evidence is to be made a part of the record. By proceeding in this manner, valuable hearing time is not taken up with the introduction of documents or with arguments over what is the appropriate procedure to introduce such evidence. Further, if the parties' prepared opening arguments are included in the brief, the arbitrator or fact finder will be able to begin the hearing with the respective parties' cases in hand.

The process by which pre-hearing briefs are used is relatively simple. Prior to the hearing date, the union and the agency set a date to exchange pre-hearing briefs. Each party is allowed sufficient time to examine the other's brief, attach objections, rebuttals, and comments, and forward the brief with attachments to the neutral. The neutral is allowed several days, at a minimum, to examine the briefs before the scheduled hearing. This process is most beneficial when there are several complicated issues at impasse, when some issues require several pieces of documentary evidence, and when few, if any, witnesses are going to be called.

The place, date, and time of hearing may be in dispute. The parties must make the neutral aware of their desires and the facts pertaining to the dispute over the logistics of the hearing. Then the neutral can make an informed decision. State statutes differ substantially as to the requirements for a time and place for the hearing and whether the hearing will be public. In some jurisdictions—some cases in Michigan, for example—there is no formal hearing; the mediator just issues an arbitral award once deciding that mediation is unlikely to resolve the dispute. Again, the logistics issue is one in which the neutral decides based on the wishes of the parties, the facts influencing their wishes, the statutory or regulatory requirements, and the neutral's preferences.

Prehearing Stipulations and Motions

The next step in the process is pre-hearing motions and stipulations. Typically, the neutral adheres to the parties' wishes concerning seques-tering of witnesses and the administration of oaths. The sequestration of witnesses is rare in interest disputes but the parties may wish to have the witnesses kept apart so that subsequent witnesses do not have the benefit of having heard prior witnesses' testimony.

If there is a dispute concerning whether an issue is properly before the fact finder or arbitrator (within the neutral's jurisdiction), this is the time that motions are made to exclude consideration of or to modify an issue.

Extension of statutory or contractual time limits for the report or award, the filing of post-hearing briefs, exchange of appearance lists, and the entering of joint exhibits are typically handled at this point in the hearing.

Stipulations of fact or joint exhibits are often entered into the record at this point in the hearing. Stipulations and joint exhibits are elements of evidence over which there is no dispute. Parties are well advised to agree on those elements and enter them into the record as mutually agreeable fact for two reasons. The most obvious reason is that such agreements save considerable time, hence expense. The second is that a clear and simple record is easier for the neutral to work with in making determinations. Rather than having two different but consistent versions of the facts in the record, an agreed upon stipulation of fact prevents trivial details from entering the record and possibly confusing the neutral.

Opening Arguments

The opening argument is precisely what it sounds like. It is an opportunity at the beginning of the hearing for each party's advocate to present what it is they want from the hearing and how they intend to justify it. It also gives each party an opportunity "to say their piece" on any issue relevant to the impasses at hand.

The opening arguments should clearly state the party's position on the issues at impasse and why its position is more consistent with the available facts and evidence than the other party's position. Many neutrals prefer to have a prepared statement of the party's position on each issue presented to them at the beginning of the hearing. This serves roughly the same purpose as a program in a play; it lets the arbitrator know what is coming next. Many advocates prefer to reserve their opening arguments for presentation with the specific issue under consideration. While this makes the case organization easier for the respective advocates, it does keep the fact finder or arbitrator in the dark during the hearing. In cases where there are package issues (for example, salary schedules, fringe benefits, and supplemental salaries), the neutral should understand the entire position of both parties as soon as possible into the presentation of evidence so as to be able to judge its relevance and its appropriate weighting.

An interesting but time-consuming compromise many advocates choose is presenting the neutral a written opening statement, then reiterating their opening statements with the presentation concerning each issue. This is time consuming, hence costly, but does provide some organization to a parties' cases. Such organization, especially with multiple issues, is well advised but can be taken to the point of redundancy. Many neutrals prefer a written opening statement, clearly outlining the party's position issue by issue. If several issues are at impasse then the written opening statement also serves as a ready guide to neutral's deliberations after the hearing is adjourned. This method of presenting opening arguments is employed by the advocates for the U.S. Postal Service, General Motors Corporation, and several other firms and public agencies as well as many unions that are well versed in arbitration advocacy and collective bargaining.

Presentation of Respective Parties' Cases

Presentation of the respective parties' cases follows the opening arguments. But who goes first, the union or the agency? A common principle in grievance arbitration is that the party requesting the affirmative action goes first. That is the party that bears the initial burden of proof. In fact finding and interest arbitration, however, clear lines of distinction are not readily apparent. In general, the party requesting a change from the previously existing contract bears the obligation to proceed first. From this perspective, if an impasse over each provision of the initial contract bargained between the parties occurs, then the union would be obligated to proceed first on each issue at impasse.

An interesting exception to this rule is that some fact finders and arbitrators will view the parties' established past practices, even before a labor contract is negotiated, as being binding elements of a contract and would require management to proceed first on any language issue that would change an established practice.[6]

The rule that the union should proceed first on each issue on initial contract negotiations is based on the theory of residual management rights.[7] Residual management rights theory is borrowed from contract law and is widely applied in grievance arbitration concerning the interpretation and application of contract language. This principle simply means that those rights not specifically vested in the union by either contract or law remain the prerogative of management. If no contract exists and the parties are bargaining their first contract, then the union would be obligated to proceed first.

The procedures utilized in fact finding and arbitration would be recognized by most jurists. However, the courtroom rules of evidence and procedure are not strictly applied in these proceedings. The states of Colorado and Georgia are exceptions requiring that the courtroom rules be applied in arbitration matters within their jurisdictions.[8] Hearsay testimony, leading questions on direct examination, depositions, and other courtroom infractions are not only permissible but are common in fact-finding and arbitration procedures.

Fairly strict procedures are followed, however, when it comes to the calling and questioning of witnesses. When witnesses are used by either party, the party calling the witness has an opportunity to examine the witness fully before yielding (this is called direct examination), then the responding party has the opportunity to examine the witness fully (this is called "cross examination"). If, after cross examination is completed, the advocate who called the witness has further questions to put to the witness, that advocate will be given an opportunity to further question the witness (this is called "redirect examination") and so forth until both advocates are satisfied that they have gleaned all relevant testimony from the witness. At that time the witness is either excused or excused subject to recall (the latter meaning the witness might be examined further by one or both of the advocates later in the hearing). Once the party obliged to proceed first has completed this procedure then the other party will be given the same opportunity to present its case.

In interest arbitration and fact finding it is common for the advocates not to call any witnesses. Rather, the advocates present the arguments and substantiate them with documentary evidence. Normally the proper courtroom procedure for introducing documentary evidence is to call a credible witness to identify, explain the source of, and explain the significance of all documentary evidence. When documents are entered into the record in most public sector interest cases, generally the advocate makes claims for the source, reliability, and proposed weight to be assigned to document. The advocate then asks the neutral to identify the document and accept it into the record. Most fact finders and arbitrators find this troubling. Even under the relaxed and informal rules of evidence used in fact finding and arbitration, a party proceeding in such a manner is not getting the most out of their documentary evidence. Again this is where there is simply no good substitute for being fully prepared. The neutral is left with evidence for which no corroboration is offered and its credibility may be in serious doubt. It is always well advised to identify the source of the documents and provide the neutral with what supporting evidence is available.

In the discussion concerning the standards applied by fact finders and arbitrators, much more will be presented concerning evidence, preparation for the hearing, and upon what, specifically, fact finders and arbitrators base their decisions.

Closing Arguments

Closing arguments are often called summations. The skillful and sophisticated advocate will summarize the arguments presented and outline the evidence supporting his or her claims. In addition, the learned advocate will unemotionally and categorically refute each of the claims of the opponent—pointing out the faults in the opponent's arguments and evidence so as to impeach (or discredit) the other party's position.

Competency is only acquired by studying the process, being fully prepared, and paying close attention to the other party's claims and evidence during the hearing. As with opening arguments and cases, the party requesting the affirmative action proceeds first with the closing arguments. Often parties will make their closing arguments, listen to the opponent's arguments, and then request an opportunity for rebuttal. Such rebuttals are time consuming and generally result in the opponent requesting the same consideration. Rebuttal should be reserved for only the most unusual circumstances.

Posthearing Stipulations and Motions

Posthearing briefs are rarely filed in either fact-finding or interest arbitration matters. Such briefs simply make for extensive time delays— in preparing and exchanging the briefs—that are contrary to the relatively expedited nature of the fact finding and arbitration in most jurisdictions. It is important to note that at this point the hearing is closed. The parties must refrain from discussing the merits of the case with the neutral until the report is issued concluding this phase of the impasse resolution process. The only exception is a request for clarification.

Clarification of an award or a fact-finding report is not uncommon. Clarification is a request for an explanation or correction of some portion of the report or award that has either an uncertain meaning or is in error. Requests for clarifications are generally not entertained by the neutral unless the parties jointly request the clarification. The Code of Ethics of the National Academy of Arbitrators requires arbitrators refrain from clarifications unless both parties request such a clarification. An interesting dilemma results because the Uniform Arbitration Act allows for clarification on the motion of either party or a court order. Most neutrals will follow the more conservative guidelines of the Code of Ethics.[9]

Parties may attempt to abuse the clarification process using it as a method of appeal or re-litigation of the issues settled. Arbitrators and fact finders generally take great care to assure the integrity of the process and will not give a losing party such a privilege.

OTHER PROCEDURAL ISSUES

There are a great number of other matters concerning the conduct of the parties and the neutrals in the arbitration of interest disputes. Many of these matters are very technical legal issues that rarely arise in fact finding or interest arbitration cases, such as vacation of arbitrator's awards, appeals to court, and enforcement orders. These matters cannot be given adequate attention here and are therefore not examined.[10]

There are, however, several issues that are not uncommon to interest arbitration and fact finding and must be examined to gain an appreciation of the total process. These issues are ex parte communications and hearings, subpoena, stays and continuances, and inspections and site visitations.[11]

Ex Parte Communications and Hearings

Ex parte means, in the literal translation, in absence (of one party). Ex parte communications are communications by one party with the neutral in the absence of the other party. An ex parte hearing is a hearing in the absence of one party. These issues are of critical importance to most neutrals. A neutral's reputation for fairness and lack of bias is the foundation upon which a career as an arbitrator or fact finder must be built. Obtaining a fair and impartial hearing is of critical importance to the parties. It should be clear then that ex parte communications should be avoided. Unfortunately, in many jurisdictions, the time constraints placed on the parties by statute require the use of the telephone for such purposes as establishing the date, time, and place for the hearing as well as other administrative issues. Both the parties and the neutrals have an obligation to minimize these ex parte communications and where they are unavoidable the parties must refrain from discussing the merits of their cases with the neutrals. Most neutrals will instruct the parties to refrain from mentioning anything about pending cases during ex parte communications.

Ex parte hearings are generally a different matter. In most cases in which proceeding ex parte becomes an issue, it does so because one party or the other refuses to participate. Some state statutes allow for such proceedings, while others strictly prohibit ex parte hearings. In most states where ex parte hearings are prohibited, failures to appear without cause or refusal to participate are unfair labor practices (failure to bargain collectively). Neutrals will generally not proceed with an ex parte hearing unless one party refuses to participate and that party understands that there will be an ex parte hearing if it continues to refuse to participate.

An ex parte hearing does not assure the participating party of a victory. Neutrals will still require the participating party to present its contentions and supporting evidence and should the evidence be inadequate to support its claims an unfavorable ruling will be forthcoming.[12] There is generally no such thing as winning by default in interest arbitration.

Subpoena

A subpoena is an order to appear issued by an official given such power and authority by statute. The appearance can be as a witness or as a keeper of records. In the later case, the subpoena can also require the keeper of the records to produce relevant specified documents for the neutral's inspection, for inspection of the other party, or for inclusion as exhibits into the hearing record.

States differ substantially in the process whereby subpoena may be issued and served.[13] Some jurisdictions require the parties to seek subpoena from a court of competent jurisdiction, while others grant the PERB or even the arbitrator the authority to compel an appearance. Subpoena are typically enforceable through the courts. If a person refuses to appear, the court can find the person in contempt, order subsequent attendance, and/or levy penalties for contempt of court.

Continuances and Stays

Continuances and stays are motions to delay the hearing or appearance of a party. It is not uncommon for a party to be subjected to something that would make attendance at a hearing or proceeding with a hearing either unfair or impossible. Weather conditions, illnesses, and other circumstances do occur making participation difficult. Neutrals view these motions in a wide variety of ways, but in general if there is good cause, clearly outside of the moving party's control, and no statutory prohibition against the continuance or stay it will be granted. It is also true that if an unanticipated argument or evidential element occurs the neutral may grant the surprised party a continuance on this basis alone, especially if the focus of the surprise could not have been reasonably foreseen. Further, if the party requesting the continuance would be denied a fair hearing if the motion would be denied, even for events within that party's control, a majority of neutrals will grant the motion.

Continuances and stays are relatively common. Abuses of these privileges do occur from time to time, but in an effort to assure a fair hearing neutrals will frequently grant wide latitude to the parties. Of course, this depends on the jurisdiction's enabling statutes and the neutral as well as the circumstances involved in the request, yet these motions are more often than not granted especially if good cause can be shown.

Inspections and Site Visitations

Occasionally an issue will be presented in interest arbitration or fact finding that focuses on a specific work location. In road maintenance, prison guards, and postal operations as well as other activities the place where the work is accomplished is important to understanding of a party's case. Safety issues in particular commonly require arbitrator inspection of the site. This can be time consuming and costly if the site is some distance from the hearing site. If the parties mutually agree to inspection, arbitrators will rarely deny a motion for inspection. If one party objects and there is a reason to believe that the other party's case in some respect depends on the inspection arbitrators will rarely deny a motion for inspection. The problem is the delay and the potential expense in such inspections. These must be balanced against the duty to give the parties a fair and impartial hearing but generally the latter will be given the greatest consideration.

SUMMARY AND CONCLUSIONS

The preparation for interest arbitration and fact finding should occur in phases. The preponderance of evidence gathering should have occurred before negotiations began. The preparation for the hearings themselves should be, for the most part, organizing documents and interviewing witnesses so as to allow for a well-organized case. Naturally there may be gaps created through the negotiations process and problem areas pointed out by the mediator that require additional gathering of evidence and maybe even some updating, but the majority of an advocate's time should be devoted to organizing the case and polishing the presentation if the negotiators did their jobs in preparation for negotiations. If the negotiators did not do their jobs, then the discovery of evidence and preparation of the case for fact finding or arbitration will be a significant task.

The procedures utilized in interest arbitration and fact finding do not significantly differ. Differences may be observed across jurisdictions, but for the most part these differences are minor. The stages of the procedures utilized in interest arbitration and fact-finding cases generally include pre-hearing conferences, pre-hearing stipulations and motions, opening statements, presentations of their cases, summations, and post-hearing stipulations and motions. There are several other issues that are common in interest arbitration and fact-finding cases, including ex parte communications and hearings, subpoena, continuances and stays, and inspections and site visitations. State statutes and the arbitrators' Code of Ethics (Appendix C) give substantial guidance on the majority of these issues. It should be remembered that the neutral is bound to give the parties an equal and fair opportunity to be heard. If there is no guidance to be found in statute or the Code of Ethics, most arbitrators and fact finders will err in favor of giving the parties every opportunity to present their respective cases.

Neutrals endeavor to give the parties a fair and impartial hearing. This means that the parties will have equal access to the stages of the procedure outlined in the chapter as well as the benefit of the doubt in requesting continuances, stays, inspections, and site visitations. Subpoena are orders requiring a person to appear and/or produce documents. States vary in how subpoena may be obtained, but they are enforceable in court. Violation of a court order enforcing a subpoena is contempt of court. Ex parte communications are generally avoided by neutrals, but where they cannot be avoided fairness requires the parties to refrain from discussing the merits of any pending cases. Ex parte hearings are generally rare, but do occur where a party refuses to participate, as long as there is no statutory prohibition of ex parte hearings and the refusing party was given a reasonable opportunity to be present for the hearing and refused to participate.

Procedures in fact finding and interest arbitration are almost indistinguishable from one another. The only significant differences in the processes are the decision making of the neutrals and the end product. In fact finding only recommendations are made, but in arbitration the award is final and binding and the neutrals generally consider these differences in preparing their decisions. These differences, however, have relatively little effect on the procedural conduct of the hearings.

This chapter serves as an introduction to the quasi-judicial methods of dispute resolution known as fact finding and interest arbitration. The following chapters are detailed discussions of how fact finders and arbitrators make their decisions. These discussions assume that the reader understands the procedural material presented in this chapter. Without an understanding of how the structural processes of fact finding and interest arbitration work then the decision-making processes will mean relatively little.

NOTES

1. Jehoshua Eliasberg, "Arbitrating a Dispute: A Decision Analytic Approach," *Management Science*, 32 (August 1986); pp. 963–974.

2. David A. Dilts and Clarence R. Deitsch, *Labor Relations* (New York: Macmillan, 1983), pp. 134–152.

3. Kansas Statutes Annotated. 72–5413 et seq.

4. Ohio Revised Code 4117.13 et seq.

5. For further discussion of these issues in general see Owen Fairweather, *Practices and Procedures in Arbitration* second edition (Washington, D.C.: Bureau of National Affairs, 1983).

6. See Arbitrator Singer's award in *Pinehaven Sanitarium* at 47 LA 482.

7. For a further discussion of this issue see Frank Elkouri and Edna A. Elkouri, *How Arbitration Works*, 4th ed. (Washington, D.C.: Bureau of National Affairs, 1985), pp. 457–463.

8. Colo. Rev. Stat. Ann. 80–4–10 (1964) and Ga. Code Ann. 7–210 (1953).

9. David A. Dilts, "Award Clarification: An Ethical Dilemma?" *Labor Law Journal*, 33 (1982), pp. 366–370.

10. See Fairweather, *Practices and Procedures in Labor Arbitration*, chapter 3 for a discussion of enforcement of arbitrator's awards under agreements to arbitrate.

11. See the Voluntary Labor Arbitration Rules of the American Arbitration Association for some general guidelines on how arbitrators will typically handle many of these issues.

12. Arbitrator's award at 71 LA 1238, 1241.

13. The Iowa Public Employment Relations Board changed its policy in October 1986 to allow fact finders and arbitrators to issue the subpoena themselves rather than have the PERB issue the order.

8

Decisional Standards of
Fact Finders and Arbitrators:
Economic Issues

> A man never feels the want of what it never occurs to him to ask
> for.
>
> Arthur Schopenhauer

The Professors Elkouri from the University of Oklahoma authored a classic text on arbitration titled *How Arbitration Works*. The first major subhead in its Chapter 18 ("Standards in Arbitration of 'Interests' Disputes") is "Do Standards Exist?"[1] While the Elkouris intended this to be a rhetorical question, some persist in addressing the Elkouris' question literally, placing critical significance on the "yes" or "no" response.

It would be nice to say that standards do exist, that neutrals are well versed in these standards, and that standards are fairly and uniformly applied to all interest disputes. Unfortunately this is not the case. Were it the case, fact-finding and interest arbitration outcomes would be nearly predictable. The parties could predictably ascertain the nature of the fact finder's recommendation or the arbitrator's award by simply examining the available evidence in an objective manner and applying objective standards. Fact finding and interest arbitration are imperfect methods of determining truth. They apply imperfect truth to competing claims to ascertain whose claims are best supported by evidence. The best-supported claims then prevail. But how are the standards determined that will allow the neutral to be objective?

DETERMINATION OF STANDARDS

The Elkouris have a well-formulated answer to this rhetorical question.[2] Although it is very similar to the authors' conclusion, it is well worth repeating here as originally written.

Sometimes the parties will specify, in their stipulation for arbitration (fact finding), the standards to be observed. Even if the parties do not stipulate the standards to be observed, the arbitrator generally will make an award (recommendation) based upon one or several of the commonly accepted standards. In such case the selection of the standards used is still determined by the parties, though less directly, since an arbitrator (fact finder) generally will not apply any given standard unless evidence has been introduced to support its application.

The standards used by arbitrators (fact finders) are not pulled out of the air— nor are they artificially created. They are, generally speaking, the very same ones that are used by the parties in their negotiations. But if the arbitrator (fact finder) and the parties all use the same bargaining criteria, how can arbitration (fact finding) successfully resolve disputes where the parties' bargaining has failed? It can do so because the arbitrator (fact finder) is much more likely to be objective and to weigh impersonally the evidence adduced with respect to the various criteria.

The neutral, when possible, should use the same standards that the parties would have used in reaching a voluntary settlement if such a settlement would have been possible. The authors refer to this approach in fact finding and arbitration as the use of inferred standards; that is, the neutral uses the standards the parties' behavior infers to be the preferred standards.

Using Inferred Standards

What does it mean to use inferred standards, in a practical sense? The parties themselves establish some standards during the give and take of negotiations. The standards they set are reflected in their own negotiating behavior. It is therefore incumbent upon the fact finder or arbitrator to ascertain what standards the parties view as important. This is akin to gleaning the intent of the bargaining parties from the written language of a contract, past practices, or their bargaining history. Under this approach, it is the mutual intent of the parties that is of significance. But this approach, to be useful, must be capable of practical application.

How does the neutral infer standards from behavior? The first method is to examine the arguments used by the parties. If both parties' arguments focus on comparability of wages with similarly situated jurisdictions then the neutral will generally focus on this standard.

The neutral may also infer standards from evidence. If both parties approach the issue of a fair wage by presenting evidence of the wages prevalent in private sector businesses in the same city, then they have inferred that such is an appropriate standard for comparison.

The neutral faces considerable problems in inferring standards when the arguments are different and the evidence is used to support competing standards. The neutral may not infer a standard when the union argument focuses on characteristics of the employee (education, dexterity, and so on) while the agency argument focuses on characteristics of the job (clerical, sales and so on). Indeed, the need for the neutral may arise precisely because of impasse over the appropriate standard to be used rather than the application of an agreed upon standard.

In many cases the standards used by the parties during negotiations are recognizable to an observer and mutually acceptable to the parties. They are using the same standards. If this is the case, then the issue of standards creates no problem for the neutral. The parties may simply stipulate the standards the neutral is to apply to each issue.

Using Stipulated Standards

Once the parties have stipulated standards, it is only the facts and the implications of those facts over which the parties disagree. Under these circumstances, the fact-finding or interest arbitration process is reduced to one of understanding how evidence is weighted (credible or relative merit or how compelling the evidence is). The application of determined standards to the evidence is deferred to a later portion of this chapter.

In some jurisdictions, the fact finder or arbitrator is not free to use only inferred and stipulated standards. Numerous jurisdictions specify standards to be used by the neutral, while several state statutes contain no specific decisional standards for interest disputes. Examination of the various state statutes that do contain standards can provide some valuable insights and demonstrate that not all jurisdictions view decision-making standards in the same manner.

Using Statuatory Standards: Lessons from Michigan

The state of Michigan's Police and Firemen's Arbitration Act provides that interest dispute arbitrators will consider the following standards in formulating their orders:

(a) The lawful authority of the employer.
(b) Stipulations of the parties.
(c) The interests and welfare of the public and the financial ability of the unit of government to meet those costs.
(d) Comparison of the wages, hours and conditions of employment of the employees involved in the arbitration proceedings with the wages, hours and conditions of employment of other employees performing similar services and with other employees generally:
   (i) In public employment in comparable communities.
   (ii) In private employment in comparable communities.

(e) The average consumer prices for goods and services, commonly known as the cost of living.

(f) The overall compensation presently received by the employees, including direct wage compensation, vacations, holidays and other excused time, insurance and pensions, medical and hospitalization benefits, the continuity and stability of employment, and all other benefits received.

(g) Changes in any of the foregoing circumstances during pendency of the arbitration proceedings.

(h) Such other factors, not confined to the foregoing, which are normally or traditionally taken into consideration in the determination of wages, hours and conditions of employment through voluntary collective bargaining, mediation, fact-finding, arbitration or otherwise between the parties, in the public service or in private employment.

This Michigan statute, while applying to only police and firemen, still provides some very useful insights into the standards utilized by arbitrators and fact finders. The Michigan legislature specifically informed the parties (including the arbitrators) what standards it saw as particularly important in this sector of public employment. But paragraph (h) allows the neutral to also consider additional unspecified standards, which might be in general use in any facet of labor relations in any sector of the economy.

In searching for the legislative intent of this section of the Michigan law, many have concluded that the legislature intended to provide general guidance with paragraphs (a) through (g) but paragraph (h) demonstrates the Michigan legislature viewed the arbitration process as second best to a voluntarily negotiated settlement.

By now the reader is well aware of a diversity of standards that exist in interest arbitration of economic issues. The standards discussed have a common goal: reasonable consideration of unsettled issues to reach a reasonable resolution of the impasse. Two further approaches are directed more at the end than the means: the acceptability standard and the equity standard.

Using the Acceptability Standard

As with numerous other issues in dispute resolution, there are competing approaches to telling the neutral how best to ascertain the standards to be used.

An acceptability standard, as the authors use the phrase, refers to both the means and the end. Fact finders and arbitrators present a discussion of the rationale used along with the final recommendation or award. For the parties to fact finding to accept the report as a basis for further negotiations, the rationale of the fact finder must seem reasonable even if preceived as less than optimal. Neither should arbitral awards strike both parties as "off the wall," lest the arbitral process be diminished in its usefulness as a resolution process. The use of inferred, stipulated, and statutory standards are clearly consistent with this approach so far.

Generally, the neutral has some latitude in choice of acceptable standards. The constraint on the neutral is that the adopted standards must not be in opposition to standards mutually held by the parties to the impasse. Put more simply, the neutral's applied standards may not be too different from that of the parties.

For the same reasons that the rationale should be reasonable, the recommendations or awards themselves should generally strike both parties as falling within a range of reasonable bounds. If wages were the single issue at impasse, the neutral acting under an acceptability standard would be limited in the range of reasonable wages. The minimum would be at least as great as the agency has offered; the maximum would be no more than the union has requested. The acceptability standard is not, by itself, sufficient to determine the recommendation or award. It merely places upper and lower bounds on the award.

Using an Equity Standard

The neutral whose considerations are controlled by an equity standard is obliged to determine what is fair within his or her own value system and base the recommendations or award on this brand of justice. The more familiar the parties are with the neutral's value system, the more serviceable the results are likely to be. The more consistent the neutral is in applying his or her own value system, the more serviceable the results are likely to be.

When there are no stipulated or statutory standards, the equity standard is almost assuredly one that will be applied either alone or in combination with other standards. For this reason, many parties facing impasse resolution procedures will attempt to use only experienced fact finders or arbitrators. Experience comes only from having been hired in the past. Neutrals quickly gain a reputation; those with a less satisfactory reputation quickly fall from demand.

Neutrals faced only with factual disputes should be so informed. The parties should specify the standards they wish utilized if they wish to avoid the application of whatever standards the neutral considers most appropriate. The more guidance jointly provided by the parties to the neutral, the more likely that the fact finding or arbitration decision will be similar to a negotiated settlement. Naturally the parties cannot expect the neutral to be without his or her own value system and opinions on the subject of fairness. Neutrals are human beings and the parties must understand that neutrality simply means that the decision maker is prepared to rule in favor of either party, depending solely upon the record made at the hearing (see Appendix C). Regardless of the standard actually applied, an interest arbitration award does settle a dispute—by the power of the award's finality. Such is not the case with fact finding.

Fact-finding recommendations should assist the parties in settling the impasse. The role of the fact finder may be to identify the strengths and weaknesses of the different standards that could be used to judge an issue. Negotiations often reach impasse because the parties differ on the method of evaluating evidence, not because of disagreements on what the evidence is. This standards problem is a common one in interest cases. Then, to the extent possible, the recommendations should be explained in light of the weight given to the different standards as well as the evidence.

STANDARDS FOR ECONOMIC ISSUES: AN INTRODUCTION

Often it is difficult to separate issues at the bargaining table or at a hearing. As fringe benefits, the salary schedule, and supplemental salaries are all economic (dollar) issues, they are highly interrelated. Since most school districts publish schedules of annual salaries, negotiators in that field are familiar with the interrelationship of economic provisions and calendar provisions. Calendar provisions include the reporting and concluding dates for the school year, which affect summertime employment options; the contract year, which shows the number of school days; the work day, which determines the hours per day worked; sick leave, maternity leave, personal days off, and sabbatical leave, which affect the number of days worked; and extracurricular duties, which may affect both hours and salary. Similar interrelationships are encountered with bargaining criteria or standards used in evaluating contract language issues—the subject of the following chapter. With these difficulties in mind, the focus of attention is now narrowed to the specific bargaining criteria for monetary issues (the economic package).

The economic package consists of issues typically viewed as compensation to the public employee for services rendered. This classification, however, does not directly translate into costs for the employer. There are many contract language issues that represent substantial monetary costs to the employer and that are not generally considered to be part of the economic package. It is perfectly permissible—in fact it is wise— to point out the interrelations between contract language issues and the economic package where such influences exist and can be properly documented. Fact finders and arbitrators are aware that packages within the total agreement exist and that a contract must be viewed in total to ascertain its meaning and assignment of relative rights (and costs).

There are three major standards used in cases involving the economic package: (1) prevailing practice or comparative norm, (2) the cost of (or standard of) living, and (3) ability of the public employer to pay and the public interest. The major standards are so named because of their wide acceptability to the negotiating parties and hence their widespread use in fact-finding proceedings. In addition to these major standards, there are several minor standards used in evaluating economic packages. The minor standards tend to be of limited applicability and are generally specialized in nature. All are discussed in the sections that follow.

Prevailing Practice (Comparative Norm) Standard

This standard is the one most widely used, though it is not used as a sole standard in most cases. The reasons for its use are multiple: Valid, reliable evidence is available; it carries connotations of fairness; and it may reflect market forces as well. Even its reputation as an acceptable standard enhances its acceptability to parties at impasse. As the name implies, this standard is concerned with what other similarly situated bargaining relations or similar employer-employee contracts have used for solutions to common problems.

Prevailing practice is synonymous with comparative norm in application to the economic package. The prevailing practice embodies the concept of the external wage structure—a relative ranking of the agency's wage/salary schedule to that of other similar employers (horizontal) or other occupations (vertical). Public employer and the counterpart union negotiators base their economic demands, at least in part, on the standards that have been established in labor-management contracts in industries and economic environments relatively similar to their own.

Public employers will attempt to avoid being at the top of the external wage structure, while unions will attempt to ensure that they won't be at the bottom either. The agency has an incentive to avoid extremely low wages also. The public employer must attempt to negotiate a wage package that is substantial enough to ensure an adequate supply of skilled public employees. With this, the union has no objection. But it is the public employer's attempt to avoid anything in excess of that minimum required that puts it into a conflict situation with the union. The union wishes, understandably, to use comparisons that support the best possible economic package.

As should be expected, the parties will introduce comparative wage packages that best support their individual positions—fact finders and arbitrators know this too. The introduction of such comparability data requires the introducing party to establish the credibility of such comparisons. Credibility means sufficient evidence is introduced to demonstrate that the comparison group is similar or relevant to the bargaining unit. Such data as budgetary information, population, demographics, growth rates for the jurisdiction, and industrial composition of the economy are commonly introduced to show that the comparisons are valid.

The key to the effective use of this standard in bargaining is the quality of evidence. School boards have, on occasion, introduced their athletic conferences as their comparability groups—this type of comparison may or may not be a valid comparability group. Athletic conferences mean virtually nothing in terms of the tax base, per capita income and wealth of the residents of a district, the financial history and status of the district, the bargaining history of the present parties, and changes in any of the aforementioned or programs offered by the district. The only ways in which schools in an athletic conference are almost always comparable is in number of faculty, student enrollment and geographic proximity. These comparisons may not be economically valid on their face.

The comparisons have to be supported with reliable and valid evidence that supports the contentions being made before an arbitrator or fact finder will give them weight. A principal's opinion that a group of four or five school districts are comparable does not necessarily sway a neutral more than any other contention. If the principal's opinion can be supported with budgets (over the last few years), student enrollment figures, demographic data about the districts, income and wealth data from the districts, and the specifics of contract settlements in those districts. Then an opinion supported by credible evidence becomes a fact, and that is what the arbitrator or fact finder is after.

Unions frequently make the same kinds of errors; what sense does it make to use as a comparability group those districts that border on the parties' own district if each of the bordering districts is at least twice as large, is at least 10 percent wealthier (on average), has an average per capita income at least 5 percent higher, and each has increasing student enrollments while the subject district has declining student enrollments? It makes no sense and cannot be mistaken by the most inept fact finder or arbitrator as anything resembling a reasonable control group for comparison purposes.

The gathering and organization of evidence concerning the comparative norm is time consuming and may be quite difficult. If the parties have done an adequate job of preparation for negotiations and the comparative norm was used at the bargaining table as a negotiations criteria, then this information should be available from the data gathered for negotiations and need not be replicated for a fact-finding or arbitration hearing. If the data need to be gathered for the purposes of fact finding or arbitration, then the lack of adequate preparation for negotiations may be the cause of the impasse.

There are several sources of comparability information. The state agencies responsible for tax collections, budgeting, and certification or licensing of professional public employees will typically have detailed information on salaries, budgets, demographics, and other useful items for comparison purposes. In addition to such state agencies, unions (for example, National Education Association state offices; American Federation of State, County, and Municipal Employees regional offices; and so on) often gather such information. On the employer side of the table, such organizations as the State Association of School Boards or the State Association of Municipalities will gather like information. Negotiators should identify the sources of such information and assure that the desired data can be made available to them. On occasion negotiators will find that no such data are gathered for their jurisdiction. To conduct one's own survey requires that the validity and reliability of such gathered information can be documented for the neutral. If such expertise is not available within the organization, there are resources such as universities and survey firms located in the area that can provide the necessary services at a reasonable cost.

Cost of Living (Standard of Living) Standard

The cost of living and the standard of living are mirror images of one another; in other words, as the cost of living goes up the standard of living must go down unless an offsetting increase in income is forthcoming. In virtually every fact-finding or arbitration hearing this standard is used by one or both parties. This is a valid consideration but the data on cost of living and standard of living are often not directly applicable to anything except the "average or typical" family or to certain standard metropolitan statistical areas or the United States in general. The standard or cost of living data for specific individual areas will vary widely across the United States. Whether rural areas are higher or lower cost of living areas than metropolitan areas is subject to debate. There are sources of cost or standard of living data for specific areas of the country that are not standard metropolitan statistical areas.[3] The basic message is, while this standard is always considered (when introduced) it is almost never given controlling weight. We say almost never because if such data were available in valid and reliable forms they could be given controlling weight. In such cases as Detroit, Los Angeles, or New York City where such data are routinely available, this evidence will generally be given weight. There is another problem with published price indices or family budgets other than simply the availability of the data. The price indices or family budget may not be representative of the public employees' households within a specific jurisdiction.

The cost of living is typically measured by the Consumer Price Index (CPI). The CPI is an index number that changes as the price of a particular market basket of goods changes. This market basket of goods consists of items that the Bureau of Labor Statistics of the U.S. Department of Labor believes is purchased in the same proportions (roughly) by a typical American family. The CPI is available for U.S. national averages and for selected standard metropolitan statistical areas.[4] There are subjective judgments about what goes into the market basket of goods to be surveyed for price and CPI allows very little inference to be drawn concerning local or even regional prices. The CPI can only serve as a rough guide to negotiators. As a matter of fact, often it is unlikely that one can say with any degree of certainty that a specific geographic region is experiencing higher or lower rates of inflation than the national average.[5]

The other type of data most frequently cited to demonstrate to an arbitrator or a fact finder what an acceptable standard of living should be is the family budget data gathered by the Bureau of Labor Statistics:

> These data are for three "adequate standards of living": lower, intermediate, and higher. The budgets described here are for a characteristic family of four: a 38 year old employed husband, a housewife (not employed outside of the home), a thirteen year old boy and an eight year old girl. The lower budget category assumes the family rents its home. For the other two categories it is assumed the family is purchasing their dwelling. The "other costs" category includes such items as gifts, charitable contributions, life insurance, and occupational expenses, (most of which are not included in lower budgets).[6] [emphasis added]

What constitutes an adequate standard of living is highly subjective and little inference can be drawn from these data concerning what a particular group of people in a specific geographic region of the country would need for an adequate budget to maintain an acceptable standard of living.

There are cases where the union or employer has made an effort to survey persons in their district concerning what an adequate budget was for the maintenance of an acceptable standard of living. Such efforts are generally a waste of time if the survey is not scientifically conducted, verified, and the results tabulated in an objective and documented manner. If such evidence were produced and its reliability and validity were documented it would be admissible and weighed for what it was worth.

Ability to Pay (Public Interest) Standard

This standard, together with the prevailing practice/comparative norm standard form the basis for the majority of fact finding recommendations and arbitration awards concerning economic issues in most jurisdictions.[7] The ability to pay and the public interest are not precisely the same concept but in the application to economic issues they overlap considerably. The ability to pay question is generally a budgetary question. The budgeting process across states typically varies and few generalizations can be made concerning how budgetary information is to be gathered and interpreted.

There are a few generalizations concerning ability to pay that should be mentioned before proceeding to the public interest aspects of this standard. In most jurisdictions a claimed inability to pay must be proven with evidence. This follows the National Labor Relations Board's decision in *Truitt Manufacturing* concerning bargaining in good faith.[8] A claim of an inability to pay is good faith bargaining if such a claim can be supported with evidence. But if the claim is not supported with credible evidence, then the employer's actions evidence bad faith bargaining. Informed employers have, therefore, become reluctant to claim an inability to pay. Rather, employers are more prone to argue that they would rather utilize limited budgetary resources for other priority items than for a wage increase.

Inability to pay has a different implication for the public sector than it does for the private sector. Revenues to a public employer are somewhat more controllable than the revenues to a private sector employer due to the public employer's ability to tax. Taxes can be raised to support various levels of spending. Whether a tax increase is politically wise or equitable are different questions from whether revenues can be increased through increased taxes. This latter question is the linkage between the ability to pay and the public interest.[9]

There must be a delicate balance struck between the tax burden imposed on the jurisdiction's residents and the revenues available to fund public safety, roads, and school programs. While this balancing act may be delicate, there is a wide variance in the amount of tax revenue that may be obtained for public services without impoverishing or significantly harming the taxpayer. The ability to pay standard in the public sector is a much less stringent test than it is the private sector where profit maximization and loss minimization are much cleaner and easily measured concepts than tax burden and quantity and quality of service in the public sector.

The ability to pay can be adduced from the public employer's budget, but this alone cannot prove the inability to pay. Further information about the present tax burden and what the proposals would do to future tax burdens within the jurisdiction need be considered. Often the school board or city commission will state that in its opinion taxes cannot be raised to pay increased salaries. This may be a legitimate claim but too often this claim cannot be shown to be valid because no evidence to support the claim was introduced into the record. In cases where the public employer is paying close to the lowest salaries of their reasonable comparability groups and the tax rates assessed are much lower than jurisdictions with comparable incomes and tax bases, a claimed inability to pay or public interest in lower taxes will generally fail. Fact finders and arbitrators will normally look disfavorably on such claims of public interest when the evidence clearly shows that an unreasonable burden will not be imposed on the taxpayer while public employees are being compensated at rates significantly lower than public employees in appropriate comparability groups. Again if the tax burden is relatively high the school board or city commission must be concerned with how it can reduce this burden. An inability to pay and unwarranted tax increase are sure arguments for the employer's economic package (or at least very close to it depending on the evidence concerning the other standards) if there is valid and reliable evidence produced to support the claims.

MINOR STANDARDS

In addition to the major standards already considered, there are several minor standards that may influence a fact finder's recommendations or an arbitrator's award. Minor standards, as the name implies, indicate that such issues would be rarely given substantial weight. The weight assigned depends on the evidence and the relative importance of the standard to the overall case for the economic issues. The most important of these standards will be reviewed in this section: (1) bargaining history; (2) changes in the risks of the job, responsibilities, and skill requirements; (3) geographic differentials; (4) steadiness of employment; and (5) changes in productivity.

Bargaining History

The historical trends in settlements negotiated between the parties will be given consideration by arbitrators and fact finders if such evidence is introduced. Should a party have consistently resisted the introduction of a particular fringe benefit over several contract negotiations then this is evidence of the unacceptability of such a benefit. The historical positioning of a particular jurisdiction's employees in a comparability group is also often given weight. Such proposals and changes during the life of a bargaining relation may provide insights concerning the intent of the parties and what has and has not been mutually acceptable over past negotiations.[10]

Changes in Job Risks, Responsibilities, and Skill Requirements

If the risks, responsibilities, or skill requirements of a position change, then the appropriate wage will follow the direction of the change if it is substantial and warrants a compensation adjustment. The demands of a particular position should be reflected in the salary or wages paid. It is inequitable for additional risks or responsibilities to be assigned to an employee and the compensation not reflect this change relative to coworkers. This presumes that the internal wage structure was reasonable before the change. Fact finders and arbitrators will normally give such equity issues some consideration if the contentions can be supported with credible evidence.[11]

Geographic Differentials

Geographic areas are sometimes given minor weight as a comparability group if it can be shown that high turnover rates, substantial quits, or other such difficulties can be shown with reliable and valid evidence. The geographic area in which a public employer operates will often determine the labor market area from which the employer draws employees. From this perspective there is an element of competition involved with this standard. If the employer is paying a competitive wage for the geographic area then this may be considered by the neutral, especially in cases where no reliable cost of living data are available.

Steadiness of Employment

This standard is often considered in the public sector because a steady job with a lower wage may produce as much annual income as a less steady job with a higher wage. This standard, however, is rarely raised and is difficult to show any significant evidence either to refute or support claims for this standard.

Changes in Productivity

Changes in the productivity of the work force will typically result in demands for changes in total compensation. Naturally, if productivity falls management will wish to pay less for the less productive labor, and if productivity increases the unions will demand more for the increased output. Productivity is sometimes difficult to measure but numerous economic studies have been quite successful in measuring value added by various skill classes of labor.[12]

Productivity increases can come from several different sources. For example, a better-trained, better-educated, and healthier work force will typically be more productive. Better equipment and better managerial techniques can also generate higher productivity. The separation of productivity gains into their true sources can often be a difficult and controversial task. Where evidence can be adduced concerning changes in productivity and what was responsible for this change arbitrators and fact finders will generally give considerable weight to such credible evidence.[13]

There are other minor standards, many of which are unique to specific occupations, areas of the country, and industries. These standards are not reviewed here and for the bulk of readers will never be encountered. It is, however, wise for the reader to bear in mind that such standards—increases in payroll taxes, government regulations, and automation for example—do exist.

SUMMARY AND CONCLUSIONS

Standards in interest disputes are those criterion used by the neutral in determining what fact-finding recommendations or arbitration awards should be entered in specific cases. There is no agreement among fact finders and arbitrators as to what the appropriate standards are for economic issues. The standards will vary between neutrals and specific cases. In general there appear to be three major schools of thought concerning appropriate standards. One school of thought suggests that neutrals ought to confine themselves to the standards the parties adopted through their negotiations. Another focuses on party acceptability of the recommendations and/or award. This particular view seems most reasonable in the case of fact-finding recommendations but is a dangerous view in the case of interest arbitration awards. The final view is that the neutral should employ his or her own view of equity. The foundation of this contention seems to be that the parties choose the neutral and when such a decision is made it is made with the knowledge of the neutral's view of the world. This founding contention seems to many arbitrators and fact finders to be rather naive, if not misleading.

Many enabling statutes impose on the neutrals what standards they must employ in making determinations in both fact-finding and interest arbitration cases. Another large group of statutes remain silent on the standards to be employed. Public policymakers, some very distrustful of the fact finding and arbitration processes, apparently believe it is the proper exercise of their legislative power to determine what standards are appropriate to collective bargaining and impasse resolution. There may be some wisdom in such legislative determinations but there are also dangers. Few, if any, legislators are experts in collective bargaining or dispute resolution, and bargaining relations vary in many respects. To provide guidance is desirable, but to fix decision-making rules by statute may create more problems than such actions cure.

In addition to numerous minor standards, there are three major standards that appear to be widely applied in fact-finding and interest arbitration cases. The major standards are the comparative norm or prevailing practice, the public employer's ability to pay and the public interest, and the cost of or standard of living. If the ability to pay an increase in compensation is shown, generally one of the other standards is given greatest weight and normally that standard is the comparative norm or prevailing practice. Normally the standard or cost of living standard is hard to quantify and support reliably and accurately with credible evidence.

The standards of decision making concerning the economic package are what give predictability to the fact-finding and interest arbitration processes. To the extent that these standards are demanded of neutrals by the parties and are used by the parties themselves the processes of fact finding and interest arbitration can be effective dispute settlement techniques. In applications where the standards are not known or the neutral applies his or her own brand of justice the fact-finding and interest arbitration processes cannot serve the parties' needs or produce serviceable results except purely by chance.

NOTES

1. Frank Elkouri and Edna A. Elkouri, *How Arbitration Works*, 4th ed. (Washington, D.C.: Bureau of National Affairs, 1985), p. 803.

2. Frank Elkouri and Edna Asper Elkouri, *How Arbitration Works*, 3d ed. (Washington, D.C.: Bureau of National Affairs, 1973), pp. 745–746.

3. These data are available from the American Chamber of Commerce Research Association located in Indianapolis.

4. These data are available from the Bureau of Labor Statistics. Each month the CPI is published in the *Monthly Labor Review*. The Commerce Department, Bureau of the Census gathers this information and publishes a quarterly report titled *Consumer Prices*, which provides even more detailed information than is made available to the Bureau of Labor Statistics.

5. For further discussion see Arthur Sloane and Fred Witney, *Labor Relations* 5th ed. (Englewood Cliffs, N.J.: Prentice-Hall, 1985), pp. 301–304.

6. David A. Dilts and Clarence R. Deitsch, *Labor Relations* (New York: Macmillan, 1983), p. 164.

7. See Elkouri and Elkouri, *How Arbitration Works*, 4th ed., pp. 807–810.

8. *NLRB* v. *Truitt Manufacturing Company*, 351 U.S. 1949 (1956).

9. State of Connecticut, 77 LA 729, 730, 732 (Healy and Seibel 1981).

10. *United Traction Company*, 27 LA 309 (Sheiber 1956).

11. *Government Printing Office*, 73 LA 1 (Bloch 1979).

12. For example, see K. Clark, "The Impact of Unionization on Productivity: A Case Study," *Industrial and Labor Relations Review*, vol. 34 (July 1980), pp. 462–470.

13. For example, see *City of Harve, Montana* 76 LA 789 (Snow 1981), as well as arbitrators' awards at 15 LA 496, 9 LA 201, and 7 LA 530.

9

Decisional Standards of Fact Finders and Arbitrators: Contract Language Issues

To follow foolish precedents, and wink
  With both our eyes, is easier than to think.
                                    William Cooper, *Tirocinium*

Language issues pose their own unique and peculiar problems in fact finding and interest arbitration. Language issues range from seniority clauses to management rights provisions to union security arrangements to grievance procedures and beyond. The one thing all of these issues have in common is an assignment of rights to the agency or union under the contract.

Most language issues are of a distributive nature, much the same as the economic issues. While some language issues are more properly classified as integrative, such issues rarely result in impasse. So most of the language issues that find their way to the fact finder or arbitrator are concerned with distributive issues.

There are often real monetary costs involved with language issues. The distinction between economic issues (addressed in the previous chapter) and language issues has arisen because the costs attributable to language issues are often very difficult to quantify. Thus, the distinction, while useful, remains somewhat artificial.

Language issues also pose a unique problem for the fact finder and arbitrator. Because economic issues are easier to quantify, disputes over economic issues tend to center on the total cost or benefit of the proposals. Language issues disputes tend to center on who should receive what right and for what purposes. As such controversies are of a more conceptual nature and difficult or impossible to quantify, it is not inaccurate to describe language issues as qualitative.

In many respects this qualitative nature of these disputes makes the fact finder's and arbitrator's job more difficult because the application of qualitative standards is less precise. The standards themselves for language issues are not totally unlike those applied to economic disputes. Since language issues involve assignment of rights that shape and govern the employee-employer relation, there are understandable differences. A one-time assignment of dollars in economic issues makes the standards applied to those issues somewhat more straightforward, but language issues that establish a continuing obligation have occasionally necessitated a different sort of standard.

Language issues are rather common to interest arbitration and fact-finding cases. A recent study of interest awards in police protection found that the mean number of issues per case was thirteen.[1] This study found that 91 percent (of the 343 awards examined) had at least one salary issue and more than 46 percent involved a union security issue. Working conditions issues were involved in another 34 percent, and individual worker security issues were involved in another third of the awards examined. These data suggest that language issues are relatively common in police interest cases. It is also likely that language issues are relatively common in other segments of the public sector.

The reduction of the parties' respective rights to a written document is a grave responsibility. In many cases the parties have a long established bargaining relation and many practices and customs have evolved concerning how things are to be done within the organization. Many of these customs and practices are never reduced to writing and included in the written labor agreement, but these items also are a portion of the contract. There are many reasons customs and practices sometimes do not find their way into the written labor agreement. What is left out of a contract is often as important as what is placed within the four corners of the document. The parties should carefully consider what items are included and what items are excluded. If there is agreement on who has rights and how these particular rights are to be exercised then the parties may be well advised to include them in the written agreement, but if there is no agreement or there is no established practice or custom then the parties may be well advised to leave such items out of the contract. The length of the written document is unimportant; what is important is that the labor agreement reflect the parties understandings and respective rights.

With this in mind it is time to examine the various standards employed by arbitrators and fact finders in language issues cases. It is important to remember that many of these standards are similar to those for economic issues, but that the concepts to which they are typically applied may differ substantially.

STANDARDS FOR LANGUAGE ISSUES

It is worth repeating that it is often difficult and sometimes unwise to attempt a separation of language from economic issues. The reason for the separation here is simply for ease of presentation and conceptualization. The bargaining criteria (standard) for language issues can be divided into major and minor standards as was done with the economic package. The major standards for language issues are (1) prevailing practice, (2) demonstrated need, (3) bargaining history, and (4) public interest and statutory limitations. Each of these major standards are discussed below and are followed by a discussion of minor standards.

Prevailing Practice

This standard is much the same as the comparative norm/prevailing practice standard discussed in the economic package section of the previous chapter. Comparability is the key to the application of this standard. What have comparable jurisdictions done in free negotiations concerning this particular issue? In other words, what have similarly situated unions and managements negotiated concerning this issue without resort to impasse resolution techniques such as arbitration? The evidence presented should be for comparable jurisdictions as the evidence must be credible for this standard to be given weight by fact finders or arbitrators.

There are several aspects of this standard that differ substantially from the comparative norm applied to economic issues. Often the nature of a public agency's mission requires that certain rights, unquestioned in the private sector, be the subject of negotiations. In such cases as the scheduling of hours, is the public employer to be compared with public employers or private employers in the area or both? The question of appropriate comparability groups for purposes of determining rights is a particularly thorny one. The public employees should not be forced to hold alternate employment simply because of their public employee status.[2] On the other hand, many public sector jobs require responsibilities, risks, and hours that are not comparable with those found in the private sector.[3] Public employees not satisfied with the rights bestowed upon them by their contracts may seek private sector employment in the same manner as they would leave the public sector for higher-paying private sector employment.

Comparability of rights within a contract also must be viewed as a whole as was true of the economic package. Union security clauses in the private sector are relatively common. This security arrangement provides the union with the ability to perform its representational function by providing the financial resources necessary for such activity. In the cases where public sector unions are prohibited from a union security clause while private sector unions have such protections, employees may view their public sector unions as less capable of defending them than their private sector counterparts.

Comparability of the jurisdictions for purposes of determining a prevailing practice concerning a specific language issue can differ somewhat from the practices found concerning economic issues. It is rare that data would be available concerning the characteristics of each labor contract within a state or particular segment of a jurisdiction's public sector. If a particular contract provision is relatively common within an area, for example, grievance arbitration for teachers, then the arbitrator or fact finder may be persuaded that this is, in fact, a prevailing practice. The control for characteristics of a city or school district is still generally applied by arbitrators and fact finders concerning those things such as population and budget for which data are available. Control for the assignment of other rights within the contract is generally not as easy as control for the expenditures on fringe benefits when considering salary.

Prevailing practice is a powerful guide to arbitral decision making. When negotiators propose an innovative demand, the neutral is faced with a situation where there is no prevailing practice. In this situation, the approach of arbitrators has been known to vary widely from the approach of fact finders. Arbitrator McCoy rejected an innovative demand claiming that such new concepts should be the product of negotiations and not arbitrators' awards if no compelling reason could be shown for the inclusion of such language in the contract.[4] Fact finder Gleeson, on the other hand, reasoned that fact finders' recommendations were a proper place to recognize the need for leadership in innovative contractual provisions.[5] Thus neutrals will sometimes be faced with situations where their recommended contract terms show more innovation than the terms they would impose on impassed parties.

Demonstrated Need

The parties to negotiations will almost always discuss whether a proposed contract provision is really needed. These discussions will often center on the relative needs of the parties. Evidence concerning the expected effect of the proposed language is typically offered into the record to show the arbitrator or fact finder that one party's needs are served by the language and the needs of the other party are not significantly influenced or are also served by the same provision. Such evidence is difficult if not impossible to produce concerning many issues.

There are, however, exceptions such as seniority provisions (for layoffs and recalls) and dues checkoff provisions. Evidence supporting (or refuting) these and some other language issues is sometimes available. One notable example involves a fire department in major midwestern city. The firefighters are entitled to vacation bids on the basis of seniority. There was no contract language governing cases where two firefighters had the same seniority or what was to happen if a firefighter was called into work on an emergency basis and lost all or part of his scheduled vacation. The union proposed to add language to the contract that required seniority ties to be broken in reverse alphabetical order and that if an employee missed a portion of his or her vacation entitlement due to emergency call back that the employee had the option of continuing to work and rebidding their vacation period or simply adding the unused vacation period (due to the call back) to the end of their present vacation period. The city objected to both provisions, claiming there was no need for such language. The union then showed the arbitrator where an average of ten firefighters per year over the last five years had lost a portion of their vacation due to call backs. The union also presented evidence of twelve employees with exactly the same amount of seniority and that hard feelings had been created because of inconsistent treatment of these firefighters in bidding for their vacation periods. The city conceded that no scheduling problems would be created by the union's proposal, but there was no need for such language since there were so few employees involved. This is a clear case of demonstrated need, and the union prevailed in that specific case since the city could show no adverse affect.

The demonstrated need standard is as difficult to apply as the cost of living standard in the economic package. What constitutes a real need as opposed to a simple desire is very subjective and cannot be specifically defined in an operational manner for fact-finding or arbitration purposes. As a result, this standard is rarely given controlling weight by either the parties or an arbitrator. On occasion fact finders are persuaded that such provisions should be included in the recommendations should a preponderance of evidence show a need for such inclusion.

Grievance arbitration is an interesting example of demonstrated need being applied to fact-finding and arbitration cases. Most grievance procedures end in final and binding arbitration. In the state of Kansas the concept of sovereignty still dominates many public employers' views of grievance arbitration. Of 304 school districts in that state, the Kansas Public Employment Relations Board reports only 9 with contracts containing final and binding arbitration of grievances. The school boards in that state prefer suit to enforce the negotiated contract rather than to allow an arbitrator to exercise final and binding authority over contract disputes. This is true even in the case of one specific school board, which has lost three law suits in as many years at substantial monetary cost. Here the need has been demonstrated for final and binding arbitration but the ideological constraints have prevented its widespread acceptance. The Kansas PERB records show that between 1984 and 1986 the issue of binding grievance arbitration went to fact finding on only eight occasions. The fact finder recommended the inclusion of such a provision in all eight cases, but the recommendation was rejected by the school board in seven of the eight cases.

Bargaining History

This standard is often given controlling weight by fact finders and arbitrators because it clearly demonstrates how the parties have viewed a particular issue over the life of their bargaining relation. Two situations are common at fact-finding and interest arbitration proceedings. The first involves a contract provision that has been proposed in several negotiations but never accepted by the other party. The second involves a contract provision that one party has been unsuccessful at "negotiating out" of the contract over several negotiations. In such situations, unless there is clearly compelling evidence under one of the other standards arbitrators will typically maintain the status quo.[6] Fact finders, on the other hand, are generally not as inhibited as arbitrators in this arena.[7] This does not mean that compelling evidence under another standard cannot be found that would result in a recommendation or an award that is counter to the bargaining history of the parties, but such situations are relatively rare.

A recent classroom teachers' case in Kansas City illustrates use of this standard. The union asked the fact finder to retain an early retirement program that management of the school district had sought to terminate for the past three years. The bargaining history clearly supported the union's case, on its face, if the historical bargaining environment was ignored. When the early retirement program was negotiated the school district had been experiencing constant declines in enrollment and had proposed the early retirement program as a method of avoiding layoffs. However, the last four years had witnessed a change; there had been substantial increases in enrollments and the district was now losing many needed teachers to this early retirement program. An incident that intensified the school district concerns involved an administrator who accepted a position in a neighboring district for a $12,000 pay increase after taking early retirement; the early retirement cost the district $25,000 per year. The bargaining history standard was deemed supportive of management's position on this issue.

The customs and past practices that have evolved during the years prior to a formal bargaining relation may still be given weight as a bargaining history by interest arbitrators and fact finders.[8] Thus, in cases where the parties have reached impasse during the negotiation of their first labor agreement, there may still be found a bargaining history. For a past practice to be given such status it must have attained the status of "past practice," that is, be a consistent treatment of the issue, mutually acceptable to the parties, and relied upon by the parties.[9]

Public Interest and Statutory Limitations

The public interest in contract language issues is just as critical as in economic issues. The hours during which public services will be available, the work rules concerning public service delivery, the job security of specific employees, and numerous other such issues may have a direct bearing on the quantity and quality of service provided by the public sector.

The confidence that the taxpayers have in their police and fire protection or public schools is another important consideration. Disciplinary rules, professional development, staffing requirements, and other such language items may have a real and direct effect on the public's confidence in any particular public agency's ability to deliver the services within its authority. In a recent bargaining session, a police negotiator asked the city manager: "Would you fly with an airline pilot who would work for the minimum wage?" The city manager responded that he would not. The policeman then asked: "Would you trust your safety or even your life to a cop who was making one dollar more than the minimum wage?" The city manager did not respond, and the police department got their requested 8 percent wage increase. Public confidence is a very powerful force in public sector collective bargaining.

Public interest is also concerned with the efficiency of the delivery of public services, as was discussed in the previous chapter. If work rules or other contractual rights require greater numbers of employees, the connection between the economic cost and language issues again becomes clear. There is a delicate balance between adequate provision of services and efficiency. This delicate balance is a matter of public opinion and perception and is often the subject of debate and too rarely the subject of scientific inquiry and objective measurement.

Public interest and public policy are not necessarily the same thing. Frequently law makers will perceive what they believe to be the public interest and enact legislation to protect that interest. Sometimes they are right sometimes they are not. The important thing to remember is that the process is of public policy formulation allows for corrections and that the elected representatives are the persons charged with the authority of making law. Pressure can be brought to bear by unions through the political arena to change public policy, but the unions are subject to the legislative enactments of the elected representatives, with whose appointees they must negotiate. This places public sector unions in a unique position relative to other labor organizations, and it also grants public employers rather unique powers relative to their private sector counterparts.

Obviously a competent arbitrator or fact finder will abide by the law. The neutral will only issue recommendations within his or her jurisdiction and will inform the parties when an issue is outside the neutral's jurisdiction. Most state statutes clearly outline the fact finder's and the arbitrator's jurisdiction, but as with many such statutes it is easy to find certain gray areas that are subject to interpretation.

Maybe of more importance and greater interest are other arenas of public policy and their effects on the fact-finding or interest arbitration processes. There has been considerable debate about whether grievance arbitrators are bound by external law, that is, whether they must interpret and apply law outside of the contract.[10] It is not uncommon in interest arbitration and fact-finding cases to find that certain rights are granted public employees by statute. Nor is it uncommon to find a union or an employer who wishes to burden the labor agreement with the reproduction of those statutes in the labor contract. While the first such experience is often amusing, the parties should be made aware that their rights, guaranteed by statute, are not made more secure by their inclusion in the contract.

Unfortunately, it is not uncommon to find a party proposing that an illegal subject of bargaining be included in a contract or that some language in direct contravention to a particular statute be included in the agreement. A fact finder or arbitrator is typically bound by statute in such cases and must apply the standards of the statute if the controversy is within his or her jurisdiction.[11] An interest arbitrator whose award is contrary to public policy risks the setting aside of his or her award by the courts. In the case of a fact finder's report, the parties are at risk of running afoul of the subject statute and the fact finder should warn the parties of that risk.

MINOR STANDARDS

Minor standards for language issues are relatively issue specific. Their applicability to impasse resolution is much less common than the major standards discussed above. Such considerations as affirmative action compliance, health and safety, building design, productivity, economic efficiency, and technological development may play a role in the bargaining of specific issues. If such criteria have been used in the negotiations, the standard used should be identified and entered into the record with supporting evidence.

These standards are referred to as minor standards because of their relatively rare individual application. But it is not uncommon for some specialized language issue to surface that requires their application. In many cases involving such standards the arbitrator will need special expertise. Arbitrators and fact finders have an ethical obligation to inform the parties if such expertise is not possessed.[12]

One final word concerning language issues. Contract language is very important in the overall meaning to be assigned to a contract. Language must be carefully phrased, tested, and proofread to assure that the language contains the meaning the parties intended. Too often, however, language issues end up in impasse proceedings only to "smoke screen" the real issues at impasse or to have additional issues available to provide a possibility for recommendation (or award) splitting. Such fact finding or arbitration tactics are costly and are often ineffective. Fact finders and arbitrators are typically well versed in collective bargaining and will quickly come to recognize smoke screens for what they are. If the neutral fails to recognize the smoke screen for what it is, you may have made a serious mistake in the selection of the neutral. The result is that these issues will be determined on their merits without the intended splitting. This could easily undermine the party's position engaging in such behavior if it utilizes a significant number of smoke screen issues. If there is really only one issue at impasse (such as an economic package) and five or six smoke screens are introduced, the opponent is probably going to have five or six favorable recommendations or awards before the economic package is examined. This sheer weight of numbers can be used to bias public and weaken constituent support. A smoke screen might then cast a shadow on substantive arguments in favor of the real issue. To summarize—smoke screens can backfire. A favorable fact-finding recommendation on the economic package might carry less bargaining weight if many other issues have been lost. Smoke screen issues can easily be interpreted as abusing the fact-finding or arbitration process because no real impasse exists over these issues. The parties should consider carefully which issues are brought to impasse to save both money and time.

DECISIONAL THINKING OF ARBITRATORS AND FACT FINDERS

A few comments concerning the decisional thinking of arbitrators and fact finders are order. There are some differences between the role of fact finder and the role of interest arbitrator. The interest arbitrator does not have to convince either party of the desirability of negotiating his or her recommendation into the contract. The interest arbitrator's award is final and binding. The fact finder must convince the parties of the appropriateness of his or her recommendations. the fact finder's report is not final and binding and therefore the recommendations frequently take on the tone of suggestions the fact finder knows will be rejected during the current round of negotiations. Other than these role differences, the decisional thinking of fact finders is much the same as that for interest arbitrators but there are some differences between rights and interest arbitrators. For example, grievance arbitrators have the benefit of a contract that specifically enunciates the parties' intent in a written contract. The interest arbitrator often has no intent to "hang his hat on" making the job of interest arbitration much more difficult and much less predictable. The basic job of the fact finder is to ascertain what the "facts" are and base recommendations for settlement on what the evidence suggests are the facts. The bargaining criteria or standards serve the sole purpose of demonstrating to the fact finder what factors the parties view as important to a determination on the merits of each issue. The determination of facts is important to both the fact finder and the interest arbitrator. There is no substitute for making a credible record before the neutral that supports your position. This is essentially the idea of building a preponderance of credible evidence necessary to prove a case in the courtroom. The only significant difference is that the courtroom rules of evidence do not apply. Fact finding or arbitration, however, are not terribly formal processes, nor are the decision-making processes utilized by fact finders or arbitrators as formal as judges sitting on a district court bench. Fact finding and arbitration are processes that rely heavily on the expertise and competence of the neutral selected or appointed to hear the case. Probably the most cogent description of the nonlegalistic approach to fact finding and arbitration is to be found in a text by Paul Prasow and Ed Peters:

> The fact-finder, however, does not sit as an impersonal spectator weighting the scales of proof pro and con without impressions of his own on how they should tilt. His evaluation of the record produced at the hearing is shaped by such knowledge and experience as he possesses. Where he perceives that a particular salary claim is especially meritorious on its face, a modest degree of proof might persuade him. If on the other hand, he perceives the salary claim to be less meritorious on its face, he might deem that same quantum of proof insufficient to sustain the burden of proof. Triers of fact who too rigorously minimize their human experience and beliefs when evaluating the record are often said to indulged in mechanical jurisprudence.[13]

Differences exist between neutrals about how mechanistic the process should be. The mechanical jurisprudential approach to fact finding and arbitration may have a role to play in specific disputes, but in general the parties are not well served by fact finders or arbitrators who will unduly allow form to control substance in such matters.

The decisional thinking of neutrals can be briefly summarized as based on the standards the parties bring to their own negotiations and the evidence entered into the record. The formality and weighting of evidence, however, is a matter of the training and background of the individual neutral, within broad limits. Little in the way of generalities can be stated here other than what has already been offered.[14] Those fact finders and arbitrators who have formal legal training and those who have survived the test of time and numerous cases will be competent in the making of a record and the weighing of evidence, but the real question is more what the parties themselves expect from the process. The parties generally select arbitrators and fact finders and there is normally a track record that will reflect how these neutrals handle such matters. If this is a serious concern for the parties they should do a little investigative homework before they select a neutral.

SUMMARY AND CONCLUSIONS

In some ways language issues are more difficult for fact finders, arbitrators, and the parties themselves to handle. The economic package can generally be quantified and measured in specific ways. The more conceptual nature of specifying the parties respective rights in written English is less precise and yet every bit as important as the economic package.

There are numerous, infrequently used, minor standards for language issues and four major standards. The four major standards were discussed: (1) prevailing practice, (2) demonstrated need, (3) bargaining history, and (4) public interest and statutory limitations. The prevailing practice standard is concerned with the solutions to certain disputes that have been freely negotiated in similarly situated public sector or private sector bargaining relations. Demonstrated need is concerned with whether the proposing party can show a need, rather than a desire, for the proposed language. The bargaining history concerns the parties behavior during prior negotiations concerning the disputed issue as well as the past practices of the parties where no prior contract exists. The public interest and statutory limitations concern the effects of the proposed language on the delivery and cost of public services and whether the proposal is consistent with the requirements of applicable statutes.

The role of the fact finder and interest arbitrator differ somewhat, but their decision-making processes are identical. The neutral is to base the award or recommendation on the credible evidence adduced by the parties. The rules of evidence, while similar to a courtroom application are less formal and tailored to the specific needs of arbitration.

The fact finder and the interest arbitrator have a decision-making role to perform that is much more than the application and interpretation of a statute or contract. The fact finder must provide recommendations and rationale that will provide the parties at impasse guidance in resolving their own dispute. The interest arbitrator must ascertain what contractual requirements are best supported by the record. This is creating for the parties the contract with which they must live for the next few months or years.

NOTES

1. John Delaney and Peter Feuille, "Police Interest Arbitration: Awards and Issues," *Arbitration Journal,* vol. 39, no. 2 (June 1984), pp. 14–24.

2. *City of Uniontown, Pennsylvania* 51 LA 1072 (Duff 1968).

3. *City of Providence, Rhode Island,* 47 LA 1036 (Seitz 1966).

4. *Twin City Rapid Transit Co.,* 7 LA 845 (McCoy 1947).

5. *Minnesota State Highway Patrol,* 56 LA 697 (Gleeson 1971).

6. *City of Dayton, Ohio,* 85 LA 325 (Heekin 1985).

7. *Perry Township Schools,* Indiana Education Employment Relations Board, Case No. F–79–5–5340 (Robert E. Dunham).

8. See Arbitrator Clark Kerr's reasoning in this regard at 6 LA 98.

9. See Owen Fairweather, *Practice and Procedure in Labor Arbitration,* 2d ed. (Washington, D.C.: Bureau of National Affairs, 1983), pp. 215–224, for further discussion of past practices.

10. See, for example, Bernard D. Meltzer, "Ruminations About Ideology, Law, and Labor Arbitration," in Dallas L. Jones, ed., *The Arbitrator, the NLRB, and the Courts; Proceedings of the Twentieth Annual Meetings of the National Academy of Arbitrators* (Washington, D.C.: Bureau of National Affairs, 1967), pp. 1–36.

11. For example, see Public Law 217, Acts of 1973 (Indiana).

12. See the code of ethics contained in Appendix C of this text.

13. Paul Prasow and Ed Peters, *Arbitration and Collective Bargaining* (New York: McGraw-Hill, 1983), p. 326.

14. For an excellent discussion of the rules of evidence see Marvin Hill and Anthony Sinicropi, *Evidence in Arbitration* (Washington, D.C.: Bureau of National Affairs, 1980).

10

The Effects of Statutory Impasse Procedures

Things are not always as they seem, Watson.

Sherlock Holmes

Earlier chapters began from a common perspective—that parties had to resort to impasse resolution procedures because they had reached a bargaining impasse. In this chapter the perspective is reversed in order to raise some questions of interest to the practitioner of collective negotiations. Answers are then offered to those questions, answers that rely heavily on extensive empirical research.

The reversal of perspective is most evident in the first question raised. Do impasse resolution procedures cause there to be more impasses? The statistical answer to the question is "yes," but that one word doesn't give a very complete description of the relationship between structure and bargaining. The impasse resolution structure—those procedures required or available—in each state influences the very nature of the collective bargaining relationships within the jurisdiction. Much of this chapter is devoted to a discussion of known influences.

It is very important to note that, while the structure influences the likelihood of particular outcomes in bargaining, it does not predetermine what will happen in any individual bargaining relationship. The parties themselves maintain ultimate control over the actual outcomes within the limits established by law.

The first major section of this chapter deals with the factors that influence the likelihood of an impasse in negotiations. The interrelationship of influential factors and resolution procedures is discussed at some length.

The second section deals with labor peace. Labor relations statutes generally state explicitly that labor peace is one of the dominant goals of the legislation. Have statuatory impasse resolution procedures eliminated strikes in the public sector? No, they haven't. The interrelationship of impasse procedures and actual labor peace experience is described. There is more to the issue of labor peace than the strike experiences of a jurisdiction. The continuing labor relationships following resolution of an impasse are an issue of very real concern.

What happens to the bargaining relationship when the parties have reached impasse? Clearly it continues just as the chapter continues with a discussion of life after impasse—more precisely, a discussion of what having resorted to impasse means for the negotiating parties and their continuing relationship. The fact-finding report and interest arbitration award each complete a step in the impasse resolution procedures, but they do not complete the labor relations process. This section guides the practitioner in continuing with that process.

The third section addresses the issue of the bargained outcome vis-à-vis the arbitration outcome. Are bargainers better off with an arbitration award or a negotiated settlement? The authors' strong bias toward contracts that reflect the desires of the parties rather than the judgment of the neutral is supported by evidence cited in this section. Neutrals perform their function well, but they can't outperform parties intent on reaching an accord.

The fourth section of this chapter then addresses the evolution of labor-management cooperation. Many lessons have been learned from successful negotiations, from negotiations resolved after resort to impasse proceedings and from negotiations that terminated with labor "warfare"—strikes, job actions, and lockouts. The evolution of labor-management cooperation is presented so that novice practitioners might learn from the experiences of the past without having to repeat those experiences.

FACTORS AFFECTING IMPASSE AND ITS RESOLUTION

Good Faith Bargaining

Nothing increases the likelihood of a negotiated settlement (avoiding impasse) more than good faith bargaining. Good faith is descriptive of both behavior and attitude. Both good faith behavior and good faith bargaining are continuums rather than yes/no descriptors. As observed in an earlier chapter, behavior is observable and attitude is not, so the PERBs and courts must infer attitude from behavior. Good faith behavior, as a minimum, means a willingness to meet at reasonable times and places, to negotiate mandatory issues, and to commit agreed upon items to a written contract. This behavior will normally be sufficient to avoid an unfair labor practice conviction.

But the good faith envisaged by most legislatures is something more; it is an attitude of good faith. It calls for an honest attempt by the parties to find a mutually acceptable package of terms and conditions of employment, a real desire to negotiate a contract that both parties can live with. It means that the parties enter negotiations with the hopes of ending with a contract. It means that both hope to be able to reach an agreement without third party intervention. It means that the parties are willing to make full use of third party assistance, when necessary, to help them reach an agreement.

A good faith attitude does not mean that one party should make concession after concession until the other party is satisfied. It does mean that each is willing to make reasonable compromises where there is room and incentive to compromise.

What can one party do when the other is not bargaining in good faith? If the other party does not exhibit good faith bargaining conduct but has a good faith attitude, the conduct is probably due to ignorance and mediation is likely to be successful. Empirical studies have confirmed the expectation that mediation is most helpful when negotiators are inexperienced.[1] If the other party lacks an attitude of good faith, little can be done without substantial evidence of bad faith behavior prior to the final step in the resolution procedure. Mediation will likely be ineffective.[2]

Bargaining Stances Based on Principle

Positions taken in negotiations that are based on a deeply held belief are unlikely to be modified in response to another party's differences in belief. For example, the union negotiator may feel that punching a time clock is demeaning, that bargaining unit members shouldn't have to punch in if management personnel don't have to. Management may see nothing demeaning about using a time clock. Each is likely to find the other's beliefs unpersuasive. Such positions based on principle (or strongly felt perceptions) are unlikely to be modified or compromised (double entendre intentional).

Therefore, issues based on principle are likely to lead to impasse. However, this kind of issue is one that mediation has a good chance of resolving.[3] Mediators are adept at helping each party better understand the other side's point of view, at helping identify alternatives, and at bringing the discussion back to being issues oriented rather than feelings oriented.

Bargaining in "Good Faith" Toward Impasse

Good faith includes an attempt to reach contract settlement. Due to the political nature of management and union positions, the negotiators may feel too politically threatened to reach settlement without impasse despite a personal desire to settle earlier. Constituents—influential management or union folks—may be insisting on a "hard line" approach in bargaining. Mediation is unlikely to settle such an impasse.

Fact finding, because of its generally public nature, stands a far better chance of leading to impasse resolution. Parties may be able to blame the fact finder for concessions they were already prepared to yield. If the hard line pressures continue, arbitration may be required to settle the dispute. Thomas A. Kochan references the empirical work of James Stern in stating that "management representatives might find the arbitrator to be a useful scapegoat for the adverse public reaction that is likely to result from higher cost settlements."[4]

Hopefully, the party facing the political imperatives has given enough clues to the counterpart in negotiations that the political necessities are understood. Though the bargaining process clearly suffers from the lack of a negotiated settlement if the issues go to arbitration, the bargaining relationship may survive the current round of negotiations relatively unscathed. There is no alternative for the negotiator when faced with this bargaining stance but to accept the reality that the impasse is going to fact finding and perhaps arbitration.

A History of Previous Impasses

As statuatory impasse resolution procedures are characteristic of public sector collective bargaining legislation, one concern of proponents is on a possible side effect of the legislation. The concern is that ready access to impasse resolution procedures might cause the parties to be less vigorous in their efforts to achieve a voluntary settlement without resort to third party intervention. A related concern voiced by the prestigious Taylor Committee is that "[d]ispute settlement procedures can become habit-forming and negotiations become only a ritual."[5] These concerns are collectively called the "narcotic effect" of impasse resolution procedures. One way to determine whether a narcotic effect really exists is to examine bargaining histories is to compare the periods before and after impasse procedure resolution were legislated for public employees. A strong narcotic effect was uncovered in a statistically thorough examination of New York police, firefighters, and teachers.[6]

So resort to impasse resolution procedures tends to cause repeated use. Why? Probably because it's easier than doing everything that can be done to prepare for and conduct healthy negotiations. Do the parties eventually realize that letting neutrals resolve disputes is not as good as negotiating a settlement themselves? Yes, but it takes some time for the parties to come to that realization. The evidence as to how long it takes is mixed. Whether the narcotic effect generally lasts for decades or for only a few years remains a matter of debate.[7]

It is important for the practitioners of collective negotiations to strive for mutually determined contract terms. A contract determined by an outsider, even by the most adept of neutrals, is likely to be inferior to a contract negotiated by two parties intent on reaching an accord.

The Structure of Legislated Impasse Procedures

The New York State study focused on a change in the collective bargaining law that applied to most jurisdictions outside New York City. The new law added arbitration as a final step in the legislated impasse procedures.[8] The executive branch (and others, presumably) were concerned that increasing the number of impasse procedure steps would increase resort to those procedures. The concern proved valid.[9] The New York State study did show a 16 percent increase in impasses and a 15 percent increase in impasses that went to the final step of the impasse procedures due to the change.[10] However, this effect was partially offset by an increase in settlements at the mediation step.[11]

The increased success of the initial step (mediation) and increased resort to the final step (arbitration) focused some attention on the intermediate step (fact finding). The study reports that parties took more extreme, inflexible positions on moving to the fact-finding step than they held in earlier negotiations. That effect was so pronounced that the study recommended elimination of the fact-finding step. Costs and time delays associated with fact finding were considered to be more burdensome than the limited benefits of fact finding warranted. This appraisal was bolstered by the similarity between fact-finding reports and final arbitration awards.[12]

Interestingly enough, an Iowa study came to a different conclusion. Gallagher and Pegnetter found that fact finding settled many disputes without resort to arbitration. The Iowa procedures in arbitration allowed the neutral to choose either of the parties' final offer or the fact finder's recommendation. This seemed to narrow the differences between the parties' final offers; that is, even when fact finding did not result in a negotiated settlement, it narrowed the differences between the parties.[13]

Conclusion

Does a set of statutory impasse resolution procedures generally effect changes in the behavior of bargaining parties? Yes. Just as expanding a highway will increase traffic on the highway, expanding resolution procedures will increase their use. Does this mean there was no need for the new highway lanes or the new resolution procedures? No, it does not. The message is that there is no panacea—no absolute cure for the difficulties that arise in collective bargaining.

For the practitioner, the change in impasse resolution procedures changes incentives facing each of the bargaining parties. Nonetheless, a mutual attitude of good faith and an understanding of the bargaining process will normally result in successful negotiation of collective bargaining agreement. It is hoped that the agreement is reached before resort to impasse procedures is required. When that is not the case, an understanding of the process greatly improves the chances of its success in providing a negotiated settlement.

LIFE AFTER IMPASSE

Impasse and Labor Peace

Most labor legislation enacted has explicitly listed labor peace as a primary purpose of the legislation. Labor peace is usually defined as the absence of industrial warfare. So labor peace usually means no strikes, work slow downs, or sick outs.

A study of Indiana teacher unionization is instructive. The Indiana legislature established mandatory mediation and fact-finding steps following impasse. It further allowed the parties to agree to interest arbitration to resolve a continuing impasse. There is no observable difference in strike activity between the prelaw and postlaw periods. The statutory impasse procedures had no noticable impact on strike activity. But it should be noted that the strike activity averaged one school day lost for each school district once every seventeen years.[14] While other states experience more public sector strike activity than this, states that prohibit strikes do not generally experience many strikes.

The New Jersey experience surrounded consideration of alternative modifications to an existing state law. "[A]lthough most unions publically advocated the right to strike, many labor leaders privately indicated ... that they 'would get clobbered' in a strike."[15] In lieu of adopting a right to strike, New Jersey adopted compulsory arbitration of interest disputes. During the next few years there were no strikes over interest issues, though some stoppages reportedly occurred over "procedural matters . . . to hurry along the dispute settlement process."[16] The state's director of conciliation and arbitration related that there

are some who say that "well there were very few [strikes] prior [to the law]." While that may be true, we cannot forget that in [the two prior years] intense feelings began to develop throughout the state over negotiations which became very lengthy without producing voluntary agreements, and there was no place for these disputes to go.[17]

The question raised here is a fairly direct one. Do statutory impasse procedures reduce strikes? The answer is less direct: The evidence is mixed but the amount of activity is small enough that the answer doesn't much matter (except to those directly affected).

Many have suggested that the best way to ensure motivation of the parties to bargain is to allow them to strike over impasses. Economics professor Charles W. Baird takes a contrary view expressing a dim view of the effectiveness of strike authorizing legislation.

The claim . . . that legalizing public sector strikes will actually decrease the incidence of strikes is counter-factual. Pennsylvania legalized public sector strikes in 1970 whereupon there followed a thirteen fold increase in such strikes. . . . Nationally, the average number of public sector strikes per state, per year was 1.34 before the adoption of collective bargaining legislation and 5.00 after the adoption of collective bargaining legislation. . . . [T]he increased incidence of strikes was not due merely to a secular increase in the propensity of government employees to strike. Except in 1961 the average number of strikes per state among employees not covered by collective bargaining legislation . . . was substantially less than among employees that were covered by such legislation. . . .[18]

Negotiating in Future Years

Becoming an informed negotiator is key to avoiding impasse. The practitioner needs to be informed on issues and the administration of bargaining and impasse resolution. Authors at University of South Carolina and Purdue University have simulated bargaining with "naive negotiators." The more training the bargainers received, the closer the parties were to reaching a settlement.[19] This book has already moved the practitioner out of the category "naive negotiator." Further experience and attention to the principles presented should reduce undesirable impasses, increase the likelihood that impasses can be resolved, and help maintain the bargaining relationship in the event the impasse goes to arbitration.

IMPASSE PROCEDURES AND ARBITRATION OUTCOMES

The question was raised earlier concerning the resort to impasse resolution procedures and the outcome resulting. It has been established that impasses are more likely to occur when there are statuatory impasse procedures. But what effect does having these procedures have on the salaries that result from their use? Can unions or agencies do better in arbitration than in negotiations? The general answer to the first question is that the availability of impasse procedures tends to cause negotiated salaries to be a little bit higher than they would otherwise be. While overall public sector legislation cannot be labelled pro-labor or pro-management, the advent of impasse resolution procedures is generally seen to have been pro-labor. Once the procedures are available, however, there is no discernible difference between the salaries that are negotiated and the salaries awarded by a neutral.[20]

This point is made so that parties who have been introduced to public sector impasse procedures through this volume will never succumb to the temptation to prefer the services of a neutral to the advantages of a negotiated settlement. The authors view the neutral as a physician called in to treat one symptom of an ailing labor relationship. The services of the physician should not be preferred to good health. The neutral should be called upon only when the labor relationship requires professional assistance.

EVOLUTION OF LABOR-MANAGEMENT COOPERATION

At the Local Level—An Attitudinal Initiative

Many labor relations observers have found that times of moderate, but not extreme, financial stress are most likely to produce increased labor-management cooperation. Professor Jacoby "concludes that unions and employers will voluntarily work together to improve productivity only within an intermediate range of economic stress."[21] The Scanlon Plans of the post–World War II era similarly saw cooperation as most likely only when the parties saw cooperation as necessary to maintain a competitive (hence operating and employing) position in the market.

The public sector has experienced moderate financial stress in recent years. Many agency budgets have not kept pace with inflation or work loads. These stresses have generally not been severe; rarely is the survivability of an agency threatened. But the stresses have made it difficult for agencies to provide their employees with anticipated improvements in salaries and benefits. One possible, and often actual, consequence of these stresses is conflict rather than cooperation. The press has discussed the increasing conflict observed in some towns and school districts as a natural outgrowth of the financial pressures. The authors feel that the public sector need not be different from the private sector, that increased financial pressures could be the catalyst for greater cooperation.

The pressing question for agencies and unions, then, is how can a relationship become more cooperative when financial pressures are increasing? Cooperation centers on negotiations. Good negotiations require good information and understanding of the process. One concrete way for negotiators to show an attitude of cooperation is to give the parties who will sit across the bargaining table a useful gift. The authors highly recommend copies of a book subtitled "Negotiating Agreement without Giving In." The formal title of this informal book is *Getting to Yes*. It's designed for a general audience, inexpensive, (in paperback), and easy reading. Before giving it away, though, it is a good idea for a negotiating team to read it for themselves.

With a subtitle that includes "without giving in," the gift is sure to be seen as a cooperative move. But the book is not about winning, it is getting bargaining process to succeed by focusing on issues. The following annecdote from the book's concluding remarks make that point.

In 1964 an American father and his twelve-year-old son were enjoying a beautiful Sunday in Hyde Park, London, playing catch with a Frisbee. Few in England had seen a Frisbee at that time and a small group of strollers gathered to watch this strange sport. Finally, one Homburg-clad Britisher came over to the father: "Sorry to bother you. Been watching you a quarter of an hour. Who's *winning*?[22]

Both parties can win when negotiations look for ways to meet both parties' concerns rather than their demands.

At the State Level—A Structural Initiative

Massachusetts, in response to an aggressive political climate, adopted a novel approach to resolve the management's dissatisfaction with mandatory interest arbitration and labor's demand for closure in bargaining. The firefighters' union represented their constituents and most police associations in negotiating an agreement with the Massachusetts League of Cities and Towns. The state legislature effectively ratified this agreement by passing a statute virtually identical in its terms.[23] This agreement established the bipartisan Joint Labor-Management Committee (JLMC): six management representatives, six labor representatives, and two neutrals (one of whom chaired the committee). The brainchild of Professor Dunlop, formerly Secretary of Labor, the JLMC

was empowered to take jurisdiction in any dispute over a police or fire fighter contract, whether or not they were petitioned by the parties for such jurisdiction. Through a variety of informal mechanisms as well formal procedures, the Committee was to seek to mediate as much as possible and was given the power to arbitrate in those instances in which a mediated solution was not possible.[24]

Professor Dunlop notes that the JLMC "was created[,] . . . is manned [, and] . . . is operated by the parties" themselves.[25] Although the JLMC was initiated in response to strong adversarial political actions previously undertaken by the parties, it is a singular example of state level labor-management cooperation.[26]

SUMMARY AND CONCLUSIONS

On the one hand, statutory impasse resolution procedures offer parties additional assistance in resolving difficulties that arise in the attempt to come to a collective bargaining agreement. On the other hand, statutory procedures that involve a cloture step, such as arbitration, offer a party the opportunity to substitute a neutral's decision for a negotiated settlement. This chapter summarized the results of modeling experiments and empirical research; five major conclusions were reached.

When practitioners bargain with a good faith attitude, mediation is likely to be a very useful tool to break the impasse. The converse is also true; mediation is rarely successful at resolving an impasse when one or both of the parties are not bargaining in good faith.

Fact finding is most likely to be successful when there are honest disagreements or when one party faces political pressures to hold to a "hard line."

Parties who have resorted to statutory procedures in the past are more likely to repeat. This narcotic effect wears off after some time as parties discover that adjudicated settlements are inferior to negotiated settlements.

Increasing the number of impasse resolution steps increases their use. No single set of procedures seems to be significantly more successful than others. It appears appropriate for jurisdictions to continue refining their procedures to match local needs.

Investigations into strike (or other job actions) show no steady pattern related to the impasse resolution structure. This is disquieting to some since strike avoidance is one of the reasons most commonly given as a reason for collective bargaining statutes. Nonetheless, public sector strikes remain rare by most measures. Practitioners are warned that the absence of a strike is hardly proof of good labor-management relations.

Considerable time has been spent to discover if arbitration awards differ systematically from negotiated agreements. Time and time again the answer is "no." Parties need to work together to shape an agreement that most closely meets their needs and individual situations. While arbitrators may fashion a package that has the same overall dollar value, the distribution of dollars may not be quite what the parties would have chosen for themselves had they been able to break the deadlock in negotiations. Arbitration remains a viable method to bring cloture to a dispute. But it is still a second best solution.

Many avenues remain open for increased labor-management cooperation. Agencies and unions can work together to become better negotiators. This will decrease the likelihood of impasse, particularly impasses unresolved by mediation or fact finding. Increased cooperation often takes the path of structural changes in the handling of disputes. Some jurisdictions allow the parties a great deal of latitude in fashioning their own dispute resolution techniques should they be so inclined. The options are plentiful. Examining those options together furthers the attitude of cooperation that must have positive consequences for the bargaining relationship.

Some alternative techniques and processes that others have tried are discussed in the following chapter.

NOTES

1. Thomas A. Kochan, Mordehai Mironi, Ronald G. Ehrenberg, Jean Baderschneider, and Todd Jick, *Dispute Resolution under Fact-Finding and Arbitration: An Empirical Analysis* (New York: American Arbitration Association, 1979), p. 54 (hereafter cited as Kochan, 1979).

2. Ibid., p. 53.

3. Ibid., p. 54.

4. Thomas A. Kochan and Jean Baderschneider, "Dependence on Impasse Procedures: Police and Firefighters in New York State," *Industrial and Labor Relations Review*, 31, 4 (July 1978), p. 434.

5. *Final Report of the Governor's Committee on Public Employee Relations* (Albany: State of New York, 1966), p. 33; as reported in Kochan, 1979, p. 6.

6. Kochan, 1979, pp. 25–26.

7. Compare a later review of the New York study and the response of the original researchers. Richard J. Butler and Ronald G. Ehrenberg's "Estimating the Narcotic Effect of Public Sector Impasse Procedures" and Thomas A. Kochan and Jean Baderschneider's "Estimating the Narcotic Effect: Choosing Techniques That Fit the Problem," *Industrial and Labor Relations Review*, 35, 1 (October 1981), pp. 3–20, 21–28. A follow-up study supported the assertion that the narcotic effect was of short or intermediate duration. James A. Chelius and Marion M. Extejt, "The Narcotic Effect of Impasse-Resolution Procedures," *Industrial and Labor Relations Review*, 38, 4 (July 1985), pp. 629–630.

8. The New York law previously allowed referral of impasse issues to the legislature for determination if fact finding was unsuccessful at the dispute.

9. This happened in Massachusetts when that state added arbitration as a final step for firefighters and police. But one author noted that the increase was temporary and offered the possibility that parties might try arbitration just to find out how well it worked. Jonathan Brock, *Bargaining Beyond Impasse: Joint Resolution of Public Sector Labor Disputes* (Boston: Auburn House, 1982), p. 38 (hereafter cited as Brock, 1982).

10. Kochan, 1979, pp. 37, 158.

11. Ibid., p. 158.

12. Ibid., p. 92.

13. Daniel G. Gallagher and Richard Pegnetter, "Impasse Resolution under

the Iowa Multistep Procedure," *Industrial and Labor Relations Review*, 32, 3 (April 1979), pp. 327–338.

14. William J. Walsh, "An Institutional and Economic Analysis of the Teacher Collective Bargaining Act," Ph.D. Dissertation, Indiana University, 1986, p. 220.

15. William M. Weinberg, "A Comment on the Legislative History," in *Interest Arbitration: Proceedings of an IMLR Conference* (Brunswick, N.J.: Institute of Management and Labor Relations, Rutgers University, 1980), p. 5.

16. Ibid., p. 7.

17. James W. Mastriani, "Compulsory Interest Arbitration: An Analysis of the First Two Years' Experience," in *Interest Arbitration*, pp. 11–12.

18. Charles W. Baird, "Strikes Against Government: The California Supreme Court Decision," *Government Union Review*, 7, 1 (Winter 1986), pp. 22–23.

19. Angelo S. DeNisi and James B. Dworkin, "Final Offer Arbitration and the Naive Negotiator," *Industrial and Labor Relations Review*, 35, 1 (October 1981), pp. 78–87.

20. Peter Feuille and John Thomas Delaney, "Collective Bargaining, Interest Arbitration, and Police Salaries," *Industrial and Labor Relations Review*, 39, 2 (January 1986), pp. 228–240; Brock, 1982, p. 38, indicates that this is the substance of the Sloane Report for the particular case of Massachusetts.

21. Sanford M. Jacoby, "Union-Management Cooperation in the United States: Lessons from the 1920s," *Industrial and Labor Relations Review*, 37, 1 (October 1983), p. 18.

22. Roger Fisher and William Ury, *Getting to Yes: Negotiating Agreement without Giving In* (New York: Penguin Books, 1981), p. 154.

23. Brock, 1982, pp. 25–26.

24. Ibid., pp. 44, 47.

25. Ibid., p. v.

26. Brock presents a guide for establishing such a joint committee for those practitioners who operate at the statewide level within their own organizations.

11

Experimental Impasse
Resolution Procedures

New opinions are always suspected, and usually opposed, without
any other reason, but because they are not already common.
John Locke, *An Essay Concerning Human Understanding*

One of the most significant differences between public and private sector
collective bargaining is how contract impasses are settled. In the private
sector, once the parties have negotiated to impasse then they may legally
threaten or actually resort to "industrial warfare": The union may call
a strike and the employer may lock out employees.

But even in the private sector there are notification requirements for
firms in interstate commerce. Mediation services are then provided
through the Federal Mediation and Conciliation Service in the hopes of
resolving impasses without industrial warfare. Section 8(d)(3) of the Taft-
Hartley Act requires that the FMCS be given notice of any dispute over
the termination or modification of a labor contract and that the contract
will continue in full force and effect for at least sixty days from the date
of that notice while the FMCS attempts to mediate the dispute. In the
health care industry impasse procedures are established that go so far
as to establish fact finding. In cases of disputes that "threaten the health
and safety of the nation" special impasse procedures are also specified.
So even in the relatively unbridled private sector there are examples of
statutory impasse procedures to be found.

Section 305 of the Taft-Hartley Act makes strikes by federal employees
unlawful. Even though fourteen states allow strikes, in varying degrees
and circumstances, and some local statutes permit public employee
strikes, the majority of state and local collective bargaining statutes pro-

hibit strike activity. Section 305 of the Taft-Hartley Act states, more directly than most, the mainstream view of public policymakers concerning public employee strikes:

Strikes by Government Employees

It shall be unlawful for any individual employed by the United States or any agency thereof including wholly owned Government corporations to participate in any strike. Any individual employed by the United States or by any such agency who strikes shall be discharged immediately from his employment, and shall forfeit his civil-service status, if any, and shall not be eligible for reemployment for three years by the United States or any such agency.[1]

The majority of state and local public sector bargaining laws also prohibit strikes to protect the public from the loss of essential public services.[2] Where strikes are permitted they are generally restricted to specific situations as in Minnesota, are de facto permitted as in Illinois, or are permitted only if the parties are willing to assume the risk of certain penalties as in New York. A delicate balance is the often stated goal of labor legislation. On the one hand, the legislature wants the continued operation of essential government operations; on the other hand, the legislature wants effective employee input into the terms and conditions of employment through the mechanism of collective bargaining. In the absence of the right to strike, impasse procedures have been structured as a substitute.

The prohibition of strike activity by public employees is founded on the concept of sovereignty. Taxpayers are required to pay for the operation of government—there is no freedom of choice for the taxpayer—and in exchange the taxpayer is given the right to elect the officials charged with the responsibility to oversee the operations of government. Management in government generally sees itself as exercising the sovereign rights of the electorate and that employees should therefore be precluded from a free choice in the matter of strikes. In other words, since there is no choice for the taxpayer in the marketplace, then there should be no choice for the public employees or their unions in whether to offer their services during a labor dispute.

Interest arbitration has, from time to time, come under fire as an effective substitute for the strike.[3] The criticisms of interest arbitration as a strike substitute have resulted in a perceived need to search for better alternatives. Some experimentation has been forthcoming from a few jurisdictions. These experiments fall into two basic categories: attempts to make the currently popular impasse procedures more effective and attempts to combine the more acceptable impasse procedures to create hybrids that may prove to be more effective dispute resolution devices. Those jurisdictions that permit public employee strikes also may be thought of as experimenting with impasse resolution since they are approximating the impasse resolution methods of the private sector.

The purpose of this chapter is to examine some of these experimental impasse resolution procedures and determine why they have evolved and what they tell us about the more commonly employed impasse procedures. Before proceeding to an examination of the experimental procedures and their implications, a few observations will be offered as to why experimentation has occurred at all to place in perspective what the role of experimentation is in the overall scheme of public sector impasse resolution.

WHY EXPERIMENT?

Any intervention in such important affairs as employee compensation, the determination of relative rights, and job security will risk hostility from the negotiating parties who typically view these issues as being within their mutual discretion. Labor-management relations is perhaps the best example of this very human reaction to outside interference in what are perceived to be critically important affairs. Mediation and fact finding require active roles by the parties to the impasse. Mediation and fact finding are far less intrusive than other forms of intervention such as courtroom litigation or interest arbitration.

To review, a mediator directly assists the parties during their negotiations and has no authority to impose a solution on them. A fact finder conducts a hearing, discovers evidence, and then formulates a set of recommendations that are simply advice to the parties on how the impasse may be resolved. An interest arbitrator has the authority to impose a solution on the parties. Interest arbitration, because of its relative intrusiveness, is typically the final step in most statutory impasse procedures and occupies the place in the bargaining queue that the strike would have otherwise occupied, allowing resolution of the impasse without the costs associated with the strike.

As is true for most things in life, the advantages of interest arbitration are not achieved free of cost. The parties yield the power of joint self-determination of the issues by becoming obligated to be bound by statutory impasse resolution machinery not directly controllable by the parties, either individually or jointly. Arbitration substitutes the judgment of an outsider who may have limited familiarity with local issues for the judgment of those closest to the situation—labor and management. This loss of self-determination is often viewed as a substantial cost by both labor and management in the public sector. Although the theoretical function of the neutral in interest arbitration is to "determine what the parties, as reasonable men, should themselves have agreed to at the bargaining table, . . . "[4] " . . . it can be expected that something new will come from the neutral and that there will be some substitution of neutral judgment for that of the respective parties."[5] Because of this substitution and the consequent loss of control of substantive contract matters (a significant cost to most negotiators), both labor and management have generally opposed the use of interest arbitration to resolve private sector disputes, preferring the self-determination associated with the strike.

This reflects the private sector attitude, where less than 3 percent of all labor agreements specifically provide for the arbitration of disputes stemming from the creation (that is, the bargaining) of new contract language. The following statement of a management representative is typical of the attitude of the private sector labor relations practitioners toward interest arbitration.

Arbitration is an abdication on the part of the union and management of any control over their situation. If the company is private, going to arbitration means giving away your responsibilities to the stockholders. If the company is public going to arbitration means giving away your responsibilities to the taxpayers.[6]

It is little wonder, then, that many public sector labor relations practitioners are equally disenchanted with the interest arbitration process and have sought less costly and ideologically repugnant alternatives that either avoid or modify the traditional or pure model of interest arbitration.

An equally serious potential cost of interest arbitration is "that the process would 'chill' interparty bargaining and/or serve as a habit forming 'narcotic' which would take its place."[7] Critics are quick to point out that union and management negotiators are aware that contract impasses will go to arbitration and that arbitrators have a propensity to use prearbitration final offers as extremes in fashioning awards. The critics are concerned that the specter of interest arbitration encourages the parties not to present—that is to say, reveal—their true offers prior to arbitration. Instead of developing and utilizing traditional interparty negotiating skills to mold a private agreement, the negotiating parties develop the requisite skills to convince the fact finder and/or arbitrator of the propriety of their own positions and thus achieve a favorable third party agreement. Recent research tends to confirm the existence of this narcotic effect where interest arbitration has been adopted and widely used.[8]

Given the lack of teeth in either mediation or fact finding and the various problems associated with interest arbitration, it is understandable that parties might search for alternatives that may reduce the known difficulties. In some cases the apparent dissatisfaction with interest arbitration, fact finding, and/or mediation in their pure forms may be justified. It does appear that in many, if not most cases, the traditional impasse procedures have served the parties well. It is unclear from the available evidence whether other methods of dispute resolution in the public sector are really needed or where alternative procedures have been adopted that they have dampened the critics' view of the traditional impasse resolution procedures.

STRIKE AS AN ALTERNATIVE

Some jurisdictions have utilized a rather interesting alternative to the traditional public sector impasse procedures; they have granted public employees the right to strike. Though that grant is often limited, any right to strike stands apart from the general prohibition of public employee strikes. Even limited strike rights can be thought of as revolutionary if not experimental.

The only state that specifically grants public employees a virtually unfettered right to strike is Montana. The state of Montana only interferes in public employee strikes if simultaneous strikes occur within 150 miles of each other. The union contemplating a strike in Montana must give written notice to the state and management specifying the strike date.

Alaska, Hawaii, Minnesota, Oregon, Pennsylvania, Rhode Island, and Vermont all permit public employee strikes for specific groups and under specific circumstances.[9] In these states, the general rule is that strikes that threaten essential public services may be enjoined. Rhode Island prohibits strikes by public employees; but Rhode Island courts may only enjoin a strike if the agency can make a specific showing of irreparable injury unless the injunction is issued.

Both Illinois and New York allow specific types of strikes. Illinois public employees may not have their strikes enjoined if they have bargained to an impasse and then exhausted the available impasse resolution procedures. New York's Taylor Act imposes fines on the participating employees and the loss of dues checkoff if the union engages in strike activity. New York public employees also run the theoretical risk of job loss; as a practical matter, though, the strike is permitted in that state.

In Michigan, Massachusetts, Wisconsin, Maine, and South Dakota the strike may have certain statutory penalties for the employees and/or union associated with it but there is no clear and outright prohibition of public employee strikes.[10]

The evidence concerning strike activity in the public sector does show that from 1960 through 1978 there was a fairly consistent upward trend in the frequency of public employee strikes. Since 1978 there has been some mitigation of this trend, due mostly to the recession of 1979–1982 and possibly the example made of Professional Air Traffic Controllers

Organization (PATCO) in the federal sector. Little inference can be drawn as to whether public employees having the right to strike has had any significant effect on either labor-management relations or the success of collective bargaining in those states permitting the strike.

EXPERIMENTS WITH INTEREST ARBITRATION

Final offer arbitration is an alternative dispute resolution mechanism that has received considerable attention and has even been adopted in several jurisdictions. Under final offer arbitration, the neutral is restricted to selecting the last offer of one of the parties; the neutral is not free to fashion a compromise agreement from the negotiation proposals of labor and management. Final offer arbitration is also called "either-or arbitration" and "best offer arbitration" since the arbitrator is restricted to one of the two parties' offers. Final offer arbitration has a couple of variants as the arbitrator may select final offers either as a package or on an issue-by-issue basis depending on the preference of the parties.[11] These variants have been applied to the fact-finding process as well.

What does final offer arbitration do for collective bargaining? Presumably the negotiating parties are more motivated to bargain in good faith. The parties may accurately fear that if their proposals appear less reasonable than those of their opponent, then the neutral will select the other party's proposals. Final offer arbitration may reduce extreme bargaining positions.

Evidence is mixed concerning the success of final offer interest arbitration in overcoming the alleged disadvantages of pure interest arbitration. Long and Feuille have found it to be "relatively successful" in Eugene, Oregon,[12] while Chandler concludes that "the new clout and centrality of the third party has a strong effect on interparty negotiating even when the procedure is designed to soften this result."[13] As for the effect on substantive contract content, recent research studies seem to indicate that final offer arbitration changes the outcome from what would have occurred without interest arbitration. Final offer arbitration initially gives weak unions a "leg up" in achieving what could not be achieved because of the union's deficiencies in either bargaining power or skills.[14] These results are consistent with the earlier findings of Witney that arbitrators' decisions tend to be artificial, unduly rigid, and generally inferior to privately negotiated settlements.[15]

Iowa presently uses a variant of final offer interest arbitration. Chapter 20 of the Code of Iowa specifies that mediation and fact finding occur before resorting to interest arbitration, except that the parties may mutually agree to other procedures consistent with the purposes of the Act. The interest arbitrator is limited to awarding either one of the parties' proposals or the fact finder's recommendation. Since the parties may

choose an alternative impasse procedure, they generally choose to eliminate the fact-finding report as an alternative for the arbitrator. Thus, in
practice the arbitrator is restricted to the parties' final offers. Ohio's
recently enacted impasse procedures also allows for privately negotiated
procedures in much the same manner as Iowa. Final offer arbitration
represents the only major experimentation that is the modification of a
single traditional impasse procedure.

MEDIATION-ARBITRATION

Mediation-arbitration (med-arb) combines the two dispute settlement
techniques of mediation and arbitration, just as the name implies. Under
med-arb, the mediator becomes the arbitrator with binding authority to
settle any issue not resolved through mediator-assisted negotiation efforts. The parties agree in advance that all decisions, whether achieved
through mediator-assisted negotiations or through arbitration by the
mediator, "become a part of the mediator-arbitrator's award and are
final and binding."[16] The essence of med-arb is that the specter of arbitration provides the parties with an additional incentive to resolve
their differences through mediator-assisted negotiations. As noted by
Kagel:

The parties for the first time really have to bare their souls, because if they are
dishonest in the sense of holding back on a particular issue, they know the med-
arbitrator is going to make the decision, and that's the whole point of med-arb.[17]

Early entrance by the neutral as a mediator also permits the neutral to
become thoroughly familiar with intricacies of the parties' bargaining
relationship and its environment, thereby lessening the chances that any
decision the arbitrator is called upon to render will be either unrealistic
or unworkable.

Med-arb has been utilized with some success in interest disputes in
several jurisdictions. There is, however, a real danger in this process.
The mediator and arbitrator are the same person, so the neutral must
have the requisite skills to accomplish both functions while maintaining
neutrality. Recall that the role of a mediator is to present the issues in
such a way that the parties will find them acceptable and the role of the
arbitrator is to decide the issues based on standards and evidence. It is
understandably difficult for the mediator to discover the parties' desired
and bottom line position on issues when the parties know that the
neutral will turn arbitrator if the issues go to impasse.

MUTUAL ANXIETY SYSTEM

One of the most innovative of externally imposed mixed impasse resolution procedures is the mutual anxiety system proposed to the California State Assembly in 1973. This system seeks to motivate public sector negotiating parties, particularly agencies, to bargain in good faith. The anxiety created is due to provisions that may make the fact-finding report binding in the absence of an agreed upon contract. The system was not adopted by the state of California, but its proposal stirred debate and actually resulted in a few local jurisdictions experimenting with the system. The multistep med-arb system proposal is presented in Exhibit 11.1.

The basic elements and steps in the mutual anxiety system are illustrated in Exhibit 11.1. Although several steps are depicted, the procedure ceases at the point of agreement. The individual steps reflect an attempt simultaneously to protect the public interest and motivate good faith bargaining. The motivation for good faith bargaining stems from the "uncertainty, the fear on both sides of the bargaining table of possible consequences if agreement is not reached . . . "; those consequences follow adoption of the fact finding report as a binding arbitration award.[18] In the words of one of the creators of the mutual anxiety system, "What we tried to do was create a structural risk, so rather than run the risk arising from nonagreement, the parties would prefer to settle."[19]

Little information is available concerning the mutual anxiety system since the California State Assembly did not adopt the procedure and only a few California municipalities have used the system. In theory it suggests that the parties negotiate out of the fear that they will be required to bear substantial costs if they fail to achieve a negotiated settlement. Costs and the fear of being forced to pay those costs are the driving mechanisms for good faith bargaining in this system. From Chapter 3 the reader will recall the resistance-concession model developed by J. R. Hicks. This model predicts the duration of strikes based on the parties' willingness to assume the costs associated with a strike. The mutual anxiety system operates in much the same manner, but assumes that the parties will avoid the structural costs involved in the system. Whether this is a good assumption is subject to considerable debate. If one party can impose substantially more cost on its opponent, will the mutual anxiety system generate the expected results? This is an empirical question for which no answer has yet to emerge, but if the experience of the private sector in the use of the strike is any indication it is doubtful that the mutual anxiety system would be as effective as its proponents contend.

In examination of Exhibit 11.1, the system begins with mediation. The next step is fact finding. These steps are traditional impasse procedures

Exhibit 11.1

Mutual Anxiety Impasse Resolution Steps

MEDIATION

If unsuccessful, then ——

FACT FINDING WITH RECOMMENDATIONS

Parties required to negotiate and consider fact finding proposals for some specified period of time.

VOTE ON FACT FINDING REPORT

At the end of the period of time specified in the previous step, both sides are required to submit the fact finding report to their respective constituencies for acceptance or rejection--prerequisite for the right to strike or lock out. If either side rejects the fact finding report, negotiation continues, or ——

STRIKE/LOCK OUT NOTICE

Any party wishing to strike or lock out must give 5 days' notice to the other side and the public.

CONSUMER/TAX PAYER--INITIATED COURT ACTION

After the strike/lock out notice, judicial relief may be sought by any consumer or tax payer. The court must decide whether (1) there is an imminent threat to public health and safety and, if so, (2) there are alternative safeguards (other than the injunction) against the threat to public health and safety. Where there is no threat, court relief is not granted and the strike/lock out continues.

INJUNCTIVE RELIEF AND CONVERSION OF THE FACT FINDING

REPORT TO A BINDING ARBITRATION AWARD

Where the court determines a threat to public health and safety to exist and that there is no alternative method of insulating the public therefrom, it will enjoin the work stoppage and convert the fact finding report to a final and binding arbitration award.

Source: David A. Dilts and Clarence R. Deitsch, *Labor Relations* (New York: Macmillan, 1983), p. 301.

common to most jurisdictions. If the negotiations that follow the fact-finding report fail to resolve the impasse, then the fact-finding report must be submitted to the respective constituencies. If both constituencies accept the report, the dispute is resolved. If either rejects the report, then either side may resort to traditional industrial warfare—strike or lockout—upon five days' notice to the other side and the public.

The next step is creative and has considerable merit. If the public health and safety are threatened by the work stoppage the taxpayers may seek injunctive relief. This process allows for the protection of taxpayer rights while guaranteeing the right to strike and lock out should no threat to public health or safety be found. If the court finds the injunction is warranted to protect the public interest, then the fact-finding report is converted to a final and binding interest arbitration award. This procedure protects the parties in essentially the same manner as the impasse procedures adopted in most jurisdictions. The logic of the mutual anxiety system has some appeal.

OTHER FORMS OF EXPERIMENTATION

There have been several recent developments in the private sector in creative impasse resolution such as the General Motors–United Auto Workers Saturn Contract and the experimental negotiations in the basic steel industry during the 1970s. Unfortunately the public sector has not produced as many creative ideas concerning impasse resolution.

One, not all that creative, suggestion has been referred to as the "new industrial relations." This is basically labor-management cooperation, a formalized version of integrative bargaining as discussed in Chapter 3. Labor-management cooperation became the rule of the day during the hard times for the smoke stack industries during the recent recession. With Gramm-Rudman and the new federalism it appears that many state and local governments and their unions may be forced to look at this concept in a more serious and urgent manner. This is not directly impasse resolution, in the sense of statutory or negotiated procedures, but is at the core of the philosophies held by the negotiating parties and therefore may be thought of as impasse prevention. As labor and management become increasingly concerned about the external bargaining environment and are forced to face common problems, cooperation may become necessary for either to survive. One interesting byproduct of labor-management cooperation is the reduction in impasses and the maturing of bargaining relations, which give rise to the reduction in impasse rates. It is therefore evident that labor-management cooperation is a dispute prevention mechanism worthy of serious consideration.

It is unfortunate from an academic standpoint that so few experimental techniques have been tested in recent history. Experimentation has the potential, in impasse resolution, of providing invaluable information about the public sector collective bargaining process, but the lack of experimentation may also provide some interesting conclusions as well.

WHAT DO THE EXPERIMENTS TELL US?

There does appear to be some dissatisfaction with the traditional approaches to impasse resolution procedures. The reliance on the strike, even in a limited form, suggests that the parties recognize that the mutual risk implicit therein is an important element in bringing cloture to the negotiations process. Both the mutual anxiety system and final offer interest arbitration appear to be based on this theme. The strike has been the traditional manner in which private sector negotiators have resolved their impasses, and the public sector seems to be discovering the fact that the strike really does motivate bargaining. The impasse procedures traditionally utilized may simply fail to motivate bargaining as effectively as the strike or lockout.

The final offer interest arbitration experiments purport to create the risk of bearing costs if a party is unreasonable in its positions. The research shows that there is still the narcotic effect and several other symptoms that may be distasteful to negotiators associated with this system. In the early 1970s Kansas experimented with final offer fact finding and rejected the system after only a couple of years of use because of many of the same criticisms that have been leveled at interest arbitration. Additionally the complexity and rigidity appeared to flaw the final offer fact-finding process sufficiently to warrant its being abandoned in favor of less rigid and complex reports that would truly aid the parties in resolving impasses rather than simply litigating them.

In general little is learned from the experiments concerning the effectiveness of impasse procedures, other than what is already known. Bargaining may not be well served by impasse procedures such as interest arbitration or fact finding. If the parties are free to strike or lock out then there is a direct motivation to negotiate that may be more effective in preventing impasses than any procedure will be at resolving them after they occur. The old adage that an ounce of prevention is worth a pound of cure may, in fact, have been supported by the types of experiments the parties have involved themselves with, but before this view of experimentation is accepted it should be noted that few experiments have been tried. This lack of experimentation may indicate that the parties are relatively satisfied with the traditional approaches of mediation, fact finding, and interest arbitration. If the parties were truly dissatisfied with the present impasse resolution procedures it seems reasonable that considerably more experimentation would be in evidence.

The med-arb process, in some measure, reflects the parties need for quick resolutions. If mediation, then fact finding, and then interest arbitration is the procedure utilized there can easily be months of delays. The med-arb process requires only one neutral, not three, and can be initiated and completed in a matter of days, not months. This process seems to support the idea that the parties have considerable faith in the present corps of neutrals, otherwise the responsibilities for mediation and interest arbitration would not be entrusted to a single neutral. This process could, however, as easily be interpreted to mean that there are a very few trustworthy neutrals and when one is found he or she should be entrusted with all neutral functions. Which of these competing views is correct cannot be ascertained from the available evidence.

SUMMARY AND CONCLUSIONS

Dissatisfaction with the traditional impasse resolution procedures has caused some jurisdictions and parties to look for alternative impasse procedures. The experimentation that has taken place has been rather limited, but there have been some notable things done in this regard. Some jurisdictions have allowed strikes and lockouts as an impasse resolution mechanism, while most of the other experiments have focused on making the parties either bear greater cost for failure to negotiate a contract or force more realistic bargaining. This suggests that collective bargaining may really be generic and that the differences in the public and private sector bargaining are artificial and center on the former's inability to either strike or lock out.

Labor-management cooperation may become increasingly important over the next decade due to several factors. Such labor-management cooperation may have the desirable byproduct of minimizing impasses. While not directly an impasse resolution procedure labor-management cooperation may operate in much the same manner as the strike in that cost may prevent impasse, if those costs are the things that require the parties to be cooperative.

NOTES

1. 73 Stat. 519.
2. Fourteen states either allow or specify minimal penalties for strikes.
3. Arnold M. Zack, "The Arbitration of Interest Disputes: A Process in Peril," *Arbitration Journal*, 41 (June 1986), pp. 38–42.
4. Arbitrator Whitley P. McCoy, 7 LA 848.
5. A. J. Lindemann, "Critical Aspects of Interest Arbitration," *Proceedings of the Eighth Annual Meeting of the Society of Professionals in Dispute Resolution* (Washington, D.C., 1981), pp. 192–198.
6. Kenneth M. Jennings, et al., *Labor Relations in a Public Service Industry:*

Unions, Management and the Public Interest in Mass Transit (New York: Praeger, 1978), p. 110.

7. Margaret Chandler, "Interest Arbitration: The Duty to Rectify Unequal Bargaining Skills," in *Proceedings of the Eighth Annual Meeting of the Society of Professionals in Dispute Resolution,* pp. 199–203.

8. Jennings, et al., *Labor Relations in a Public Service Industry,* p. 120.

9. Benjamin J. Taylor and Fred Witney, *Labor Relations Law* (Englewood Cliffs, N.J.: Prentice-Hall, 1983), pp. 648–651.

10. Ibid.

11. Final offers by package means that the neutral must award the entire position of one party or the other, issue-by-issue final offer arbitration allows the parties to win in some issues but lose in others.

12. Gary Long and Peter Feuille, "Final-Offer Arbitration: 'Sudden Death' in Eugene," *Industrial and Labor Relations Review,* 27 (January 1974), pp. 186–203.

13. Chandler, "Interest Arbitration," p. 202.

14. Mary McCormick, "A Functional Analysis of Interest Arbitration in New York City Municipal Government, 1968–75," in Marvin Levine and Eugene Hagbury, eds., *Labor Relations in the Public Sector* (Salt Lake City: Brighton, 1979).

15. Fred Witney, "Final Offer Arbitration: The Indianapolis Experience," *Monthly Labor Review,* 96 (May 1973), pp. 20–25.

16. Sam Kagel, "Combining Mediation and Arbitration," *Monthly Labor Review,* 96 (September 1973), p. 62.

17. Ibid.

18. Donald H. Wollett, "Mutual Anxiety: A California Proposal," *Monthly Labor Review,* 96 (September 1973), pp. 51–52.

19. Ibid.

12

Impasse Resolution in the Public Sector: A Summary

"IF I MESS THIS UP, MY NAME'LL BE MUD FOREVER!"
"You mean like Captain John Smith?"
"WHO'S HE?"
"T'was captain of the Titanic."

COLLECTIVE BARGAINING IN THE PUBLIC SECTOR

The private sector union experience began some two centuries ago. American unions were primarily formed in response to financial concerns and working conditions, rather than along ideological grounds as was often the case in Europe. The totally adversarial relationships of the 1800s can be viewed as a pitting of combinations of labor against corporations which are combinations of capital.

Without strong legal or popular support, unions rose and fell with the cyclical economy of that century. As the nation became less agrarian, popular support for unions grew. The legislature, sometimes with considerable delays, accommodated popular sentiment with labor legislation during the early 1900s. Unions experienced rapid growth. Following World War II, many felt that union conduct required additional legislative restraints. In the 1940s, federal legislation further defined union conduct in dealing with management. In the 1950s, federal legislation further defined union conduct in dealing with union members. Today, with very few exceptions, unions are exemplary models of democratic institutions.

Public sector unionism lagged that of the private sector considerably. This lag is largely reflected in the legal environment. Unionism of government employees was quite often illegal. The greatest single impetus to public sector collective bargaining was an executive order of President John Kennedy.[1] He directed government agencies to bargain with majority unions on a restricted set of issues. Today federal collective bargaining is a matter of legislation.[2] However, prohibited subjects of bargaining include wages, overtime, holidays, and most elements of the typical fringe package; these subjects are all a matter of law, thus removed from managerial discretion. The exclusion of economic issues from federal sector bargaining is the principal reason that this book has focused on state and local collective bargaining.

Within the public sector, unionism of state and local employees lagged that of federal workers. This too was a reflection of the legislative environment. Although some states preceeded the federal government, the federal government actions generally legitimized collective bargaining by public employees. The subsequent state statutes have been far from uniform. Developed in different years in response to different political pressures and different local circumstances, state statutes have a variety of scopes, coverages, and impasse procedures. This book has emphasized the aspects of collective bargaining procedures and process common to most jurisdictions.

The two principal theories—the Hicksian resistance-concession model and the behavioral theory—of collective bargaining presented a comprehensive survey of the basis for most bargaining literature. Both describe the way that bargaining impasses can come about.

In preparing for contract bargaining, a negotiating team should develop a strategy: identifying, categorizing, prioritizing, and scheduling goals. Then the team should review issue-oriented table tactics as well as style-oriented bargaining tactics. A thorough preparation for bargaining is the best insurance against negotiation of a "poor" contract. It also minimizes the likelihood of unnecessary impasses.

IMPASSE RESOLUTION IN THE PUBLIC SECTOR

Impasses occur through lack of adequate preparation for bargaining, through inexperience, through misunderstandings, through honest differences of opinion, and by design. The impasse resolution procedure used by the impassed parties may be voluntary or compulsory depending on local statute. The most common structure provides for mediation of disputes, fact finding of unsettled disputes, and arbitration of issues of contracts remaining at impasse.

Mediators are neutrals with education or experience in labor relations, labor law, economics, and the psychology of negotiations. The purpose of mediation is to find contract terms acceptable to the parties and to remove any emotional barriers to their acceptance.

Fact-finding procedures involve setting up the ground rules for the proceedings, gathering evidence, determining standards to be applied to the evidence, and presenting the final report to the parties for consideration. There are a great variety of decisional standards that can be applied to economic and to contract language issues. As described in some detail in Chapters 7 and 8, the standards have been established in legislated statute, by history of the sector, through the custom of the parties, and by consent of the negotiators. Some standards are easily understood and applied; others, inferred with some degree of difficulty.

Fact-finding reports are often released publicly some weeks after presentation to the parties if no negotiated settlement has taken place. This public release will normally bring some pressure on one or both of the parties to settle. If no agreement is in sight, many jurisdictions specify interest arbitration as the last step of the resolution procedure.

Information is presented to the arbitrator in much the same manner as is the case in fact finding. The essential difference is that the arbitration decision is final. Arbitration's main benefit is in bringing cloture to disputes. Arbitration's main flaw is that the award is the neutral's judgment instead of the parties' consensus. While the award is an expert judgment, few would favor outside intervention to a negotiated settlement. That is why every effort is made to resolve disputes prior to reaching the arbitration step.

Interest arbitration is almost unique to the public sector. The private sector is generally free to resort to industrial warfare—strike or lockout— to resolve disputes. Although the incidence of strikes is relatively low in the private sector, the strike-lockout threat still serves as a strong inducement to modify extreme bargaining stances and reach settlement.

Impasse resolution procedures do bring about settlements to contract bargaining disputes in the public sector. But, like medicine, there are side effects to their use. Impasses are somewhat more likely to occur when parties know that there is an established procedure to follow. Resort to the procedures induces a narcotic effect in some bargaining relationships; there is an increased likelihood that future disputes will go to impasse. Fortunately the narcotic effect wears off eventually, although the length of time it takes varies considerably across studies.

Some negotiators may be inclined to take disputes to interest arbitration rather than negotiate a settlement in the hopes that the arbitration award will be preferable. There is no evidence to support those hopes; studies have consistently shown the similarity between negotiated and awarded settlements. Some studies have even suggested that the fact finders' reports are a reliable predictor of what an arbitration award will look like. Thus, empirical studies support the authors' preference for negotiated settlements and the authors' respect for the quality of services provided by neutrals.

Most negotiations reach a settlement without impasse. The majority of impasses are settled through mediation. Most remaining disputes are settled through fact finding. Of those disputes going to interest arbitration, most parties are able to narrow their areas of disagreement to a handful of issues having already resolved most troublesome areas. It might be tempting to say that the current impasse resolution systems work and be satisfied with the status quo.

Fortunately, most jurisdictions are not stagnant. States continuously monitor each other's successes and difficulties to see if their own systems can be improved. Experimentation has continued; more novel approaches usually in response to what are perceived as more novel situations. This results in an "everybody wins" competition among jurisdictions to see which will develop a system of dispute resolution superior to others. While it is not anticipated that a single system will become universal in the public sector, the future will probably see an eventual narrowing of mandatory statutory procedures and a growth of optional procedures available to meet local needs.

Increasing experience and expertise of the practitioners of labor negotiations will bring about a maturation of bargaining relationships. It will become easier for parties to reach settlements. Impasses over misunderstanding or due to a failure to recognize alternatives will become increasingly less common. The authors hope that this book is a key in achieving those ends.

NOTES

1. Executive Order 10988.
2. Title VII of the Civil Service Reform Act of 1978.

APPENDIX A

Fact Finder's Report

FACT FINDER'S REPORT

In the Matter of the Fact Finding Between	David A. Dilts Fact Finder
Employees represented by International Brotherhood of Electrical Workers, AFL-CIO, Local 53	PERB Case 75-I-12-1987
and	
Water Pollution Control Department, of the City of Kansas City, Kansas	September 14, 1987

APPEARANCES:

For the Union:

James R. Waers, Attorney-at-Law
Keith Querry, Business Manager
John Morasch

For the City:

Daniel Denk, Attorney-at-Law
George Johnson
Lewis Levin
Eugene Andrisevic
Burdette Cavin

Hearings in the above cited case were conducted on Wednesday, September 2, 1987 in the ninth floor conference room in the City Hall of Kansas City, Kansas. The parties stipulated that five issues remained at impasse and were therefore properly before this Fact Finder. The parties also agreed to grant this Fact Finder the seven day extension for the filing of the report in this matter. The record was not closed on September 2, 1987, but remained open until receipt of the one additional document agreed upon by the parties.

TABLE OF CONTENTS

ISSUES AT IMPASSE

The parties stipulated the following issues are impasse:

1. The wage package;
2. Paid personal business leave in lieu of paid holidays;
3. Union dues checkoff;
4. Overtime pay; and
5. Call-in pay.

BACKGROUND

The Water Pollution Control Department of the City of Kansas City, Kansas was originally formed in 1966. It was formed in response to the Federal Government's growing concern for the collection and treatment of sewage. The Department has grown over the years and currently has 152 authorized positions of which 101 are bargaining unit jobs. The

Department is divided into six sections; the Treatment Section which is responsible for collection and treatment of all sewage in the City and for the operation of the City's flood pumps; the Sewer Maintenance Section is responsible for all sewer cleaning and emergency backups and the maintenance of the sewer system; the Laboratory Section is responsible to conduct all treatment plant analysis, prepare reports to the State of Kansas, inspect the efficiency of the treatment plants and for pretreatment operations; the Engineering Section provides the in-house engineering service to the Water Pollution Control Department; and the Administrative Section provides all administrative services to the Water Pollution Control Department.

In August of 1985 the International Brotherhood of Electrical Workers, Local 53 petitioned the Kansas Public Employment Relations Board for a unit determination for certain of the employees in the Kansas City, Kansas Water Pollution Control Department. The Public Employment Relations Board, on April 1, 1986, entered its order determining the appropriate bargaining unit. [see PERB order of April 1, 1986, in Case no. 75-UDC-1-1986].

The present negotiations are for the initial contract between the parties. The parties have been able to resolve all issues except for those contained in the respective declarations of impasse. The parties have agreed to an initial contract of three years duration.

The parties have also agreed to phase out the various steps in the Public Administration Service (PAS) compensation plan. While agreement has been reached on phasing out the PAS's steps, the method by which these steps are to phased out has not been agreed upon.

POSITIONS OF THE PARTIES

Before proceeding to the Fact Finder's recommendations and supporting rationale, a brief review of the parties respective positions will be offered. The Union is the moving party and its positions on each issue will be summarily examined before turning the City's positions on each issue.

Union's Positions

1. Wages

The major difference between the City and the Union wage proposals is that the City's proposal provides for relatively small wage increases (less than 10 percent over three years) for senior employees. The Union's proposal defers increases in the step rates for employees until they reach the final step in the progression. Thus, until the top step is reached, each employee, under the Union proposal, receives a 5 percent cost of living wage increase per annum. Only upon attainment of the top level, does an employee receive the step increases that he would have received under the PAS system. The Union is not seeking retroactive pay for those years of wage deferral, the Union is only asking that this percentage wage increase be included when the employee reaches the journeyman level.

Under the Union's proposal, all employees currently in Step 4 or above would attain the highest classification rate by the end of the agreement. It is hoped that in successor agreements, similar provisions will be made to allow employees in Step 1 through 3 to move to the higher classifications. In this way, senior employees are rewarded for years of service and acquired skills while less senior employees still receive a fair wage increase. This is consistent with Union wage proposals submitted throughout the course of negotiations. The Union has consistently proposed to gradually eliminate the seven step progression system.

The cost of the Union's proposal is only 2.4 percent more, over three years, than the City's proposal. The Union's proposal would produce an 18.4 percent increase over the life of the three year agreement. This proposal is certainly affordable. The City's budget is over $100 million and $250,000 was already budgeted for salary increases in the Water Pollution Control Department.

The comparability data show that the City's wages are relatively low for some classifications, but relatively high in others when compared with similar jurisdictions. In comparisons with other jurisdictions, it must be remembered that most of the employees in these other jurisdictions have been receiving their step increases, while in Kansas City, Kansas the employees have not. This means that step and classification comparisons are dangerous, since the Kansas City employees would have been advanced through the steps in the other jurisdiction's pay schemes.

The Union also contends that the employees of the Water Pollution Control Department are relatively poorly paid when compared to other Kansas City, Kansas employees. The Water Pollution Control Department received relatively poor wage increases in 1985 and 1986, thus creating a need for a catch-up wage increase.

The City has not argued that it has an inability to pay the Union's wage increase. The comparability and cost of living data clearly show the need for the Union's proposal to be adopted. The Union put its final and best offer on the table and asks the Fact Finder to recommend it.

2. Paid Personal Days in Lieu of Paid Holidays

The City requested at the start of negotiations to reduce the number of paid holidays from twelve to eight. The Union's initial proposal was to increase the holidays by one, for a total of thirteen paid holidays. The Union also proposed to change the personal leave policy from three days charged to sick leave to forty hours personal leave not charged to sick leave. Through the course of negotiations, these two items become intertwined through a proposal by the Union.

The Union agreed it would accept eleven paid holidays if personal leave days were increased from three to four days per year charged to sick leave. The City rejected this proposal.

The Union's proposal herein is not a cost item. The additional day of personal leave is charged against the employees accumulated sick leave, thus the Union is proposing to give up one paid holiday in exchange for one additional personal leave day, which is charged to sick leave. The agreement between the City and the Fraternal Order of Police provides for five paid personal days.

3. Union Dues Checkoff

In negotiations, the Union proposed standard language and a form for checkoff of Union dues. The Union sought dues checkoff for obvious reasons. Dues checkoff is the most convenient way for members to meet their financial obligations to the Union. The employees are saved the time and the inconvenience of contacting a Union steward to make direct payments, going to the Union hall to pay dues, or mailing dues in on a monthly basis. Dues checkoff also is a costs savings item to the Union in that there is less bookkeeping and time expended on receiving and receipting for dues.

The Union is not seeking to break new ground with this issue, as numerous other agreements between the City and labor organizations contain Union dues checkoff. Further, the City currently provides for checkoff from Water Pollution Control employee's wages for a number of items including, medical, credit union, savings bonds, and charitable contributions. It should therefore be apparent that there is no significant cost factor to the City in adding Union dues to its current list of payroll deductions.

4. Overtime Pay

The Union's initial proposal called for the payment of overtime for any hours worked over eight in one day or forty in a week. The Employer's proposal has remained consistent that overtime be paid only after forty hours worked in a week. The Union subsequently moved from its initial position and proposed overtime at time and one-half for all hours paid for in excess of forty hours in one week. The Union believes this position is reasonable. For example, under the City's proposal, if an employee during a holiday week works a sixth day, no overtime would be paid in that the eight hours of holiday pay was not for time actually worked. However, the Union submits that holidays, vacation, and sick leave are contractual benefits enjoyed by the employee. An employee should not be penalized by being denied overtime merely because the employee has utilized a contractual benefit. The Union therefore request the Fact Finder to recommend its proposal on this issue to assure other employee rights are protected.

5. Call-in Pay

The Union's final proposal with respect to call-in pay was a four hour guarantee at the applicable wage rate when an employee is called into work. The Union's proposal is necessary to protect an employee from such abuses as calling him in during the middle of the night and then after the employee dresses and travels to work finding the employer has changed his mind.

Clearly, employees are entitled to be compensated for such inconvenience and time expenditures. Other agreements between the City of Kansas City and other labor organizations all provide for some type of guarantee pay for call-ins. The current practice of the Water Pollution Control Department is difficult to ascertain. Call-in pay varies significantly across the various divisions of the Water Pollution Control Department. However, it is clear that most employees receive some type of guarantee for call-in work.

The Union respectfully submits that its positions on all of the issues at impasse are the most reasonable and are supported by the preponderance of credible evidence. The Union, therefore urges the Fact Finder ought to recommend its positions on each of these issues.

City's Positions

1. Wages

The City proposes to annually increase the rate of all steps 3.2 percent and to eliminate Steps 1, 2, and 3 in progressive years of the agreement. The elimination of these steps is proposed by raising the lowest existing step to the next highest step in each successive year. The effect of this approach is that the lower paid employees will receive at least an 8.45 percent increase and the higher paid employees receive at least a 3.2 percent increase. The overall cost is 5 percent for 1987, 5.41 percent for 1988 and 5.92 percent for 1989.

The City has had the greatest turnover at the lower steps of the lower paying jobs. This approach addresses the need for the greatest improvements in the lower paying positions to reduce these relatively high turnover rates. High turnover rates impose significant selection and training costs and need to be brought down.

The City's comparison data show that the Employer provides an excellent fringe benefit package and its wages are comparable with or
exceed the comparable jurisdictions offered by the City into evidence
[see City exhibits 7 and 8]. Further the City has shown that it receives
more than adequate applications from qualified candidates for positions
which become open in the Department [see City exhibit 6].

The Consumer Price Index data [City exhibit 10] show that the City's
proposal will maintain the purchasing power of the employees' wages.
The CPI (U) for the first half of 1987 shows a 3.2 percent increase while
the CPI (W) indicates a 3.4 percent increase in the cost of living [see
City exhibit 10]. The City's wage proposal is certainly sufficient to maintain the purchasing power of current wages.

The City does not claim any inability to pay the Union's wage demands, but the City has present tax rates which are of concern. In fact,
the City has observed that some taxpayers have formed organizations
to determine if some political solution is available to what they believe
are relatively high taxes. The City wishes to provide the necessary public
service at the most reasonable cost. Since this Department is funded
primarily through service charges, there is a need to keep costs from
accelerating beyond what is necessary to provide good sewage treatment
service. The City is in the process of building a new sewage treatment
facility [as required by a consent decree] and the demand on the present
facilities is declining. In simple terms, this means that the per unit cost
of treatment will increase while revenues are declining.

It has also been shown through evidence that Kansas City, Kansas
has a relatively high proportion of low income households. The City is
losing younger more affluent households, while the elderly population
is increasing. This simply means that the taxpaying public is becoming
less able to shoulder reasonable tax burdens, while the demand on public
services is increasing. The City must be careful to assure that it is being
as cost efficient as possible. It is the City's considered opinion that its
proposal for wages is consistent with this obligation. The City has provided the Fact Finder a detailed analysis of the demographic and financial
constraints faced by the City in its exhibit 11.

The City respectfully requests the Fact Finder to recommend its position on the issue of wages.

2. Paid Personal Business Leave in Lieu of Paid Holidays

The difference between the parties in the holidays and personal leave
rests solely in the number of personal leave days. The City originally
proposed that the number of paid holidays be reduced to eight. This
position was modified, but the City modified its original position under
the realization that this issue had been resolved as a portion of a package.
The Union now proposes four personal business leave days and the City

has remained with three such days each year in its final proposal. The evidence will show that the Union agreed to three days of personal leave earlier in the negotiations in exchange for a section which they desired in the agreement. They have regressed from this agreed position to preserve this issue. The City urges the Fact Finder to reject the Union's proposal on this issue.

3. Union Dues Checkoff

The Union's proposal that the contract contain a dues checkoff provision is rejected by the City. The Union wants the City to perform its work for it. This the City is unwilling to do. The City believes that the collection of Union dues is something the Union should do, not the City. The City believes the Union has failed to provide a compelling reason for the inclusion of a checkoff provision in the collective bargaining agreement. The City therefore requests the Fact Finder to reject this Union proposal.

4. Overtime Pay

The City's position on the overtime issue is that it comply with the requirements of the Fair Labor Standards Act. This federal statute requires that the Employer pay an overtime rate of time and one-half for all hours *worked* in excess of forty in one week. The Union wants to improve upon that and be allowed time and one-half pay after forty *paid* hours in a week. This would mean that if an employee were on sick leave, personal leave, funeral leave, vacation or a holiday, but was paid for those hours, he would be entitled to be paid for any hours worked in excess of forty hours paid, whether or not he was absent four out of five days in a work week.

The City's position is simply that it comply with the Fair Labor Standards Act and believes there is no reason to improve upon this public policy. The Employer urges the Fact Finder to recommend its position on this issue.

5. Call-in Pay

The overtime call-in issue is simply stated that the Union wants the bargaining unit to be guaranteed four hours pay if they are called in to work overtime. The City again feels that the Fair Labor Standards Act provides for pay at time and one-half the employee's regular rate of pay for hours worked in excess of forty and that this required provision is sufficient. Call-in pay is a cost item, and the City does not wish to assume any additional costs over this issue.

The Union has shown no compelling reason to include any call-in pay provision in the collective bargaining agreement. The City's position is reasonable and therefore the Fact Finder should recommend its proposal on this issue.

FACT FINDER'S RECOMMENDATIONS AND RATIONALE

The Fact Finder will present the recommendations, followed by a supporting rationale on each issue. The order of presentation will be the same as found in the preceeding sections of this report. A summary of the recommendations will also be presented as the final section of this report.

1. Wages

Recommendation

The Fact Finder recommends a compromise position between the City and the Union on the issue of wages. The Fact Finder recommends the reduction of the PAS pay grid from the present seven steps to two for the final year of the three year contract.

For the first year of the contract the Fact Finder recommends that the parties elevate step 1 to step 2 and step 5 to step 6; with steps 1 and 5 being eliminated from the pay grid. For the second year of the contract the Fact Finder recommends that all employees now at step 2 be elevated to step 3 and that all employees now at step 6 be elevated to step 7; with steps 2 and 6 being eliminated from the pay grid. For the final year of the agreement the Fact Finder recommends that all employees now at step 3 be elevated to step 4; with step 3 being eliminated from the pay grid.

In addition to the recommended step increases and changes in the pay grid the Fact Finder recommends that a cost of living increase of 3.2 percent be applied to the wage rates for steps 1 through 4 for each of the three years; and that a cost of living increase of 3.4 percent be applied to the wage rates for steps 5 through 7 for each of the three years.

The Fact Finder further recommends that those employees currently in a step 4 and a step 7 position on the pay grids be given a one-time payment of 10 hours pay in recognition of their not receiving a step increase over the life of the contract. This payment should be made as soon as possible after the ratification of the collective bargaining agreement. The one-time payment is intended to be made on the basis of the 1987 wages recommended by this Fact Finder.

Rationale

This Fact Finder expended a great deal of time and effort examining the respective positions of the parties and the supporting evidence. Both of the parties' positions have merit and are lacking in several respects.

A Compromise Is Dictated by the Evidence

The City's proposal provides for larger percentage increases at the lower salary steps, while the Union's proposal focuses on improving the wages of more senior employees. The turnover rates at the lower salary steps provides support for the City's position, while the avoidance of salary compression provides considerable support for the Union's position.

The City has shown, to this Fact Finder's satisfaction, that General Maintenance Workers [Range 22, Step 1 being the majority] have presented considerable turnover rate problems for the Water Pollution Control Department [see City exhibit 6]. There is also evidence that turnover exists in the other lower paying classifications.

The City's proposal, however, fails to provide adequate salary differentials between the more senior and skilled employees and those with less seniority and skill. This is a matter of equity as well as market considerations. The Union's position that the more senior and skilled employees are deserving of pay raises which are not out of line with the raises for entry level employees is also meritorious.

The Current Pay System

The problem is that the PAS salary scheme contains 7 steps, with 5 percent differentials between the steps. To reduce the number of steps will require that compression, in some form, occurs at the targeted steps. In the present case, the Fact Finder recommends the elimination of all but step 4 and step 7 of the PAS system. This, unfortunately, means that these two steps will suffer from lower raises than will the steps immediately below them.

The geometry of the pay grid is cruel in another important respect. The higher the raises granted these two steps the greater must be the raises in the steps below them to finally catch-up and eliminate the lower paying steps. Neither the City's nor Union's proposal contemplated salary reductions in any ranges or steps, so the acceleration of lower steps' raises results in an inherent problem in the reduction in steps.

The City proposed that only steps 1 through 3 be eliminated. The Union, on the other hand, proposed that only steps 4 through 6 be eliminated. The Union envisioned an elimination of steps from the top. In other words, step 6 would be elevated to step 7 with a chain reaction below. With the employees' not receiving the step increases until they actually reached the higher paying step. This would result in relative large increases as the lower steps are eliminated. In order to afford the Union's proposed 5 percent increases, the Union proposed the deferral mechanism. This, however, has the potential for massive pay increases as steps 1, 2, and 3 are phased out.

The Recommendation

The Fact Finder has worked out a compromise solution that allows both the City and the Union to accomplish some of their goals. It is clear that the parties mutually intend to significantly reduce the steps in the PAS system, preferably to 2 or 3 steps. Neither party's proposal accomplishes this mutually contemplated goal. The geometry of the grid system allows the reduction of the number of steps to 2, without significant problems in the three year period. In fact the money expended for the reduction in steps, with the 3.2 and 3.4 percent cost of living increases for the respective groups is only about 1.0 percent more than what is necessary to fund the City's proposal and is 1.2 percent less than the cost of the Union's proposal, [by the Fact Finder's own calculations]. It is the Fact Finder's considered opinion that the cost differences cited by the parties cannot be directly compared, since they are working with different numbers. Even so, the parties' respective data are not so different as to cause problems in following the analysis herein contained. The Fact Finder's calculations are based on the data contained in City exhibits 3 through 5 and Union exhibits A1 and L.

There is no doubt that without the step increases being funded over the past two years that the Water Pollution Control Department has fallen somewhat behind employees in similarly situated employment are paid. This is particularly true for the more senior and skilled employees. In examining the various comparability groups offered by the parties the Fact Finder notices that City exhibit 7 shows only ranges for various job classifications. The data for the Wastewater Plant Operator classification shows that Kansas City, Kansas pays the second lowest wage at the maximum wage level of the City's comparability group. In examining City exhibit 3, this Fact Finder notes that Kansas City's Wastewater Plant Operators are mostly at the lower steps. In fact, 16 of the 20 people in this classification are in steps 3 or below. Union exhibit L shows that only 18 people are in this classification. Union exhibit L shows the seniority dates of employees by classification. This exhibit shows that 13 Wastewater Plant Operators have 5 or more years of seniority with the City. Other classifications have essentially the same difficulties. General Maintenance Workers in Kansas City, Kansas enjoys a third place position of the six comparable jurisdictions at the maximum pay range. At the minimum pay level Kansas City, Kansas drops to fourth. The majority of General Maintenance Workers in Kansas City, Kansas have five or less years of seniority [29 of 34 employees shown in this classification on Union exhibit L]. These examples can be cited throughout the wage classifications. What they clearly show is that the more skilled positions are filled by higher seniority employees in relatively low steps in the pay grid. The less skilled classifications are populated with low seniority employees, who again are in the lower steps of the grid. This is indicative of rather poor general comparability of pay levels with similarly situated jurisdictions.

It is this Fact Finder's conclusion that some attention must be paid to both the upper and the lower steps in each range. In fact, this is what the parties contentions are, in sum. The City has focused on the turnover problems and has proposed improvement in the lower steps. The Union, on the other hand, has focused its efforts on the need to improve wages for the more skilled and senior employees. It is clear to this Fact Finder that both needs are supported by the record.

The Fact Finder's recommendation that employees currently on steps 4 and 7 be afforded a one-time payment of 10 hours pay at the 1987 wage amounts to a one-half percent addition to their incomes for the first year of a contract in which they will not gain as much relative to their fellow employees [10 hours is roughly .5 percent of a standard 2,000 hour work year]. To add to these employees' hourly wage causes difficulty in reducing the number of steps in the pay grid. To include the recognition of the sacrifice these employees will make by a one-time payment of 10 hours pay is little more than a token for the City, which will cost less than $1,550 for the approximately 20 employees in these two steps. Such a one time payment will assure that all employees will have an increase in their total compensation over the ten percent figure the Union cites as unacceptable, for the life of the collective bargaining agreement.

Improvement at the Higher and Lower Steps

The Fact Finder is convinced that any recommendation must address the two identifiable problems in the present pay grid. The result of this need to improve wages at both the lower and the higher steps will result in relatively lower cost of living adjustments.

It is the considered opinion of this Fact Finder that the City's estimates for the CPI (W) and CPI (U) are reasonable estimates. The Fact Finder has no crystal ball and cannot improve on what the data show. City exhibit 10 shows that the cost of living is increasing at an annual rate of between 3.2 percent (CPI-U) and 3.4 percent (CPI-W).

To assist in eliminating wage compression and hence future bargaining difficulties, the Fact Finder recommends that the lower CPI estimate be used as the cost of living adjustment for the lower wage step [1 through 4] and that the higher estimate be used for the higher wage steps [5 through 7]. This allows a marginally higher increase for the top of the scale employees [in step 7]. Over the three years of the life of the parties' contract this difference in will amount to an almost two-thirds of one percent increase in the wage differential between step 4 and step 7. This is recognition of long service to the City, even though it is not substantial.

It is this Fact Finder's opinion that such recognition of long service is warranted, not only by the comparability data, but also to maintain good employee morale and acceptance of the recommended wage package.

Wage Steps

The Fact Finder has calculated the wages generated from his recommendation. For the lower steps [1 through 4], the Fact Finder's recommendation produces the same wage as proposed by the City for each of the three years of the collective bargaining agreement. For steps 5 through 7, the Fact Finder's recommendations produce wages higher than those proposed by the City, but lower than those proposed by the Union. In the lower pay ranges for step 7 the difference between the City's proposal and the Fact Finder's recommendation is only a penny or two per hour. For example, a Construction Worker I, at range 28, step 7, will make $9.56 per hour under the Fact Finder's recommendation rather than the $9.55 proposed by the City for the first year, but by the third year of the contract this difference increases to five cents per hour [Fact Finder's recommendation of $10.23 versus the City's proposed wage of $10.18]. For employees at step 5 of range 32, however, the difference is substantial. For the first year of the contract the City's proposal generates a wage for this range and step of $9.55, but the Fact Finder's recommendation generates a wage of $10.04. By the end of the contract the difference between the Fact Finder's recommendation and the City's proposal is $.72 and is only $.54 less than the Union's proposal. It is clear that those employees in Step 7 will receive higher raises than those in step 4. Steps 1, 2, 5, and 6 will receive the greatest benefit from the Fact Finder's recommendation. The City intended that employees in steps 1 and 2 should benefit, while the Union intended that employees in step 5, 6, and 7 should benefit most from the negotiated wage package. This Fact Finder's recommendation addresses each of the parties' concerns. The recommendation also does not produce deferrals of pay raises, but provides increased wages to the effected employees through the life of the agreement. The Fact Finder has prepared a table to illustrate the effects of the recommendations on employee hourly wages through the life of the contract. See the following table.

These recommended reductions in steps within the ranges, still leave the parties with a significant number of wage ranges. With only two steps, however, any identified inequities in the relative levels of compensation can be addressed in future negotiations. In this respect, the Fact Finder is convinced that the reduction of the number of steps to only two will remove this issue from the bargaining table in future negotiations and allow the parties to focus their attentions on the equity of the internal wage structure and market considerations.

Naturally the reductions of steps within the ranges produce significant

Table 1
Fact Finder's Recommended Wages for 1987—89

1986 Class	1986 Wage	1987 Recommend	1988 Recommend	1989 Recommend
15/1	4.97	5.39	5.85	6.34
18/1	5.36	5.81	6.31	6.84
19/4	6.38	6.58	6.79	7.01
21/1	5.77	6.25	6.79	7.36
21/4	6.70	6.91	7.13	7.36
21/3	6.38	6.58	6.79	7.36
21/7	7.77	8.03	8.30	8.58
22/1	5.92	6.42	6.96	7.54
22/3	6.53	6.74	6.96	7.54
22/4	6.86	7.08	7.31	7.54
22/7	7.97	8.24	8.52	8.81
26/4	7.58	7.82	8.07	8.33
28/1	6.86	7.45	8.08	8.76
28/2	7.22	7.45	8.08	8.76
28/3	7.58	7.82	8.08	8.76
28/4	7.97	8.24	8.52	8.76
28/5	8.37	9.10	9.89	10.23
28/6	8.80	9.10	9.89	10.23
28/7	9.25	9.56	9.89	10.23
32/5	9.25	10.04	10.90	11.27
32/6	9.71	10.04	10.90	11.27
33/1	7.77	8.42	9.13	9.92
33/2	8.16	8.42	9.13	9.92
33/3	8.58	8.85	9.13	9.92
33/4	9.02	9.31	9.61	9.92
33/6	9.95	10.29	11.19	11.57
33/7	10.46	10.82	11.19	11.57
34/6	10.20	10.55	11.45	11.85
39/3	9.95	10.27	10.60	11.50
39/5	10.99	11.93	12.96	13.40
39/6	11.54	11.93	12.96	13.40

variations in the percentage raises this recommendation yields across the various classifications. It should be noted by the parties that since both the step increases and the cost of living increases are percentage increases, the relative position of salary ranges do not change, except slightly between step 4 and 5, due to the difference in the cost of living percentage applied to the higher and lower steps. These percentage wage increases are presented in table 2 for the three year period of the contract.

The range and step is identified as class, the difference noted in column two of the table is the third year wage minus the 1986 wage, and the final column is the percentage difference over the life of the contract.

The Fact Finder's recommendations produce approximately a 5.34 percent increase for the first year [excluding the one-time payment portion of the recommendation]. For the second year the percentage increase in wages will be 6.69 percent, and the final year's increase will be about 5.97 percent.

The Fact Finder recognizes that the Union would have preferred to have the highest steps rewarded more. That is, rather than to adjust the wage scale from the bottom up, as the City has proposed and the Fact Finder has recommended. The Union would have had the Fact Finder move step 6 to step 7 and step 5 move up to step 6 at the top end, and move step 3 to 4 then step 2 to 3, and so on for each year, until the requisite number of steps were achieved. The deferral scheme offered by the Union keeps the total wage bill within reason over the life of the contract. The problem is that as the lower steps come to the journeyman level the wage increases would be very large. This could inhibit further step elimination, or create a situation where future cost of living adjustments would have to be very small to accommodate the elimination of the lower steps. The Fact Finder examined this possibility, along with numerous others. To achieve the elimination of a significant number of steps and to keep the cost of such a scheme within the range of the parties' proposals would have required such a small cost of living increase for the top step in the grid as to make this approach certainly unacceptable to the Union. The Fact Finder is convinced from the data available that elimination of steps at both the upper and lower ends is necessary and addresses both parties expressed concerns. With this as one of the primary goals of the recommendation, together with generating step 7 increases in excess of ten percent [which are necessary to maintain those steps purchasing power], the Fact Finder believes the recommended method is the only rational option.

The Fact Finder believes that the wage recommendation contained herein is a fair and equitable settlement. It is clearly within the City's ability to fund and restores the comparability of wages, evidenced in

Table 2

1987—89 Percentage Increases—Steps/Ranges

1986 Class	Wage Increase	Percentage Increase
15/1	1.37	27.6
18/1	1.48	27.6
19/4	.63	9.9
21/1	1.59	27.6
21/4	.66	9.9
21/3	.98	15.4
21/7	.81	10.4
22/1	1.62	27.4
22/3	1.01	15.5
22/4	.68	9.9
22/7	.84	10.5
26/4	.75	9.9
28/1	1.90	27.7
28/2	1.54	21.3
28/3	1.18	15.6
28/4	.79	9.9
28/5	1.86	22.2
28/6	1.43	16.3
28/7	.98	10.6
32/5	2.02	21.8
32/6	1.56	16.1
33/1	2.15	27.7
33/2	1.76	21.6
33/3	1.34	15.6
33/4	.90	10.0
33/6	1.62	16.3
33/7	1.11	10.6
34/6	1.65	16.2
39/3	1.55	15.6
39/5*	2.41	21.9
39/6	1.86	16.1

*Includes one budget line identified as 39/2/5 indicating an equity [green circle] adjustment, this percentage not applicable to that employee.

**Excludes the recommended one-time payment of 10 hours pay for employees in currently in steps 4 and 7.

similarly situated jurisdictions. The Fact Finder's recommendations should therefore be acceptable to both parties.

2. Paid Personal Business Leave in Lieu of Paid Holidays

Recommendation

The Fact Finder recommends that the current personnel policy of allowing three (3) days of personal leave charged against sick leave be adopted for the collective bargaining agreement. Further, the Fact Finder recommends that the current twelve (12) paid holidays be adopted.

Rationale

This particular issue has been confounded by its bargaining history. The bargaining history clearly shows that an agreement had been reached on a package of issues, to which the City believed elements of this issue were tied. The Union does not refute this City contention. The Union argues that this issue was given new life simply in an attempt to resolve other issues still on the bargaining table.

All of this aside, the Fact Finder has carefully examined the contract provisions for other City workers and the other comparable jurisdictions cited by both parties. It is clear to this Fact Finder that there are differences in the holiday, sick leave, and personal business day provisions. It is impossible for this Fact Finder to state with certainty that a clear standard has developed between the City and its other bargaining units or that an accepted practice has evolved in public employment.

The bargaining history is limited to the current negotiations, therefore, this Fact Finder only has the current practice to illustrate the parties past mutually acceptable resolutions for this issue.

In examining the parties respective contentions this Fact Finder is unable to find anything which indicates a compelling reason for changing the current policy. Neither does the record contain evidence of a compelling need to change the current practice. It is therefore the Fact Finder's considered opinion that the current practice should be adopted into the parties' collective bargaining agreement.

3. Union Dues Checkoff

Recommendation

The Fact Finder recommends the Union's proposed dues checkoff language [exhibit K] be included in the collective bargaining agreement.

Rationale

The City offered the argument that it preferred not to do the Union's job for it in support of its position on this issue. In other

words, the City argues, since dues collection is a portion of the
function performed by unions the City ought not agree to a checkoff
provision. All other things equal, this Fact Finder believes the City's
position is accurate. However, the record of the City's negotiations
with the Fraternal Order of Police, International Association of Fire
Fighters, and Public Service Employees Union [see contracts between
the City and FOP, IAFF, and PSEU, Union exhibits E2, E3, E4, and
E5] shows clearly that the City has negotiated checkoff provisions
with its other bargaining unit representatives. This comparability evidence is sufficient to convince this Fact Finder that the Union's position should be recommended.

Further supporting this position is two other facts. The City has
adopted checkoff for employee medical insurance premiums, charitable
contributions, and for the credit union. These payroll deductions are
clearly a convenience for the City's employees. The deduction of union
dues is also a convenience to employees. True, the Union benefits from
these automatic deductions. However, if the convenience of deductions
is offered for reasons unrelated to the City's mission, then the contention
that Union dues somehow differs is strained.

It is clear to this Fact Finder that the checkoff of Union dues, as
proposed by the Union, is consistent with all of the evidence found in
this record.

4. Overtime Pay

Recommendation

The Fact Finder recommends that the overtime rate of one and one-
half times the regular wage be paid for hours worked in excess of 40 in
a week. The Fact Finder further recommends that, for purposes of overtime calculation, that paid holidays (excluding paid personal business
leave) be considered hours worked.

Rationale

In examining the City's collective bargaining agreements with the
Fraternal Order of Police, International Association of Fire Fighters, and
Public Service Employees Union [Union exhibits E2, E3, E4, and E5] the
Fact Finder finds no standard for the payment of overtime premiums.
This is not surprising since both the police and fire fighters work irregular
hours. The bargaining unit closest to the Water Pollution Control De-
partment in their work schedules is the Public Service Employees Union.
This contract specifies that overtime shall be paid in excess of 8 hours
worked in a day.

The Union's proposal was that overtime be paid after forty hours of pay is earned. This is a different proposal than overtime being paid for hours worked in excess of 8 in a day, a position once held by the Union. The logic for this proposal is to include hours of vacation, sick leave, and paid holidays in the calculation of overtime entitlements. The City, however, objects to the payment of the overtime premium when hours not worked are included in the calculations for determining an employee's right to overtime premium payments.

Again, this Fact Finder is left with no comparability data which clearly demonstrates what the appropriate recommendation should be. In examining the results of the parties' respective positions the Fact Finder believes that simple logic suffices to determine what the appropriate recommendation should be.

The City contends that overtime should be paid for hours of work. The Union contends that its bargaining unit ought not be penalized for exercising contractual rights. Both contentions have considerable merit.

Vacations, personal business leave, and sick leave are contractual rights. These contractual rights are typically provided throughout industry for very specific reasons. Vacations are generally negotiated in to contracts and provided in personnel policies to give workers an opportunity to be away from the job, to relax and engage in non-work activities. This benefit, when it provides for pay, is to allow employees to be absent from work without loss of pay. Essentially the same reasoning is used for the inclusion of personal business leave.

Sick leave is generally provided so that employees do not lose income when they are unable to be at work due to an illness or injury. This benefit is the provision of time-off and when it is paid allows the employee to maintain his normal levels of income while injured or ill.

Holidays are periods which business and government typically do not conduct business. The rationale for providing paid holidays is somewhat different. Since legal holidays are typically non-work days, the issue is simply the protection of income.

This Fact Finder cannot determine, with certainty, the rationale used for providing these benefits prior to the bargaining relation between the parties. The Fact Finder also recognizes that the conceptual difference becomes less clear as a result of payment for vacation time and sick leave, but the conceptual difference does exist in the majority of collective bargaining motivations for negotiating such language.

The Fact Finder recognizes this difference for the provision of the respective time-off benefits and recommends that holidays should be included as time worked for pay purposes. In examining this issue from a different perspective it may be even more clear. Vacations and sick leave are relatively long term authorized absences. In the case of sick leave an employee will likely be incapacitated and cannot work. Vacations are often planned around some activity, frequently trips out of town, and employees will generally be unavailable for work. Holidays are a different matter. Holidays are generally one day periods and employees could be called-in or scheduled for work. In the case that an employee is required to work 8 hours during a holiday, no premium rate would accrue, under the City's proposal, for the loss of the holiday. Assuming holiday pay would be paid the worker even though the employee worked the holiday he would receive only the 40 hours of pay for hours worked plus his holiday pay, for a total of 48 hours pay. If overtime were required then the worker would receive 32 hours pay, for hours worked at the straight time rate, plus 8 hours of holiday pay, and 8 hours pay at the overtime premium rate of time and one-half. This results in 52 hours pay and therefore protects the employees' holiday rights.

It is clear to this Fact Finder that if the City's position that only the minimum requirements of the Fair Labor Standards Act are to be incorporated into the contract, then at least holiday pay must be calculated as hours worked to protect this negotiated right. The negotiated right to holiday pay becomes relatively meaningless without such consideration. Vacations, personal business leave, and sick leave are rights to time off and are still meaningful without being included in overtime calculations.

5. Call-in Pay

Recommendation

The Fact Finder recommends that a call-in guarantee provision be incorporated in the parties' collective bargaining agreement. The Fact Finder recommends that 4 hours work, or in lieu thereof 4 hours pay be guaranteed to employees who are called-in on vacation periods, holidays, or their regularly scheduled days off. For employees called-in on their regularly scheduled days of work, they are guaranteed 2 hours of work, or in lieu thereof 2 hours pay. It is also recommended to the parties that the call-in be defined, as work requested or required of an employee outside of his normal work schedule and when the employee must be notified to return to duty.

The Fact Finder further recommends that the overtime premium should be paid for call-ins, when applicable.

Rationale

The Union has proposed 4 hours of call-in pay for each incidence of an employee being called-back to work. The City proposes that no guarantee be included in the contract. The Fact Finder is unconvinced that either proposal is realistic.

The Union contends that the City has offered the 4 hour call-in guarantee and that the City's current proposal is offered in hopes that the Fact Finder will split his recommendation. This may, in fact, be the City's motivation for its final offer, but there is no evidence to support this position. The Fact Finder has therefore recommended a compromise position, one which is very close to what the Union has requested.

The rationale for the Fact Finder's recommendation is simple. Call-ins are very disruptive to an employee's off-duty hours. It is clear that the normal work day can only be protected if call-in provisions are included in the contract. In examining the AFSCME Local 500 contract and the Public Service Employees Union this Fact Finder notices that both contracts contain call-in provisions. This Fact Finder is also convinced that since Blue Valley is non-union, little inference can be drawn from this contract. The FOP and IAFF bargaining units have different demands and expectations placed upon them. These contracts are of little value to this Fact Finder in determining the appropriate recommendation for this issue.

The recommendation that 4 hours work or in lieu thereof, pay be guaranteed employees for days of vacation, holidays, and regularly scheduled days off is necessary to protect these days from unwarranted intrusion. On the other hand, the employer should not be placed in a situation where call-ins become excessively burdensome with respect to pay, that necessary work or emergencies cannot be responded to appropriately. From this perspective the Union's proposal is clearly the most reasonable of the two proposals before the Fact Finder and is recommended to the parties, with a modification for call-ins on a regularly scheduled duty day.

For regularly scheduled duty days, employees' rest time may be jeopardized by a call-in. To provide the Employer an economic incentive to retain employees four hours may present situations where the best interests of neither the Employer or its employees are served. For regularly scheduled duty days a 2 hour call-in pay requirement is adequate to protect the other provisions of the contract and provides the Employer with the ability to respond to emergencies and work requirements.

It is not the intent of this Fact Finder to split his recommendation, but simply to provide employees with the protections of the contract, while providing the City with adequate flexibility to assure proper sewer service.

CONCLUDING REMARKS

The purpose of Fact Finding is to provide the parties with recommendations which, hopefully, will assist the parties in arriving at a mutually acceptable negotiated settlement. The wage issue was complicated by the multi-year contract and the mutual goal of reducing the number of steps in the PAS system. The remaining issues, while less complicated, provided some interesting challenges for the Fact Finder.

There are only two issues which one party or the other won outright, the remaining recommendations are compromises. These are not aimed at splitting the recommendations. The Fact Finder searched earnestly through the lengthy record to determine what the needs and desires of the parties were. To the extent possible this Fact Finder attempted to address those primary concerns. The Fact Finder was impressed with the parties' sincerity and honesty in their respective case presentations and only wishes that both sides could have all they requested, but, in fact, most of the issues are concerned with the distribution of rights and resources. The recommendations contained herein provide the parties with a fair and reasonable settlement of the current impasse and are proffered with the hope that further good-faith negotiations will resolve the remaining issues.

The Fact Finder also reminds the parties that they are required to meet and confer in an attempt to negotiate a mutually acceptable agreement within ten days of the receipt of this report.

SUMMARY OF RECOMMENDATIONS

1. Wages

The Fact Finder recommends a compromise position between the City and the Union on the issue of wages. The Fact Finder recommends the reduction of the PAS pay grid from the present seven steps to two for the final year of the three year contract.

For the first year of the contract the Fact Finder recommends that the parties elevate step 1 to step 2 and step 5 to step 6; with steps 1 and 5 being eliminated from the pay grid. For the second year of the contract the Fact Finder recommends that all employees now at step 2 be elevated to step 3 and that all employees now at step 6 be elevated to step 7; with steps 2 and 6 being eliminated for the pay grid. For the final year of the agreement the Fact Finder recommends that all employees now at step 3 be elevated to step 4; with step 3 being eliminated from the pay grid.

In addition to the recommended step increases and changes in the pay grid the Fact Finder recommends that a cost of living increase of 3.2 percent be applied to wage rates for steps 1 through 4 for each of the three years; and that a cost of living increase of 3.4 percent be applied to the wage rates for steps 5 through 7 for each of the three years.

The Fact Finder further recommends that those employees currently in a step 4 or step 7 position on the pay grids be given a one-time payment of 10 hours pay in recognition of their not receiving a step increase over the life of the contract. This payment should be made as soon as possible after the ratification of the collective bargaining agreement. The one-time payment is intended to be made on the basis of the 1987 wages recommended by this Fact Finder.

2. Paid Personal Business Leave in Lieu of Paid Holidays

The Fact Finder recommends that the current personnel policy of allowing three (3) days of personal leave charged against sick leave be adopted for the collective bargaining agreement. Further, the Fact Finder recommends that the current twelve (12) paid holidays be adopted.

3. Union Dues Checkoff

The Fact Finder recommends the Union's proposed dues checkoff language [exhibit K] be included in the collective bargaining agreement.

4. Overtime Pay

The Fact Finder recommends that the overtime rate of one and one-half times the regular wage be paid for hours worked in excess of 40 in a week. The Fact Finder further recommends that, for purposes of over-time calculations, that paid holidays (excluding paid personal business leave) be considered hours worked.

5. Call-in Pay

The Fact Finder recommends that a call-in guarantee provision be incorporated in the parties' collective bargaining agreement. The Fact Finder recommends that 4 hours work, or in lieu thereof 4 hours pay be guaranteed to employees who are called-in on vacation periods, holidays, or their regularly scheduled days off. For employees called-in on their regularly scheduled days of work, they are guaranteed 2 hours of work, or in lieu thereof 2 hours pay. It is also recommended to the parties that the call-in be defined, as work requested or required of an employee outside of his normal work schedule and when the employee must be notified to return to duty.

The Fact Finder further recommends that the overtime premium should be paid for call-ins, when applicable.

Arbitrator's Award

ARBITRATION AWARD[1]

In the Matter of Arbitration
Between

Board of Supervisors, Sioux City, Iowa	David A. Dilts Arbitrator
and	
American Federation of State, County and Municipal Employees Local 1774	July 21, 1986

APPEARANCES:

For the Employer:

Harvey Wiltsey, advocate

For the Union:

Jerry Beers, advocate

ISSUES

The issues at impasse are the percentage wage increase and the medical insurance to be included in the successor agreement.

1. From *Labor Arbitration Reports* 86 LA 1178. Reprinted by permission from *Labor Arbitration Reports*, published by The Bureau of National Affairs, Inc., Washington, D.C. 20037.

PARTIES' POSITIONS

Wages

Union's Position: The Union proposes a 3.5 percent increase in wages for each classification in the bargaining unit.

The Union claims that its wage proposal is supported by the standards of comparability, cost of living, and the County's ability to pay.

In examining Union exhibit 1 the Arbitrator will find that the counties cited from the northwestern quadrant of Iowa have an average wage settlement of 2.54 percent. If the comparability group is broadened to include counties in western Iowa and other similarly situated counties within Iowa the average wage settlement increases to 3.19 percent. The percentage wage increase proposed by the Union is clearly similar to the experiences of these similarly situated counties.

The Union would have the Arbitrator note that there has been inflation over the past year. The County's own exhibit shows that the CPI (W) increased by 1.1 percent from May 1985 through May 1986. If comparisons are to be made with specific metropolitan areas the Union believes that Minneapolis-St. Paul, above average cost of living area, should be the basis of comparison. This area is not found on Board exhibit 18. The Union contends that this standard also supports its position that the 3.5 percent wage increase it has requested is more reasonable than the zero increase proposed by the Board.

The County has not argued that it has an inability to fund the Union's proposed wage increase. The County has simply argued that it would rather spend its scarce resources in other ways. The union rejects this County contention. The County has the ability to fund the Union's proposal and ought to pay its employees a reasonable and decent wage.

The Union further contends that its comparability group should be the basis for comparisons. The County's comparison group contains many counties which are much smaller than Sioux County and at least one county which is not organized.

The Union respectfully requests that its position be awarded on the issue of wages.

County's Position: The County proposes no wage increase be included in the successor agreement.

The County contends that the same standards relied upon by the Union proves its case for its position. The County notes that those employees with which the present AFSCME Local 1774 members ought to be compared are not receiving wage increases for next year. The cost of living data do not show that a wage increase is in order, and that the County has a responsibility not to make expenditures which are neither necessary nor advisable.

The County would preface its case by pointing out to the Arbitrator that his decision must be based on the standards required under Chapter 20 of the Code of Iowa. The County is suspicious of the statutory impasse procedures when Arbitrators' awards and Fact Finder's recommendations are based on little or no sound reasoning and cannot be correlated with the evidence in the record. The Arbitrator should base his decision on the evidence before him and not administer an independent brand of justice.

The record clearly shows that Sioux County pays its secondary road employees a wage which is more than the average for the comparable Iowa counties. The average hourly rate for the comparable counties is $8.21 while the average rate in Sioux County is $8.23. Of the comparable counties, only Lyon County employees will receive an hourly wage increase of but 2.0 percent. Cherokee, O'Brien, Osceola, and Plymouth Counties will not observe an hourly wage increase for their secondary road employees for next year. Further, none of the elected Sioux County officials will receive a salary increase for next year. This evidence strongly suggests that a zero wage increase is appropriate for the Local 1774 bargaining unit.

If the wage history is examined for the past seven years it becomes obvious that the County's secondary road employees have received greater percentage increases than its elected officials. The increase in wages for secondary road employees since 1979 was 51.6 percent (including the cost of 50 percent of dependent insurance) while the elected officials have gained only 47.0 percent in compensation since 1979.

Board exhibit 18 shows that the national average CPI (W) has increased only 1.1 percent from May 1985 through May 1986. This same document shows that for areas geographically close to Sioux County, Iowa the increase in prices has been below the national average. Chicago has witnessed only a .9 percent inflation rate, Milwaukee only a .1 percent rate, and St. Louis has experienced only .4 percent inflation. This suggests that a zero increase in this bargaining unit's wages would not adversely affect the purchasing power of the wages earned by these employees.

The County's unwillingness to add to its expenses at this time is responsible fiscal management. The Iowa farm economy has been in crisis for the past few years and farmers cannot afford to nor do they wish to increase this bargaining unit's burden on the tax payers.

The Board contends that its comparability group and not that of the Union should be the basis for the Arbitrator's analysis. Many of the counties included in the Union's comparability group are much larger than Sioux County and are located throughout the State of Iowa. Proper comparisons must be made if a reasonable award is to be issued. The County Board of Supervisors believes that a just wage is being paid at present and requests the Arbitrator to award a zero increase.

Insurance

Union's Position: The Union proposes that the same medical insurance plan be retained in the successor agreement, but also proposes that the employer's contribution for dependent coverage be increased to 75 percent from the present 50 percent while maintaining the 100 percent payment for single employee premiums.

Union exhibit 2 shows that O'Brien County pays 80 percent of the dependent coverage, Clay County pays 92 percent, and Cherokee County pays the total premium for medical insurance for dependents. All of the comparable counties pay higher wages than does Sioux County and if the total compensation package is to be brought into line with these comparable counties then Sioux County should be paying at least 75 percent of the premium for dependent health insurance.

The County can afford this proposal and the Union requests that its proposal be awarded by the Arbitrator.

County's Position: The County proposes to change the present insurance plan to include provisions for a $100 deductible and 20 percent co-payment for the next $2,000. The plan would pay 100 percent of expenses over the deductible and co-payment amounts. The County proposes to pay $69.00 for the single premium and $45.00 for dependent premiums.

The County contends that the rapidly escalating costs of health care insurance require that cost saving techniques be found if the program is not going to become an excessive burden. The increase in deductible and the co-payment provisions are such cost saving mechanisms. The deductible and co-payment provisions are common and are not going to be a burden to the members of the bargaining unit. The proposed program will save the County approximately $1,300 but will save out-of-pocket expenses to each bargaining unit member as well. If the current program is maintained the rate for family coverage will increase to $108.27 per month, of which each employee will pay $54.14 per month or $572.68 per year. Under the County's proposal the first $45 of the family premium will be paid by the County. The rate for family coverage will decrease to $71.10 leaving each employee only $26.10 per month to come out of earnings. The total cost of the family coverage, under the County's proposal, is only $313.20 per year or $259.48 less than under the Union's proposal. This represents a savings of $59.48 if the full $200 is paid by the employee and the employee would have to have $259.48 under the co-payment provision before the savings would disappear.

The County has proposed an insurance alternative which has an incentive for employees to conserve on health care expenditures which has the potential of putting money directly into the employees' pockets, while at the same time saving the County money. Here is a proposal that makes both the employees and the County better off and the Arbitrator ought to award this proposal.

ARBITRATOR'S OPINION

The Arbitrator's opinion is divided into three sections. The first major section is a general analysis concerned with the evidence presented by the parties. Each party contends that the other's comparability group is without merit and there is a controversy over the cost of living evidence. The remaining sections will focus, in turn, on each of the issues at impasse.

General Analysis: The evidence adduced by the parties focuses primarily on comparisons and changes in the CPI (W) since May 1985. Little weight can be given the CPI (W) since specific information for the Sioux County, Iowa area is unavailable. The Union argues that Sioux County is subject to the same economic forces that have produced some unspecified high rate of inflation in Minneapolis-St. Paul than to forces found in the areas suggested by the Board. The Board contends that since Sioux County is a rural area that low inflation, if not deflation, would be observed if the change in prices were documented for this area. Whatever the case may be cannot be deduced by either this Arbitrator or the parties. This Arbitrator is therefore left with little more than comparability data from which to draw conclusions.

The parties have not agreed on an appropriate comparability group and have each suggested what counties ought to form the basis for comparisons to be made by the Arbitrator. The Arbitrator is therefore faced with the issue of credibility of the competing comparability groups. The parties have, between them, offered 24 counties which they believe are similarly situated, but neither party presented much evidence to corroborate the comparability of these counties with Sioux County. The Board contends that those counties located in close geographic proximity to Sioux County ought to be those included in the analysis. There is merit to this contention since a close geographic proximity may signal certain shared characteristics such as climate, avenues of transportation (e.g., rail service), and possibly socio-political values of the population. Yet close geographic proximity is more important and a more tangible standard in that labor markets tend to have geographic boundaries. A person may travel by car as much as 50 or 60 miles (and even farther) to a place of employment. Such mobility of the work force means that what occurs in other counties within this range may be expected to effect the ability of Sioux County to employ or retain workers and may effect the nature of the duties of secondary road employees. The only other data available in the present record are the populations of the counties offered by each party and whether the secondary road employees are organized or are not represented by a union.

The population of a county may be of some value in determining the credibility of a comparability group. Those counties with metropolitan areas will typically have a larger tax base, and may have greater diversity of industry while smaller counties may be totally agrarian. The implications of this analysis within the state of Iowa should be obvious. Population may therefore be an important determinant of whether a county is comparable with another with respect not only to ability to pay but also to the nature of duties required of secondary road employees.

Employees represented by a union have an effective vehicle by which to present their views on such issues as salary and fringe benefits, that being collective bargaining. Employees without such representation cannot be said to be similarly situated and therefore are not truly comparable for present purposes without specific evidence to the contrary. Work rules and other important aspects of employment may be presumed to be quite different under collective bargaining contracts than in their absence. Nonunion jurisdictions must be compared with union jurisdictions only under the greatest caution.

In examining the comparability groups offered by the Union and the Board it is clear that several of the counties are not comparable with Sioux County with respect to one or more of the standards of comparability for which evidence is available to this Arbitrator. As with any other arbitration matter the Arbitrator must ascertain the credibility of evidence. To accept comparability groups simply because they are offered is to disregard of the trust of the parties and is counter to the requirements of Paragraph 20.22, Sections 9 (a) and (b) of the Code of Iowa. It is necessary that if the Arbitrator is to compare Sioux County's employees with other public employees he must determine whether there are bases to determine, whether the work is comparable and what factors are peculiar to the area and the classifications involved.

The standard deviation for the array of 25 counties offered by the parties was calculated by this Arbitrator and a 99 percent confidence interval constructed around the population of Sioux County to determine which counties were comparable by population. From the Union's offering, only Hardin, Lee, and Crawford Counties fell within the range of 17,936 to 43,691 which allows any inference of comparable populations to be drawn at the 99 percent confidence level. The Board's proposed group of comparable counties contains only one county which is comparable by population, that is Plymouth. Of the counties that are comparable by population, Plymouth (the only Board proposed county meeting this criterion) has no union, hence wages and benefits are determined outside of the collective bargaining arena and working conditions may significantly differ. Crawford County is the only county of the three remaining which is in the western Iowa area. Crawford County is located some 60 miles to the south-southeast of Sioux County and may be characterized as being in the general vicinity of Sioux County. Lee County is the most southeast county in Iowa and Hardin County is located some 50 miles north-northeast of Des Moines. It is fair to say that neither Lee nor Hardin Counties are in the proximity of Sioux County. This leaves but one credible comparison to be made with Sioux County, but there remains problems with this comparison. Crawford County is approximately the size of Sioux County in square miles, but has fewer miles of secondary roads than does Sioux County. Further, there is nothing in the record which indicates the relative financial positions of these counties or in their bargaining histories. Population is only one indicator of the comparability of the work of secondary road crews. Population density will dictate the order and urgency of snow removal, road repair, and may indicate the miles of secondary roads.

The parties failed to challenge the credibility of comparison groups offered by the opposing party except on the grounds of union-nonunion status, population, and geographic proximity. Without challenges on other grounds this Arbitrator is not obliged to question the credibility of comparisons on these other grounds and must focus on these challenges of credibility.

Crawford County has different union representation than the sort observed in Sioux County. Sioux County secondary road employees are represented by AFSCME Local 1774, an AFL-CIO affiliate. Crawford County secondary road employees are represented by a local association which is not affiliated with a national labor organization. Futher, Crawford County went to impasse with its union this year and the Fact Finder recommended a 2 percent increase in wages and that the employer increase contributions for family health insurance from 55 percent (from union exhibit, 1, but the Iowa Local Government Salary and Benefit Survey, 1985 indicates this figure should be 66 percent) to 100 percent. This evidence alone would suggest that the Fact Finder's recommendation of a 2.5 percent wage increase and the Union's proposal of increasing the employer's contribution for the family health insurance premium, retaining the present insurance plan, would be most consistent with the present situation in Crawford County. Yet this is but one county and that jurisdiction went to impasse. Further complicating the analysis is the fact that there is little information in the record concerning the nature of the relative merits of the health insurance programs within these two counties. If the 1985 Iowa Local Government Salary and Benefit Survey is credible, which the Board claims it is not, then the premiums paid by the two counties can be identified. In 1985 Crawford County paid $76 for single premiums, Sioux County paid $4 less, and Crawford County paid $194 for family premiums, Sioux County paid $31 less. These figures for Sioux County are corroborated by Board exhibit 5. Whether the bargaining histories of Sioux and Crawford Counties are sufficiently similar to draw inference is suspect since they have different representational structures. This evidence can only be considered indicative without corroboration.

One credible comparison from the 24 offered by the two parties is insufficient for a finding in favor of either party. One comparable county does not allow for confidence in an award. The Arbitrator must have further information to be confident in the accuracy of inferences drawn from this record. There are no northwestern Iowa counties offered by the Union which approximate the population of Sioux County. Two such counties are found in the Board's comparability group. Cherokee County (16,238 population) and Plymouth County (comparable at 99 confidence with a population of 24,743 but nonunion) may be brought into the analysis even though limitations must be recognized in their comparability with Sioux County. Cherokee County pays an average hourly wage of $7.54 with longevity increases at 5, 10, and 15 years of service. The insurance premiums paid by this County approximate those currently paid in Sioux County. Plymouth County pays an hourly wage of $8.52 but the insurance premiums paid approximate those under the current Board proposal. Plymouth County also pays for longevity after 5, 10, and 15 years of service. Both Plymouth and Cherokee Counties will not experience increases in wages or insurance coverage for next year; the economic packages for the next fiscal year in those counties were frozen at the current year's level (Board exhibits 9 and 10). In examining the total cost of compensation Cherokee County pays $8.70, according to Board exhibit 9, for the relevant portions of the economic package while Plymouth County pays $9.33. Under the Board's proposal Sioux County would pay $8.91 for this portion of the economic package which is $.105 less than the median paid by Cherokee and Plymouth Counties. This additional evidence suggests that the award indicated by comparisons with Crawford County would be excessive.

Comparisons with O'Brien County are inappropriate. O'Brien County employees are not represented by a Union and its population is below the 99 percent confidence interval. Osceola County is much smaller than Sioux County in both square miles and population. Lyon County is directly north of Sioux County but again is much smaller than Sioux County in both square miles and population. The appropriate comparability group is therefore Crawford, Cherokee, and Plymouth Counties, recognizing there are limitations with respect to the comparisons between each of these counties.

Wage Issue: The wage issue cannot be viewed as unrelated to the insurance issue. The Board pays wages for hours worked but this sum is not the only labor cost. The Board must also pay workers through providing insurance and paying a portion of the premiums for such coverage. The total cost of the economic package includes both wages and insurance. Likewise employees receive the benefit of the hourly wage and the insurance coverage. The parties' proposals on insurance both include a requirement that employees pay a portion of family insurance coverage and the Board's proposal includes a deductible and co-payment feature which has obvious implications for the take-home earnings of employees. It is this Arbitrator's considered opinion that the wage and insurance issues are so interrelated that a separation may be unduly artificial.

The comparability evidence suggests that the counties bordering on Sioux County have economic constraints which have, for the most part, resulted in zero wage increases. Whether these constraints are real economic phenomenon or political-economic constraints cannot be ascertained from this record. The fact is that both counties from which any credible inference can be drawn which border on Sioux County have opted for zero increases for next fiscal year. Crawford County, the most comparable of the counties in either comparability group, was required to go to fact finding due to an impasse over at least wages and insurance. The Fact Finder in the Crawford County case recommended a 2 percent wage increase. In 1985 Sioux County listed 27 Equipment Operator IIs (Iowa Local Government Salary and Benefit Survey) and Crawford County identified 36 operators across three classifications. The earnings range for Sioux County was from $16,078 to $17,118; in Crawford County the earnings range was from $15,704 to $17,430. It is apparent that Crawford County's earnings range falls 2 percent below the minimum for Sioux County and exceeds Sioux County's maximum by almost 1.8 percent. A 2 percent salary increase for Crawford County employees will not significantly alter the present relation between the two counties. The same inference may be drawn for a 3.5 percent increase for Sioux County employees. Since the percentage increases under analysis are so small and the Crawford County earnings range extends about 2 percent on each end of the Sioux County range, a 2 percent increase for Crawford County will simply catch-up the bottom of their ranges with Sioux County and will not significantly disrupt comparisons at the upper end of the range. It should be further noted that Sioux County has only Equipment Operator II classification but Crawford County differentiates among three classifications of operators, one above and one below Sioux County.

The preponderance of evidence suggests that up to a 2 percent increase for Sioux County employees would be comparable with Crawford

County, but if the Plymouth and Cherokee Counties are considered, then a zero increase would be appropriate. The Union has proposed a 3.5 percent wage increase which is not within the appropriate feasible set of awards. The Fact Finder recommended a 2.5 percent wage increase. This is one-half of a percent above that increase observed in Crawford County but would extend the lower end of comparable Sioux County wages above those observed in Crawford County and would not significantly effect comparisons at the upper range of earnings. The preponderance of evidence suggests that the Board's proposal or the Fact Finder's recommendation would be most appropriate.

If the cost of living is considered, a 1.1 percent inflation rate would further support the Board's position if such evidence could be given weight as credible. This Arbitrator cannot ascertain the inflation rate for Sioux County and therefore cannot rely on this evidence except for marginal corroboration.

Had the Fact Finder given a convincing rationale for his recommendation of 2.5 percent the present Arbitrator may have been persuaded to recommend this position. After close examination of the Fact Finder's report in the present impasse it is clear that the Fact Finder formulated a set of recommendations based on compromise in an attempt to gain the parties' support for an intermediate solution. This is a legitimate and honorable strategy for a Fact Finder, but not for an Arbitrator. It is the case that parties have left this Arbitrator with a judgment call. This Arbitrator, while unconvinced of the absolute merits of either parties' case, believes that the simple preponderance of evidence suggests that a zero increase should be awarded, but only if the Union prevails on the issue of health insurance. The issue of health insurance is much clearer and the evidence suggests that the Union should clearly prevail.

Insurance: Crawford County has paid 66 percent of family health insurance benefits during 1985, and the Fact Finder in that case recommended an increase in employer contributions to 100 percent for family coverage. This 66 percent paid in Crawford County represented $31 per month more than was paid in Sioux County for the same period. In examining the other two comparable counties Plymouth County pays less than Sioux County for insurance but pays more in wages. If Plymouth and Cherokee Counties are combined it is obvious that Sioux County still paid 10.5 cents less for its economic package than these two comparable counties. This evidence suggests that if Sioux County's economic package is to be brought to the level of Plymouth and Cherokee Counties at least 10.5 cents must be added to the economic package. Further support for this position is to be found in the comparisons with Crawford County. Sioux County's employees will lose ground relative to Crawford County employees under the fact finding recommendations in Crawford County's impasse and were already behind the coverage extended to Crawford County employees under the 1985 contract. It is this Arbitrator's considered opinion that the employer should pay at least the 66 percent of the family premium in evidence in Crawford County. This is 16 percent above the Fact Finder's recommendations in the present impasse but only 9 percent below the Union's proposal. The Union's proposal is therefore the most reasonable, especially in light of the wage award and is awarded.

The Board's proposal on insurance is commended and this Arbitrator is not unsympathetic to what the Board proposed. Health insurance costs are escalating and the Board must be concerned about the control of these costs. The Board's proposal was well intentioned and a creative solution to a legitimate concern. The proposal, in fact, had the potential of making both employees and the Board better off if use of the benefit was limited to an amount of approximately $250 into the co-payment range. Had this been the only change in the insurance provisions of the successor agreement this Arbitrator may have awarded the Board's position on this issue, especially if some small wage increment had been added to the wages of the employees (to cover at least the Board's savings from the program and to limit the potential financial burden of the increased risk of the co-payment provisions). The Board's proposal, however, implicitly created another change which is inconsistent with what evidence was available concerning the bargaining history of the parties. Article IX, Section 2 of the current contract states that " . . . the employer shall contribute an amount equal to the single premium cost and fifty percent of the dependent cost for employees . . . " and the Board's proposal was that it would pay $69 for single premiums and $45 for dependent premiums. This is an important consideration since the standard for determining the amount of Board contributions would significantly change. The percentage to be paid places the burden of insurance premium increases on the Board unless such a burden is negotiated away. By specifying a dollar amount of Board contributions the burden is then shifted to the Union to negotiate at least the increase in the insurance premiums if it is to retain the protections currently enjoyed under the parties' current contract. This is a basic and fundamental change in the parties relative rights under the contract and not simply a money issue. The Board presented little credible supporting evidence for such a change. This Arbitrator would have expected to see substantive evidence of the history of premium increases over the past several years and evidence of the issue being negotiated without avail before interceding on behalf of the Board.

CONCLUSIONS

The Arbitrator has awarded an approximately 2.7 percent increase in the total economic package. A zero increase in wages and the Union's insurance proposal results in an approximately 2.7 percent increase in costs to the employer. The employer benefits from this award in that payroll taxes are avoided to some extent since this increase comes in the form of non-taxable fringe benefits and not taxable wages. Employees who are eligible for dependent insurance coverage benefit from this award while those who are not will reap none of the benefits. Employees who were contributing $45.36 per month will contribute only $27.06 per month; a savings of approximately $18.30 per month. The employees' reduced income tax liability will also increase disposable income since for most employees there are insufficient medical expenses to deduct them on the Federal Tax Schedule A. Assuming an effective income tax rate of 12 percent, employees will save approximately $2.19 per month in taxes they would otherwise have had to pay above and beyond the amounts they contributed to health insurance premiums.

Board exhibit 5 shows that only 3 employees in this bargaining unit do not benefit from employer contributions to dependent insurance coverage. This indicates that 90 percent of the bargaining unit will benefit from this Arbitrator's award.

The Board has contributed to premiums for dependent health insurance for this bargaining unit while not making such contributions to its other employees' insurance programs. The comparisons offered by the Board with employees doing dissimilar work and private sector employees are not factors the Iowa Legislature specified in Chapter 20 for this Arbitrator to consider, but the happenstance consistency generated by this award should please the Board. The increase in the economic package awarded here is in an area not made available to other of the Board's employees, while a zero increase in wages is consistent with the treatment of the Board's other employees in the portions of the economic package these other employees do receive. While this was not a consideration for the Arbitrator it does answer one of the Board's questions concerning comparability with other County employees.

AWARD

Wages: The Board's position of a zero increase in wages is awarded.

Insurance: The Union's proposal of retaining the current insurance program and the Board increasing its dependent premium contribution to 75 percent of the premium is awarded.

Code of Ethics

**CODE
OF PROFESSIONAL
RESPONSIBILITY
FOR ARBITRATORS OF
LABOR-MANAGEMENT
DISPUTES**

OF THE
NATIONAL ACADEMY OF ARBITRATORS
AMERICAN ARBITRATION ASSOCIATION
FEDERAL MEDIATION AND CONCILIATION SERVICE

FOREWORD

This "Code of Professional Responsibility for Arbitrators of Labor-Management Disputes" supersedes the "Code of Ethics and Procedural Standards for Labor-Management Arbitration," approved in 1951 by a Committee of the American Arbitration Association, by the National Academy of Arbitrators, and by representatives of the Federal Mediation and Conciliation Service.

Revision of the 1951 Code was initiated officially by the same three groups in October, 1972. The Joint Committee named below was designated to draft a proposal.

Reasons for Code revision should be noted briefly. Ethical considerations and procedural standards are sufficiently intertwined to warrant combining the subject matter of Parts I and II of the 1951 Code under the caption of "Professional Responsibility." It has seemed advisable to eliminate admonitions to the parties (Part III of the 1951 Code) except as they appear incidentally in connection with matters primarily involving responsibilities of arbitrators. Substantial growth of third party participation in dispute resolution in the public sector requires consideration. It appears that arbitration of new contract terms may become more significant. Finally, during the interval of more than two decades, new problems have emerged as private sector grievance arbitration has matured and has become more diversified.

JOINT STEERING COMMITTEE

Chairman
William E. Simkin

Representing American Arbitration Association
Frederick H. Bullen
Donald B. Straus

Representing Federal Mediation and Conciliation Service
Lawrence B. Babcock, Jr.
L. Lawrence Schultz

Representing National Academy of Arbitrators
Sylvester Garrett
Ralph T. Seward   November 30, 1974

TABLE OF CONTENTS

PREAMBLE

Background

Voluntary arbitration rests upon the mutual desire of management and labor in each collective bargaining relationship to develop procedures for dispute settlement which meet their own particular needs and obligations. No two voluntary systems, therefore, are likely to be identical in practice. Words used to describe arbitrators (Arbitrator, Umpire, Impartial Chairman, Chairman of Arbitration Board, etc.) may suggest typical approaches but actual differences within any general type of arrangement may be as great as distinctions often made among the several types.

Some arbitration and related procedures, however, are not the product of voluntary agreement. These procedures, primarily but not exclusively applicable in the public sector, sometimes utilize other third party titles (Fact Finder, Impasse Panel, Board of Inquiry, etc.). These procedures range all the way from arbitration prescribed by statute to arrangements substantially indistinguishable from voluntary procedures.

The standards of professional responsibility set forth in this Code are designed to guide the impartial third party serving in these diverse labor-management relationships.

Scope of Code

This Code is a privately developed set of standards of professional behavior. It applies to voluntary arbitration of labor-management grievance disputes and of disputes concerning new or revised contract terms. Both "ad hoc" and "permanent" varieties of voluntary arbitration, private and public sector, are included. To the extent relevant in any specific case, it also applies to advisory arbitration, impasse resolution panels, arbitration prescribed by statutes, fact-finding, and other special procedures.

The word "arbitrator," as used hereinafter in the Code, is intended to apply to any impartial person, irrespective of specific title, who serves in a labor-management dispute procedure in which there is conferred authority to decide issues or to make formal recommendations.

The Code is not designed to apply to mediation or conciliation, as distinguished from arbitration, nor to other procedures in which the third party is not authorized in advance to make decisions or recommendations. It does not apply to partisan representatives on tripartite boards. It does not apply to commercial arbitration or to other uses of arbitration outside the labor-management dispute area.

Format of Code

Bold face type, sometimes including explanatory material, is used to set forth general principles. Italics are used for amplification of general principles. Ordinary type is used primarily for illustrative or explanatory comment.

Application of Code

Faithful adherence by an arbitrator to this Code is basic to professional responsibility.

The National Academy of Arbitrators will expect its members to be governed in their professional conduct by this Code and stands ready, through its Committee on Ethics and Grievances, to advise its members as to the Code's interpretation. The American Arbitration Association and the Federal Mediation and Conciliation Service will apply the Code to the arbitrators on their rosters in cases handled under their respective appointment or referral procedures. Other arbitrators and administrative agencies, may, of course, voluntarily adopt the Code and be governed by it.

In interpreting the Code and applying it to charges of professional misconduct, under existing or revised procedures of the National Academy of Arbitrators and of the administrative agencies, it should be recognized that while some of its standards express ethical principles basic to the arbitration profession, others rest less on ethics than on considerations of good practice. Experience has shown the difficulty of drawing rigid lines of distinction between ethics and good practice and this Code does not attempt to do so. Rather, it leaves the gravity of alleged misconduct and the extent to which ethical standards have been violated to be assessed in the light of the facts and circumstances of each particular case.

1. ARBITRATOR'S QUALIFICATIONS AND RESPONSIBILITIES TO THE PROFESSION

A. General Qualifications

1. Essential personal qualifications of an arbitrator include honesty, integrity, impartiality, and general competence in labor relations matters.

An arbitrator must demonstrate ability to exercise these personal qualities faithfully and with good judgment, both in procedural matters and in substantive decisions.

   a. Selection by mutual agreement of the parties or direct designation by an administrative agency are the effective methods of appraisal of this combination of an individual's potential and performance, rather than the fact of placement on a roster of an administrative agency or membership in a professional association of arbitrators.

2. An arbitrator must be as ready to rule for one party as for the other on each issue, either in a single case or in a group of cases. Compromise by an arbitrator for the sake of attempting to achieve personal acceptability is unprofessional.

B. Qualifications for Special Cases

1. An arbitrator must decline appointment, withdraw, or request technical assistance when he or she decides that a case is beyond his or her competence.

   a. An arbitrator may be qualified generally but not for specialized assignments. Some types of incentive, work standard, job evaluation, welfare program, pension, or insurance cases may require specialized knowledge, experience, or competence. Arbitration of contract terms also may require distinctive background and experience.

   b. Effective appraisal by an administrative agency or by an arbitrator of the need for special qualifications requires that both parties make known the special nature of the case prior to appointment of the arbitrator.

C. Responsibilities to the Profession

1. An arbitrator must uphold the dignity and integrity of the office and endeavor to provide effective service to the parties.

a. To this end, an arbitrator should keep current with principles, practices, and developments that are relevant to his or her own field of arbitration practice.

2. An experienced arbitrator should cooperate in the training of new arbitrators.

3. An arbitrator must not advertise or solicit arbitration assignments.

a. It is a matter of personal preference whether an arbitrator includes "Labor Arbitrator" or similar notation on letterheads, cards, or announcements. *It is inappropriate, however, to include memberships or offices held in professional societies or listings on rosters of administrative agencies.*

b. *Information provided for published biographical sketches, as well as that supplied to administrative agencies, must be accurate.* Such information may include membership in professional organizations (including reference to significant offices held), and listings on rosters of administrative agencies.

2. RESPONSIBILITIES TO THE PARTIES

A. Recognition of Diversity in Arbitration Arrangements

1. An arbitrator should conscientiously endeavor to understand and observe, to the extent consistent with professional responsibility, the significant principles governing each arbitration system in which he or she serves.

a. Recognition of special features of a particular arbitration arrangement can be essential with respect to procedural matters and may influence other aspects of the arbitration process.

2. Such understanding does not relieve an arbitrator from a corollary responsibility to seek to discern and refuse to lend approval or consent to any collusive attempt by the parties to use arbitration for an improper purpose.

B. Required Disclosures

1. Before accepting an appointment, an arbitrator must disclose directly or through the administrative agency involved, any current or

past managerial, representational, or consultative relationship with any company or union involved in a proceeding in which he or she is being considered for appointment or has been tentatively designated to serve. Disclosure must also be made of any pertinent pecuniary interest.

    a. The duty to disclose includes membership on a Board of Directors, full-time or part-time service as a representative or advocate, consultation work for a fee, current stock or bond ownership (other than mutual fund shares or appropriate trust arrangements) or any other pertinent form of managerial, financial, or immediate family interest in the company or union involved.

2. When an arbitrator is serving concurrently as an advocate for or representative of other companies or unions in labor relations matters, or has done so in recent years, he or she must disclose such activities before accepting appointment as an arbitrator.

An arbitrator must disclose such activities to an administrative agency if he or she is on that agency's active roster or seeks placement on a roster. Such disclosure then satisfies this requirement for cases handled under that agency's referral.

    a. It is not necessary to disclose names of clients or other specific details. It is necessary to indicate the general nature of the labor relations advocacy or representational work involved, whether for companies or unions or both, and a reasonable approximation of the extent of such activity.

    b. *An arbitrator on an administrative agency's roster has a continuing obligation to notify the agency of any significant changes pertinent to this requirement.*

    c. When an administrative agency is not involved, an arbitrator must make such disclosure directly unless he or she is certain that both parties to the case are fully aware of such activities.

3. An arbitrator must not permit relationships to affect decision-making. Prior to acceptance of an appointment, an arbitrator must disclose to the parties or to the administrative agency involved any close personal relationship or other circumstance, in addition to those specifically mentioned earlier in this section, which might reasonably raise a question as to the arbitrator's impartiality.

    a. Arbitrators establish personal relationships with many company and union representatives, with fellow arbitrators, and with fellow members of various professional associations. There should be no attempt to be secretive about such friendships or acquaintances but disclosure is not necessary unless some feature of a particular relationship might reasonably appear to impair impartiality.

4. If the circumstances requiring disclosure are not known to the ar-

bitrator prior to acceptance of appointment, disclosure must be made when such circumstances become known to the arbitrator.

5. The burden of disclosure rests on the arbitrator. After appropriate disclosure, the arbitrator may serve if both parties so desire. If the arbitrator believes or perceives that there is a clear conflict of interest, he or she should withdraw, irrespective of the expressed desires of the parties.

C. Privacy of Arbitration

1. All significant aspects of an arbitration proceeding must be treated by the arbitrator as confidential unless this requirement is waived by both parties or disclosure is required or permitted by law.

a. Attendance at hearings by persons not representing the parties or invited by either or both of them should be permitted only when the parties agree or when an applicable law requires or permits. Occasionally, special circumstances may require that an arbitrator rule on such matters as attendance and degree of participation of counsel selected by a grievant.

b. *Discussion of a case at any time by an arbitrator with persons not involved directly should be limited to situations where advance approval or consent of both parties is obtained or where the identity of the parties and details of the case are sufficiently obscured to eliminate any realistic probability of identification.*

A commonly recognized exception is discussion of a problem in a case with a fellow arbitrator. *Any such discussion does not relieve the arbitrator who is acting in the case from sole responsibility for the decision and the discussion must be considered as confidential.*

Discussion of aspects of a case in a classroom without prior specific approval of the parties is not a violation provided the arbitrator is satisfied that there is no breach of essential confidentiality.

c. *It is a violation of professional responsibility for an arbitrator to make public an award without the consent of the parties.*

An arbitrator may request but not press the parties for consent to publish an opinion. Such a request should normally not be made until after the award has been issued to the parties.

d. It is not improper for an arbitrator to donate arbitration files to a library of a college, university, or similar institution without prior consent of all parties involved. When the circumstances permit, there should be deleted from such donations any cases concerning which one or both of the parties have expressed a desire for privacy. As an additional safeguard, an arbitrator may also decide to withhold recent cases or indicate to the donee a time interval before such cases can be made generally available.

e. *Applicable laws, regulations, or practices of the parties may permit or even require exceptions to the above noted principles of privacy.*

D. Personal Relationships with the Parties

1. An arbitrator must make every reasonable effort to conform to arrangements required by an administrative agency or mutually desired by the parties regarding communications and personal relationships with the parties.

a. *Only an "arms-length" relationship may be acceptable to the parties in some arbitration arrangements or may be required by the rules of an administrative agency. The arbitrator should then have no contact of consequence with representatives of either party while handling a case without the other party's presence or consent.*

b. *In other situations, both parties may want communications and personal relationships to be less formal. It is then appropriate for the arbitrator to respond accordingly.*

E. Jurisdiction

1. An arbitrator must observe faithfully both the limitations and inclusions of the jurisdiction conferred by an agreement or other submission under which he or she serves.

2. A direct settlement by the parties of some or all issues in a case, at any stage of the proceedings, must be accepted by the arbitrator as relieving him or her of further jurisdiction over such issues.

F. Mediation by an Arbitrator

1. When the parties wish at the outset to give an arbitrator authority both to mediate and to decide or submit recommendations regarding residual issues, if any, they should so advise the arbitrator prior to appointment. If the appointment is accepted, the arbitrator must perform a mediation role consistent with the circumstances of the case.

a. Direct appointments, also, may require a dual role as mediator and arbitrator of residual issues. This is most likely to occur in some public sector cases.

2. When a request to mediate is first made after appointment, the arbitrator may either accept or decline a mediation role.

a. *Once arbitration has been invoked, either party normally has a right to insist that the process be continued to decision.*

b. *If one party requests that the arbitrator mediate and the other party objects, the arbitrator should decline the request.*

c. *An arbitrator is not precluded from making a suggestion that he or she mediate. To avoid the possibility of improper pressure, the arbitrator should not so suggest unless it can be discerned that both parties are likely to be receptive. In any event, the arbitrator's suggestion should not be pursued unless both parties readily agree.*

G. Reliance by an Arbitrator on Other Arbitration Awards or on Independent Research

1. An arbitrator must assume full personal responsibility for the decision in each case decided.

a. *The extent, if any, to which an arbitrator properly may rely on precedent, on guidance of other awards, or on independent research is dependent primarily on the policies of the parties on these matters, as expressed in the contract, or other agreement, or at the hearing.*

b. When the mutual desires of the parties are not known or when the parties express differing opinions or policies, the arbitrator may exercise discretion as to these matters, consistent with acceptance of full personal responsibility for the award.

H. Use of Assistants

1. An arbitrator must not delegate any decision-making function to another person without consent of the parties.

a. *Without prior consent of the parties, an arbitrator may use the services of an assistant for research, clerical duties, or preliminary drafting under the direction of the arbitrator, which does not involve the delegation of any decision-making function.*

b. *If an arbitrator is unable, because of time limitations or other reasons, to handle all decision-making aspects of a case, it is not a violation of professional responsibility to suggest to the parties an allocation of responsibility between the arbitrator and an assistant or associate. The arbitrator must not exert pressure on the parties to accept such a suggestion.*

I. Consent Awards

1. Prior to issuance of an award, the parties may jointly request the arbitrator to include in the award certain agreements between them, concerning some or all of the issues. If the arbitrator believes that a suggested award is proper, fair, sound, and lawful, it is consistent with professional responsibility to adopt it.

a. *Before complying with such a request, an arbitrator must be certain that he or she understands the suggested settlement adequately in order to be able to appraise its terms. If it appears that pertinent facts or circumstances may not have been disclosed, the arbitrator should take the initiative to assure that all significant aspects of the case are fully understood. To this end, the arbitrator may request additional specific information and may question witnesses at a hearing.*

J. Avoidance of Delay

1. It is a basic professional responsibility of an arbitrator to plan his or her work schedule so that present and future commitments will be fulfilled in a timely manner.

 a. *When planning is upset for reasons beyond the control of the arbitrator, he or she, nevertheless, should exert every reasonable effort to fulfill all commitments. If this is not possible, prompt notice at the arbitrator's initiative should be given to all parties affected. Such notices should include reasonably accurate estimates of any additional time required. To the extent possible, priority should be given to cases in process so that other parties may make alternative arbitration arrangements.*

2. An arbitrator must cooperate with the parties and with any administrative agency involved in avoiding delays.

 a. *An arbitrator on the active roster of an administrative agency must take the initiative in advising the agency of any scheduling difficulties that he or she can foresee.*

 b. *Requests for services, whether received directly or through an administrative agency, should be declined if the arbitrator is unable to schedule a hearing as soon as the parties wish. If the parties, nevertheless, jointly desire to obtain the services of the arbitrator and the arbitrator agrees, arrangements should be made by agreement that the arbitrator confidently expects to fulfill.*

 c. *An arbitrator may properly seek to persuade the parties to alter or eliminate procedures or tactics that cause unnecessary delay.*

3. Once the case record has been closed, an arbitrator must adhere to the time limits for an award, as stipulated in the labor agreement or as provided by regulation of an administrative agency or as otherwise agreed.

 a. *If an appropriate award cannot be rendered within the required time, it is incumbent on the arbitrator to seek an extension of time from the parties.*

 b. If the parties have agreed upon abnormally short time limits for an award after a case is closed, the arbitrator should be so advised by the parties or by the administrative agency involved, prior to acceptance of appointment.

K. Fees and Expenses

1. An arbitrator occupies a position of trust in respect to parties and the administrative agencies. In charging for services and expenses, the arbitrator must be governed by the same high standards of honor and integrity that apply to all other phases of his or her work.

An arbitrator must endeavor to keep total charges for services and expenses reasonable and consistent with the nature of the case or cases decided.

Prior to appointment, the parties should be award of or be able readily to determine all significant aspects of an arbitrator's bases for charges for fees and expenses.

a. *Services Not Primarily Chargeable on a Per Diem Basis*

By agreement with the parties, the financial aspects of many "permanent" arbitration assignments, of some interest disputes, and of some "ad hoc" grievance assignments do not include a per diem fee for services as a primary part of the total understanding. *In such situations, the arbitrator must adhere faithfully to all agreed-upon arrangements governing fees and expenses.*

b. *Per Diem Basis for Charges for Services*

(1) *When an arbitrator's charges for services are determined primarily by a stipulated per diem fee, the arbitrator should establish in advance his or her bases for application of such per diem fee and for determination of reimbursable expenses.*

Practices established by an arbitrator should include the basis for charges, if any, for:

(a) hearing time, including the application of the stipulated basic per diem hearing fee to hearing days of varying lengths;

(b) study time;

(c) necessary travel time when not included in charges for hearing time;

(d) postponement or cancellation of hearings by the parties and the circumstances in which such charges will normally be assessed or waived;

(e) office overhead expenses (secretarial, telephone, postage, etc.);

(f) the work of paid assistants or associates.

(2) *Each arbitrator should be guided by the following general principles:*

(a) *Per diem charges for a hearing should not be in excess of actual time spent or allocated for the hearing.*

(b) *Per diem charges for study time should not be in excess of actual time spent.*

(c) *Any fixed ratio of study days to hearing days, not agreed to specifically by the parties, is inconsistent with the per diem method of charges for services.*

(d) *Charges for expenses must not be in excess of actual expenses normally reimbursable and incurred in connection with the case or cases involved.*

(e) *When time or expense are involved for two or more sets of parties on the same day or trip, such time or expense charges should be appropriately prorated.*

(f) *An arbitrator may stipulate in advance a minimum charge for a hearing without violation of (a) or (e) above.*

(3) *An arbitrator on the active roster of an administrative agency must file with the agency his or her individual bases for determination of fees and expenses if the agency so requires. Thereafter, it is the responsibility of each such arbitrator to advise the agency promptly of any change in any basis for charges.*

Such filing may be in the form of answers to a questionnaire devised by an agency or by any other method adopted by or approved by an agency.

Having supplied an administrative agency with the information noted above, an arbitrator's professional responsibility of disclosure under this Code with respect to fees and expenses has been satisfied for cases referred by that agency.

(4) *If an administrative agency promulgates specific standards with respect to any of these matters which are in addition to or more restrictive than an individual arbitrator's standards, an arbitrator on its active roster must observe the agency standards for cases handled under the auspices of that agency, or decline to serve.*

(5) *When an arbitrator is contacted directly by the parties for a case or cases, the arbitrator has a professional responsibility to respond to questions by submitting his or her bases for charges for fees and expenses.*

(6) *When it is known to the arbitrator that one or both of the parties cannot afford normal charges, it is consistent with professional responsibility to charge lesser amounts to both parties or to one of the parties if the other party is made aware of the difference and agrees.*

(7) *If an arbitrator concludes that the total of charges derived from his or her normal basis of calculation is not compatible with the case decided, it is consistent with professional responsibility to charge lesser amounts to both parties.*

2. An arbitrator must maintain adequate records to support charges for services and expenses and must make an accounting to the parties or to an involved administrative agency on request.

3. RESPONSIBILITIES TO ADMINISTRATIVE AGENCIES

A. General Responsibilities

1. An arbitrator must be candid, accurate, and fully responsive to an administrative agency concerning his or her qualifications, availability, and all other pertinent matters.

2. An arbitrator must observe policies and rules of an administrative agency in cases referred by that agency.

3. An arbitrator must not seek to influence an administrative agency by any improper means, including gifts or other inducements to agency personnel.

   a. It is not improper for a person seeking placement on a roster to request references from individuals having knowledge of the applicant's experience and qualifications.

   b. Arbitrators should recognize that the primary responsibility of an administrative agency is to serve the parties.

4. PREHEARING CONDUCT

1. All prehearing matters must be handled in a manner that fosters complete impartiality by the arbitrator.

   a. The primary purpose of prehearing discussions involving the arbitrator is to obtain agreement on procedural matters so that the hearing can proceed without unnecessary obstacles. If differences of opinion should arise during such discussions and, particularly, if such differences appear to impinge on substantive matters, the circumstances will suggest whether the matter can be resolved informally or may require a prehearing conference or, more rarely, a formal preliminary hearing. When an administrative agency handles some or all aspects of the arrangements prior to a hearing, the arbitrator will become involved only if differences of some substance arise.

   b. *Copies of any prehearing correspondence between the arbitrator and either party must be made available to both parties.*

5. HEARING CONDUCT

A. General Principles

1. An arbitrator must provide a fair and adequate hearing which assures that both parties have sufficient opportunity to present their respective evidence and argument.

a. *Within the limits of this responsibility, an arbitrator should conform to the various types of hearing procedures desired by the parties.*

b. An arbitrator may: encourage stipulations of fact; restate the substance of issues or arguments to promote or verify understanding; question the parties' representatives or witnesses, when necessary or advisable, to obtain additional pertinent information; and request that the parties submit additional evidence, either at the hearing or by subsequent filing.

c. *An arbitrator should not intrude into a party's presentation so as to prevent that party from putting forward its case fairly and adequately.*

B. Transcripts or Recordings

1. Mutual agreement of the parties as to use or non-use of a transcript must be respected by the arbitrator.

a. *A transcript is the official record of a hearing only when both parties agree to a transcript or an applicable law or regulation so provides.*

b. An arbitrator may seek to persuade the parties to avoid use of a transcript, or to use a transcript if the nature of the case appears to require one. *However, if an arbitrator intends to make his or her appointment to a case contingent on mutual agreement to a transcript, that requirement must be made known to both parties prior to appointment.*

c. If the parties do not agree to a transcript, an arbitrator may permit one party to take a transcript at its own cost. The arbitrator may also make appropriate arrangements under which the other party may have access to a copy, if a copy is provided to the arbitrator.

d. Without prior approval, an arbitrator may seek to use his or her own tape recorder to supplement note taking. The arbitrator should not insist on such a tape recording if either or both parties object.

C. Ex Parte Hearings

1. In determining whether to conduct an ex parte hearing, an arbitrator must consider relevant legal, contractual, and other pertinent circumstances.

2. An arbitrator must be certain, before proceeding ex parte, that the party refusing or failing to attend the hearing has been given adequate notice of the time, place, and purposes of the hearing.

D. Plant Visits

1. An arbitrator should comply with a request of any party that he or she visit a work area pertinent to the dispute prior to, during, or after a hearing. An arbitrator may also initiate such a request.

a. Procedures for such visits should be agreed to by the parties in consultation with the arbitrator.

E. Bench Decisions or Expedited Awards

1. When an arbitrator understands, prior to acceptance of appointment, that a bench decision is expected at the conclusion of the hearing, the arbitrator must comply with the understanding unless both parties agree otherwise.

a. If notice of the parties' desire for a bench decision is not given prior to the arbitrator's acceptance of the case, issuance of such a bench decision is discretionary.

b. When only one party makes the request and the other objects, the arbitrator should not render a bench decision except under most unusual circumstances.

2. When an arbitrator understands, prior to acceptance of appointment, that a concise written award is expected within a stated time period after the hearing, the arbitrator must comply with the understanding unless both parties agree otherwise.

6. POST HEARING CONDUCT

A. Post Hearing Briefs and Submissions

1. An arbitrator must comply with mutual agreements in respect to the filing or nonfiling of post hearing briefs or submissions.

a. An arbitrator, in his or her discretion, may either suggest the filing of post hearing briefs or other submissions or suggest that none be filed.

b. When the parties disagree as to the need for briefs, an arbitrator may permit filing but may determine a reasonable time limitation.

2. An arbitrator must not consider a post hearing brief or submission that has not been provided to the other party.

B. Disclosure of Terms of Award

1. An arbitrator must not disclose a prospective award to either party prior to its simultaneous issuance to both parties or explore possible alternative awards unilaterally with one party, unless both parties so agree.

a. Partisan members of tripartite boards may know prospective terms of an award in advance of its issuance. Similar situations may exist in other less formal arrangements mutually agreed to by the parties. In any such situation, the arbitrator should determine and observe the mutually desired degree of confidentiality.

C. Awards and Opinions

1. The award should be definite, certain, and as concise as possible.
   a. When an opinion is required, factors to be considered by an arbitrator include: desirability of brevity, consistent with the nature of the case and any expressed desires of the parties; need to use a style and form that is understandable to responsible representatives to the parties, to the grievant and supervisors, and to others in the collective bargaining relationship; necessity of meeting the significant issues; forthrightness to an extent not harmful to the relationship of the parties; and avoidance of gratuitous advice or discourse not essential to disposition of the issues.

D. Clarification or Interpretation of Awards

1. No clarification or interpretation of an award is permissible without the consent of both parties.
2. Under agreements which permit or require clarification or interpretation of an award, an arbitrator must afford both parties an opportunity to be heard.

E. Enforcement of Award

1. The arbitrator's responsibility does not extend to the enforcement of an award.
2. In view of the professional and confidential nature of the arbitration relationship, an arbitrator should not voluntarily participate in legal enforcement proceedings.

Index

About the Authors

DAVID A. DILTS is Professor of Business Administration at Indiana University, Purdue-Fort Wayne. A widely published author in labor relations matters, he has written four books, including *Getting Absent Workers Back on the Job* (Quorum Books, 1985), and more than forty articles. He also serves as a labor arbitrator and is listed on the rosters of the American Arbitration Association and the Federal Mediation and Conciliation Service, as well as several state agencies. As a member of the National Academy of Arbitrators, he has heard over 200 cases in the last eight years.

WILLIAM J. WALSH earned his Ph.D. from Indiana University. He is also an arbitrator and fact finder in the public sector and has performed government-sponsored research in personnel administration and compensation.